textiles

COMPLETE CONTEMPORARY CRAFT

textiles

MURDOCH BOOKS

contents

knitting

crochet

quilting

feltmaking

weaving

knitting

Yarns

The choice of yarn is most important. Every type of yarn has distinct properties; different yarns knitted to the same pattern can produce vastly different effects, so you need to match the yarn to the project. For example, for a hard-wearing sweater that can be machine washed, a specially treated wool is the best choice. A baby's garment is better made in cotton, which can stand up to repeated washing and is also cool, so the baby won't overheat.

If your local craft or specialist yarn store doesn't stock the yarn you want, or can't order it in for you, internet mail order is a convenient way of finding and ordering yarns that might otherwise be unobtainable. The freight fees are generally modest, and it's worth the extra expense to get just the right yarn.

Knitting is usually done with commercial yarns, but any continuous piece of material can be knitted, including strips of plastic or fabric (whether knitted or woven), ribbon, tape and wire.

smooth yarns in wool or wool blends
Clockwise from top: plain 8-ply (DK) pure wool; plain 8-ply (DK) pure wool; 8-ply (DK) tweed pure wool; 10-ply (worsted/aran weight) pure wool; flecked 8-ply (DK) pure wool; (centre) variegated acrylic/wool mix.

Yarn types

When choosing yarn, you need to consider its content and thickness (or ply) and how the manufacturer has treated the fibre. Yarns may be natural, synthetic or a mixture of both. Natural yarns are obtained either from animals or plants. Yarns of animal origin include wool, from sheep; cashmere and mohair, from goats; angora, from angora rabbits; and alpaca, from a relative of the llama. Plant-derived yarns include cotton, linen and hemp. Synthetic yarns, such as acrylic, polyester and nylon, are often mixed with natural yarns to improve their texture and performance.

Yarns can also be treated and spun to make them hairier, heavier, denser, more twisted, fluffier, flatter or knobblier. Some ways in which manufacturers treat yarns to change their intrinsic characteristics are by giving a shrink-resist treatment to wool to make it machine washable, and mercerizing cotton to give it a lustre.

Some terms used to describe yarn (such as silk, cotton, cashmere) refer to the yarn's content; others (such as aran, tweed, bouclé) to its texture, appearance and/or thickness.

Smooth, plain yarns are best for fancy patterns such as cables and lace, as these yarns enable the beauty and intricacy of the stitches to be easily seen. Fashion or novelty yarns are best used with simple garter stitch or stocking stitch designs; the lovely details of more complicated patterns will be lost in these busy yarns.

yarns in other fibres and finishes Clockwise from top: Mohair; slubby pure wool; wool/silk/angora mix; variegated bouclé mohair; alpaca/silk/polyamide mix.

When starting out, you may be tempted by the intriguing textures, bright colour mixtures or sensual feel of novelty yarns, but it's best to practise on smooth, plain yarns, which are easiest to knit with. Choose pale or mid-toned yarns; these show stitch details better than dark yarns, which is especially useful if you're practising more complicated stitch textures or patterns.

Reading a ball band

On the paper band around the ball of yarn is printed useful information such as the manufacturer and composition of the yarn, the recommended needle size to use, the recommended gauge (tension) that the wool should knit up to, the weight of the ball, care instructions, and the shade and dye lot. All balls for the same garment should come from the same dye lot. Different dye lots can vary in tone; a variation that is undetectable between individual balls can be quite noticeable in the finished garment. If you are forced to mix dye lots, you can make the transition between the two less obvious by alternating two rows of one dye lot with two rows of the other throughout the garment.

Yarn weights

Yarns come in many thicknesses, from thread-like yarns used for traditional lace to super-chunky yarns that knit up thickly (and gratifyingly quickly). Not all countries use the same terms for types and weights of yarn. Also, some weights of yarn are very popular in some countries and little used in others. The following table lists some of the most popular weights of yarn and their names in different parts of the world, and how many stitches they yield per 10 cm (4 in) when knitted on the recommended needle size.

novelty yarns Clockwise from top: hairy yarn in acrylic–polyamide mix; chunky velvet-look yarn in exoline; tufted yarn in polyester–polyamide mix; velvet ribbon yarn in nylon–acrylic mix; silky-look 'eyelash' yarn in polyester.

International yarn equivalents (note that figures given are approximate and will vary between manufacturers)

Australia/NZ	USA	UK and Canada	Tension (gauge) per 10 cm (4 in)	Needle
5-ply	Sport/Baby	Baby	24 sts	3.75 mm (US 5/UK 9)
8-ply	Double knitting (DK)	Double knitting (DK)	22 sts	4 mm (US 6/UK 8)
10-ply	Worsted weight	Aran	18–20 sts	5 mm (US 8/UK 6)
12-ply	Chunky	Chunky	14–18 sts	5 or 5.5 mm (US 8 or 9/UK 6 or 5)
Novelty	Bulky	Bulky	9–12 sts	8 mm (US 11/UK 0) or up

Equipment

Knitting needles

Knitting needles may be either straight (two or more separate needles) or circular (two needles joined by a length of round plastic or nylon). Needles may be made from various materials, including aluminium, wood, bamboo and plastic.

A piece of knitted fabric can be made either flat or in the round. For example, if making a sweater using flat knitting, the back and front pieces are made separately then joined up the sides. If making a sweater in the round, all the stitches for both the back and the front are cast on at the same time and the body of the sweater is knitted in one piece, in what is effectively a spiral. This eliminates side seams. To do flat knitting, you can use either straight or circular needles; for circular knitting, you will need circular needles and/or a set of double-pointed needles.

Circular needles come in various lengths; if knitting in the round, choose a length that is shorter than the circumference of the piece you are knitting. For example, you cannot knit a piece with a 50 cm (20 in) circumference on 60 cm (24 in) needles, as the knitting will be stretched.

Circular needles are particularly useful when knitting large items, such as shawls or rugs; the length of the needle easily accommodates a large numbers of stitches, and the weight of the garment stays centred over your lap rather than awkwardly weighing down one end of the needle, as is the case with straight needles.

Double-pointed needles come in sets of four or five needles about 20 cm (8 in) in length. The stitches are cast on as normal then divided roughly equally between three or four needles. The last needle in the set is then used to knit off the stitches. Double-pointed needles are useful when knitting parts of garments that may be too narrow for circular needles, such as the collars of sweaters.

Cable needles are short needles used to hold stitches while making a cable. They may be straight, or kinked in the middle to prevent the stitches from slipping off.

Needle sizes

There is no universal guide for knitting needle sizes; they are expressed differently from country to country. Sizes many also vary slightly from one manufacturer to the next. The patterns in this book give needle sizes in metric (millimetres), followed by the equivalent US and UK/Canadian sizes. For conversions, see the chart at left.

Needle size conversion chart

Metric (mm)	US	UK/Canada
2	0	14
2.25	1	13
2.75	2	12
3	–	11
3.25	3	10
3.5	4	–
3.75	5	9
4	6	8
4.5	7	7
5	8	6
5.5	9	5
6	10	4
6.5	10½	3
7	–	2
7.5	–	1
8	11	0
9	13	00
10	15	000
12	17	–
15–16	19	–
19	35	–
25	50	–

Accessories

The following handy tools may be purchased at craft or yarn stores, or improvized.

Crochet hooks These are useful for picking up dropped stitches or for casting off. The crochet hook does not have to be the same size as the needle you are using for the work; it can be a little smaller or larger without affecting the fabric too much.

Metal ruler Used for checking tension; more accurate than a cloth tape measure.

Needle gauge Used for checking the size of knitting needles; some also have metric and imperial measurements marked on the sides, for measuring tension squares.

Pins For marking out tension squares, pinning garments into shape before blocking or pressing, and pinning knitted pieces together before sewing up.

Row counter A cylindrical gadget that fits on the end of the needle; it has numbered tumblers that can be turned at the end of each row to record how many rows you have done. Useful, but not essential; you can improvise with pen and paper.

Stitch holders Made of metal and resembling large safety pins, these come in various sizes and are used to hold stitches that will be picked up again later, for example at a neck edge. For small numbers of stitches, you can improvize with safety pins.

Stitch markers Small plastic rings slipped onto the needle to mark the start of a pattern repeat or, in circular knitting, the start of a row; you can improvise with small loops of contrasting yarn (see at right).

Tape measure For measuring garment pieces.

Wool needle For sewing up seams and darning in ends of yarn on finished pieces; it should have a blunt end so as not to split the strands of yarn.

Using stitch markers

Commercially produced stitch markers are small plastic rings of varying diameters, for different-sized needles (see the centre photograph below). Alternatively, you can make your own. Using short lengths of contrast-coloured yarn, make a small slipknot in each and slip one loop onto the needle where required. As you come to each marker on successive rows, simply slip it off the left needle and onto the right.

When casting on a lot of stitches, you may find it useful to put a marker after every 20 stitches to assist in counting.

Markers can also help you keep track of pattern repeats, for example in lace, aran or other complex patterns. Place a marker at the start of each pattern repeat; then, if you make a mistake, it will be easier to trace where it occurred.

If working in the round on circular or double-pointed needles, slip on a marker to show where each new round begins.

needles (from top right) Double-pointed, straight, circular, and cable needles (straight and kinked).

accessories (from top left) Wool needle, crochet hook, stitch markers, row counter, pins.

accessories (from top) Tape measure, ruler, needle gauge, safety pin, stitch holders, scissors.

Casting on

Casting on is the term given to making the first row of stitches; these form the foundation of your knitting. There are several methods of casting on. The following are two of the most versatile. The golden rule of casting on is to do so loosely; even if you think your cast-on is too loose, it probably isn't.

step four Insert the point of the right needle into the loop around your thumb.

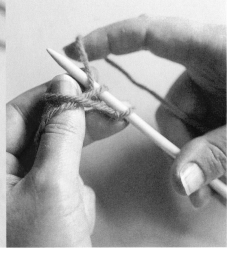

step five Wrap the ball end of yarn around the needle.

step five continued Pull the ball end of yarn through the thumb loop to make a stitch.

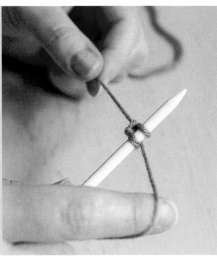

step six Pull on the ball end of the yarn until the loop is firm but not tight.

Thumb method

This gives a very flexible edge and is especially good for rib edges of garments and for garter stitch fabric.

1 Start with a length of yarn measuring a little more than three times the width of the edge to be cast on. Make a slipknot (see opposite) at this point.

2 Transfer the slipknot to a knitting needle. Draw it up until it is close to the needle, but not tight; you should be able to easily insert a second needle into the loop.

3 With the tail end of the yarn, make a clockwise loop around your thumb.

4 Insert the point of the right needle from front to back into the thumb loop.

5 Wrap the ball end of yarn around the needle and pull this loop through the thumb loop. You have now cast on a stitch.

6 Pull on the ball end of yarn until the stitch is firm, but not tight; you should be able to easily insert a second needle into the loop.

7 Repeat Steps 3–6 until you have cast on the required number of stitches. (Remember that the loop of the slipknot counts as one stitch.)

Cable method

Also known as the two-needle method, this gives a smooth edge and is particularly compatible with stocking stitch. It is not as flexible as the thumb method, so tension it loosely if it is to become the bottom, neck or sleeve edge of a garment.

1 Leaving a tail of yarn about 15 cm (6 in) long, make a slipknot on the left needle.

2 Holding the other needle in your right hand, insert its point from left to right into the loop of the slipknot.

3 Hook the yarn around the tip of the right-hand needle and pull it through the loop of the slipknot.

4 Put the loop just made onto the left-hand needle. You have now cast on a stitch. *Gently* pull the ball end of the yarn to secure the loop. If a needle will not pass easily through the loop with almost no resistance, the loop is too tight.

5 Insert the right-hand needle between the previous loop and the loop you just made. Hook the yarn around the tip of the right-hand needle and draw it through. Place the loop just made onto the left-hand needle and gently tighten.

6 Repeat Step 5 until you have the required number of stitches. (The slip loop counts as one stitch.)

Making a slipknot

Make a loop in a piece of yarn. Bring the yarn up from back to front through the loop and pull to tighten. You have now made a slipknot. Place the loop on the knitting needle or crochet hook. You can now begin casting on or making a crochet chain. Remember that the loop of the slipknot counts as the first cast-on or chain stitch.

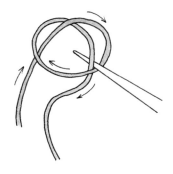

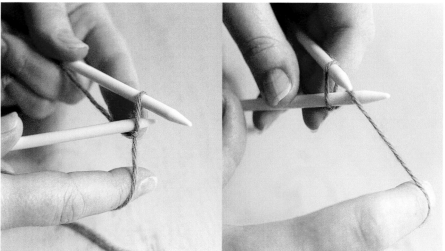

step two Insert the point of the right needle into the loop of the slipknot.

step three Hook the yarn around the tip of the right needle and pull the yarn through.

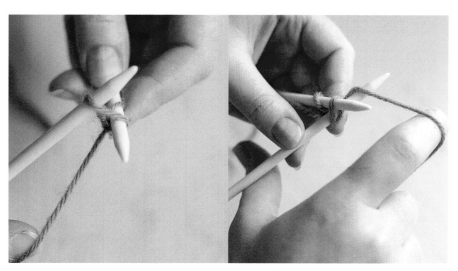

step four Put the loop just made onto the left needle and gently tighten.

step five Insert the tip of the right needle between the two loops and draw the yarn through.

The basic stitches

Knitting has just two basic stitches, the knit stitch and the purl stitch. Many different stitch patterns, including textures, cables, twists, bobbles and ribs, can be made from these alone.

Garter stitch

If you knit every row, the resulting fabric is known as garter stitch (above). It has a ridged appearance, and both sides of the fabric are identical. The fabric lies flat, without curling up at the edges.

Hint

If you look closely at the stitches on a knitting needle, you will see that they do not lie at right angles to the needle. Instead, the front 'leg' of the stitch lies slightly to the right and the back leg slightly to the left. Keep this in mind, especially if knitting a stitch that you have picked up; if you knit into the back (left leg) rather than the front (right leg) of the stitch, you will twist the stitch and it will look different to all the other stitches in the row.

The knit stitch

1 Insert the point of the right needle from left to right through the front of the first stitch on the left needle.

2 Wrap the yarn around the tip of the right needle.

3 With the tip of the right needle, draw the yarn through the stitch on the left needle.

4 Slip the original stitch off the left needle. You have now made a knit stitch.

5 Repeat Steps 1–4 until you reach the end of the row. To start the next row, you need to turn to the work. To do this, transfer the needle in your right hand, with the work on it, to the left hand; the empty needle is held in the right hand. You are now ready to begin knitting the second row.

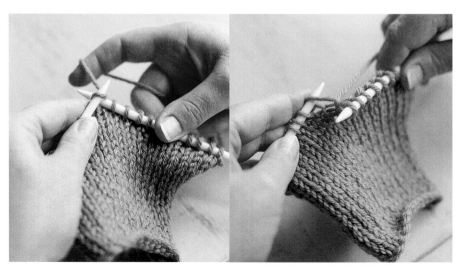

step one Insert the point of the right needle through the stitch on the left needle.

step three With the tip of the right needle, draw the yarn through the stitch on the left needle.

The purl stitch

The purl stitch is, in effect, the reverse of the knit stitch.

1 Insert the point of the right needle from right to left into the front of the first stitch on the left needle.

2 Wrap the yarn around the tip of the right needle.

3 With the tip of the right needle, draw the yarn through the stitch on the left needle.

4 Slip the original stitch off the left needle. You have now made a purl stitch.

5 Repeat Steps 1–4 until you reach the end of the row, then turn the work and begin the next row.

Stocking stitch (stockinette)

If you knit and purl alternate rows, the resulting fabric is known as stocking stitch, or stockinette. One side of the fabric is smooth, with stitches looking like little Vs. The other side is knobbly and looks similar to garter stitch. Usually the smooth side is used as the right side. If the knobbly side is used, the fabric is known as reverse stocking stitch. The difference in using reverse stocking stitch rather than garter stitch when you want a knobbly look on the right side is that reverse stocking stitch fabric is thinner than garter stitch fabric, giving a less bulky garment.

If you purl every row, you get garter stitch, but as purl stitch is slower to make than knit stitch, there is no advantage to making a garter-stitch fabric by purling every row.

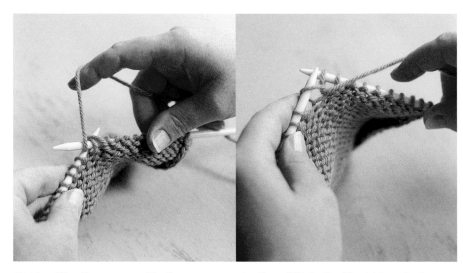

step two Wrap the yarn around the tip of the right needle.

step three With the tip of the right needle, draw the yarn through the stitch on the left needle.

Increasing

Increasing and decreasing are ways of shaping the fabric. There are several methods of increasing; the following are two of the most useful. Increasing is usually, but not always, done on a right-side row. It may be done at the edge or in the body of the piece of knitted fabric.

knit fabric, step one Knit a stitch as usual, but do not slip the stitch off the left needle.

knit fabric, step two Knit into back of same stitch, then slip the stitch off the left needle.

purl fabric, step one Purl a stitch as usual, but do not slip the stitch off the left needle.

purl fabric, step two Purl into back of same stitch, then slip the stitch off the left needle.

Working into the back and front of a stitch (inc)

Working into both the back and front of the same stitch produces a neat but slightly visible increase. This increase can be done on either knit or purl fabric. Both versions are shown here. This increase is usually abbreviated simply as inc, but you may also see it as kfb (knit into front and back) or pfb (purl into front and back).

INC ON KNIT FABRIC

1 Knit a stitch as usual, but do not slip the stitch off the left needle.

2 Insert the tip of the right needle into the back of the same stitch, from front to back and right to left. (You may need to wriggle the needle about a little to enlarge the loop, especially if your tension is tight.) Knit the stitch, then slip the stitch off the left needle. You have now made an extra knit stitch.

INC ON PURL FABRIC

1 Purl a stitch as usual, but do not slip the stitch off the left needle.

2 Insert the tip of the right needle into the back of the same stitch, from back to front and left to right. Knit the stitch, then slip the stitch off the left needle. You have now made an extra purl stitch.

Making a stitch (M1)

Another method of increasing is by working into the running stitch — that is, the thread that lies between two stitches. Working into the back of the stitch (rather than the front, as is usual) twists the stitch and prevents a hole from forming, making the increase almost invisible. This is particularly useful if you need to increase in the body of the garment. This increase is usually abbreviated as M1 (make a stitch), and can be done on either knit or purl fabric; both versions are shown here.

M1 ON KNIT FABRIC

1 With the tip of the left needle, pick up the loop that lies between the first stitch on that needle and the first stitch on the right needle. Make sure that the front of the loop slopes to the right.

2 Knit into the back of the loop. You have now made an extra knit stitch.

M1 ON PURL FABRIC

1 With the tip of the left needle, pick up the loop that lies between the first stitch on that needle and the first stitch on the right needle. Make sure that the front of the loop slopes to the right.

2 Purl into the back of the loop. You have now made an extra purl stitch.

knit fabric, step one With tip of left needle, pick up the loop lying between the two stitches.

knit fabric, step two Knit into the back of the loop that you have just picked up.

purl fabric, step one With tip of left needle, pick up the loop lying between the two stitches.

purl fabric, step two Purl into the back of the loop that you have just picked up.

Decreasing

By working one or more stitches together, thus decreasing the number of stitches in a row, you can shape a knitted piece. Decreasing may be done at either the edge or in the body of the knitting, and on both knit and purl fabric.

Hints

The number of normal rows worked between one decrease row and the next determines how steep the angle of the decrease will be. Decreasing every row produces a steep angle; decreasing less often, for example every fourth or sixth row, produces a shallower angle.

Perfecting your decreases

The most rudimentary decrease is made by working together the first or last two stitches in a row. However, a much neater look is achieved by making 'fully fashioned' decreases; these are worked a consistent number of stitches (usually two or three) in from each end of the knitting.

To make the decreases at each end mirror each other, you will need to make one of them slope to the right and the other to the left. To make a right-sloping decrease, work two stitches together through the front of the stitch as explained at right. To make a left-sloping decrease, work two stitches together through the back of the stitch.

Working in this way emphasizes the way the knitting is shaped, or 'fashioned'. It results in a decorative effect at the decreased edge, and will add a professional touch to your knitting.

KNITTING TWO STITCHES TOGETHER (ABBREVIATED AS K2TOG)

Insert the tip of the right needle into the first two stitches on the left needle, from left to right and front to back as normal. Pass the yarn around the right needle and knit a stitch, slipping both original stitches off the left needle. You have now decreased by one stitch. (It is usual to decrease by one stitch at a time, but sometimes you may be instructed to k3tog, thus decreasing two stitches.)

PURLING TWO STITCHES TOGETHER (ABBREVIATED AS P2TOG)

Insert the tip of the right needle into the first two stitches on the left needle, from right to left and back to front as normal. Pass the yarn around the right needle and purl a stitch, slipping both original stitches off the left needle. You have now decreased by one stitch. (It is usual to decrease by one stitch at a time, but sometimes you may be instructed to p3tog, thus decreasing two stitches.)

k2tog Two stitches are knitted together, then the original stitch is slipped off the left needle.

p2tog Two stitches are purled together, then the original stitch is slipped off the left needle.

Picking up stitches along edge

An edging, border or collar can be added to the main piece of knitting by picking up stitches from a cast-on, cast-off or side edge. This can be done with a knitting needle or a crochet hook. In some patterns, you may see this technique referred to as 'pick up and knit' or 'knit up'.

1 With right side of work facing, insert the tip of the right needle (or the crochet hook) into the edge of the knitting. Work one stitch in from the edge on a side or shaped edge, or under both loops of a cast-on or cast-off edge.

2 Draw through a loop of yarn; you have now picked up a stitch.

Repeat Steps 1–2 until you have picked up the required number of stitches.

If using a crochet hook, pick up as many stitches as will comfortably fit along the length of the hook, then slip these off the end of the crochet hook onto a knitting needle of the specified size. Repeat this process until you have picked up the required number of stitches.

When picking up along a slanting cast-off edge (for example a V-neck edge), you will need to insert the needle into the stitches one row below the decrease, not between the stitches, as this may form a hole. Always make sure the stitches are evenly spaced along the edge.

step one Insert the tip of the right needle from front to back into the edge of the work.

step two Draw through a loop of yarn; you have now picked up (or knitted up) a stitch.

Crochet hook method, step one Insert hook into edge of fabric and draw a loop through.

Crochet hook method, step two Transfer picked-up stitches from hook to knitting needle.

Picking up dropped stitches

Even the best knitter will occasionally drop a stitch or make it incorrectly. The mistake can easily be rectified using the following methods. A dropped or incorrectly made stitch can be traced back and fixed in this manner for several rows, if need be.

Hint

You may not notice that you have dropped a stitch until several rows after it has occurred, when you stop to look at your work or to count stitches. A dropped stitch will form a ladder in the fabric, and should be stopped as soon as possible, or it will unwind further down the work.

If you notice a dropped stitch but are in the middle of a complicated pattern that you don't want to lose track of, put a safety pin through the dropped stitch to keep it from unravelling further, then come back to it once you have finished the row you are on.

To pick up a dropped stitch on stocking stitch fabric, with RS facing you, insert a crochet hook into the dropped stitch from the front. Pick up the first horizontal bar of unravelled yarn above the dropped stitch and draw it through the stitch to the front. Repeat until all dropped bars of the ladder have been picked up. Transfer the final stitch from the crochet hook to the left knitting needle, making sure the stitch is not twisted (see page 16). When you have picked up the stitch, look at the back of the work; if there is a bar of unravelled yarn still showing, you have missed a bar somewhere along the way. In this case, deliberately unravel the ladder and retrace your steps.

To pick up a dropped stitch on purl fabric, you will need to insert the crochet hook in the stitch from back to front, then draw the bar through.

If in a patterned fabric you notice a wrongly made stitch a few rows back, you can deliberately unravel the ladder, rework that stitch correctly, then remake all the stitches above.

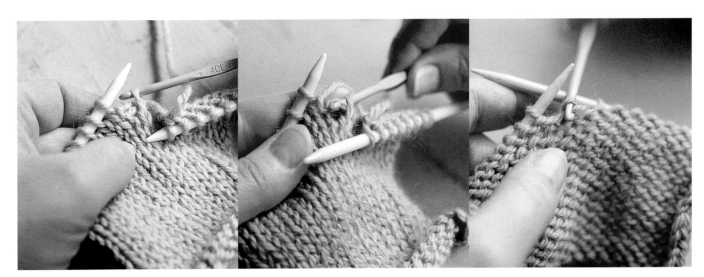

on knit fabric, step one Insert crochet hook through fabric from front to back.

on knit fabric, step two Draw bar of dropped stitch through the stitch on the hook.

on purl fabric The bar will need to be drawn through the stitch from back to front.

Casting (binding) off

Casting (or binding) off is how you finish a piece of knitting. It can be done either knitwise or purlwise, and is usually done on the right side of the fabric. Unless otherwise specified, casting off should be done in pattern; that is, each knit stitch should be cast off knitwise and each purl stitch purlwise.

casting off knitwise, step one Loosely knit two stitches as normal.

casting off knitwise, step two Lift the first stitch on the right needle over the second and off the needle.

casting off purlwise, step one Loosely purl two stitches as normal.

casting off purlwise, step two Lift the first stitch on the right needle over the second and off the needle.

When casting off, do so loosely; an otherwise beautifully knitted piece can be ruined by a too-tight cast-off, especially at the neck, cuff or lower edge of a garment. If unsure, cast off a few stitches and then stretch the fabric; the cast-off edge should stretch almost as much as the rest of the fabric.

CASTING OFF KNITWISE

1 Knit two stitches as normal.

2 From the front of the work, insert the tip of the left needle into the first stitch on the right needle and lift this stitch over the second stitch and off the needle. You have now cast off one stitch knitwise.

3 Knit another stitch and then repeat Step 2. Continue in this manner until one stitch remains on the left needle. Remove the needle, bring the end of the yarn through the last stitch and pull firmly to fasten. The cast-off is now complete.

CASTING OFF PURLWISE

1 Purl two stitches as normal.

2 From the back of the work, insert the tip of the left needle into the first stitch on the right needle and lift this stitch over the second stitch and off the needle. You have now cast off one stitch purlwise.

3 Purl another stitch and then repeat Step 2. Continue until one stitch remains, then fasten off.

Pressing and blocking

These methods of shaping finished knitted pieces are not always necessary; check the pattern instructions and do not press or block unless directed to. Acrylic yarns should never be pressed, as they will melt.

pressing Press on the wrong side using a warm iron, a pressing cloth and light pressure.

Pressing

Follow the pressing instructions given in the pattern or, if you have substituted a yarn, on the ball band. When in doubt, press a test swatch to see the result.

Before pressing, pin out the knitting to the right shape and dimensions on the ironing board. For most natural yarns (wool, cotton, linen, but not mohair), lay a damp cloth over the knitting then steam without allowing the iron to rest on the fabric. Wholly synthetic yarns should never be pressed. Yarns that are a mixture of natural and synthetic fibres can be pressed with a cool iron over a dry cloth.

Pressing is not the same as ironing. To press, put the iron on the fabric, leave it for a few seconds, then lift it up, place it on another part of the fabric, and repeat. Don't move the iron back and forth, as when ironing; this can distort the fabric.

Note that ribbed edges of garments should never be pressed. Nor should mohair, fluffy and synthetic yarns; instead, damp-finish these yarns (see opposite).

Blocking

Blocking should be done before sewing seams. Follow the instructions given in the pattern; not all knitted items require blocking. However, it is essential for most lace knitting, as it improves stitch definition and makes the fabric smoother.

To block, lay a clean, colourfast towel or sheet on a padded surface such as carpet. Lay the item to be blocked on top of this and pin it out to size, easing and gently stretching where necessary and making sure the sides and ends are completely straight. Spray with water and leave to dry completely. When the pins are removed, the piece should be flat and the stitch pattern clearly defined.

If blocking a large garment, rather than pinning every 1 cm (⅜ inch) or so, it is easier to use a series of straight knitting needles along the edges. Weave the needles through the stitches along the sides and at the ends of the piece, then pin the needles into place. If you block a lot of large pieces, it will be worth your while buying long, thin, stainless steel rods for this purpose.

blocking Pin the piece to shape, spray with water and leave to dry naturally.

Making up

'Making up' means sewing together the finished pieces. The following two methods are the most common. The yarn used to knit the garment is not always the best choice for seaming; highly textured yarns, or those that break easily, are unsuitable for sewing up. In these cases, use a smooth yarn in a matching shade.

Backstitch

This method makes a strong seam, but one that is visible and not as elastic as mattress stitch (see page 26). This method is best used only with yarns that are 8-ply (DK) at the heaviest. For garments knitted in thicker yarns, use a matching shade in a finer yarn for sewing up. Backstitch is worked a consistent whole stitch or half stitch in from the side of the piece for the whole seam. Bring the needle up between the stitches rather than through them, so as not to split the yarn.

Thread a wool needle with appropriate yarn. Hold the pieces right sides together. Fasten the end of the yarn at the bottom of the seam with a couple of small overlapping stitches. Insert the needle through both layers from back to front two rows along from where you started. Take it to the right, across the front of the work, for one row, then take the needle to the back again. *Take it across the back of the work for two rows, then bring it to the front and across to the right for one row, then to the back again.* Repeat from * to * for the entire seam, then fasten off.

Damp finishing

Mohair, fluffy and synthetic yarns, or textured patterns, should not be pressed, as their fibres or texture may be damaged by the heat. Instead, damp finish them: lay the pieces on a damp colourfast towel, roll up and leave for about an hour to let the knitting absorb moisture from the towel. Unwrap, lay the towel on a flat surface and place the damp pieces on top of it. Gently ease the pieces into shape and pin as explained in 'Blocking', opposite. Lay another damp towel on top, pat all over to make contact between the layers and let dry naturally, away from direct sunlight or heat sources.

backstitch Work a consistent distance (one stitch or a half stitch) in from the edge.

sewing up two side edges in mattress stitch (see page 26) Work one stitch in from the edge.

the finished seam Once the stitches are pulled firm, the seam is virtually invisible.

Hints

When sewing together two side edges or two cast-off or cast-on edges, you are working with pieces that have the same number of stitches or rows, so you can match the sewing row for row or stitch for stitch. However, if you are sewing a side edge to a cast-on or cast-off edge, you will be working with different numbers of stitches and rows. Because a knit stitch is wider than it is long, a square of knitted fabric will have more rows up and down than stitches across. This means that when you are attaching a side edge to a cast-on or cast-off edge, there are more rows on the side edge than there are stitches on the other edge. To match the two pieces evenly, make a mattress stitch through each stitch on the cast-on or cast-off edge but skip a row occasionally on the side edge.

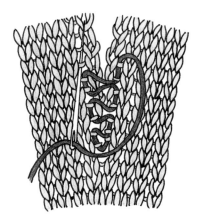

diagram 1 Sewing up two side edges using mattress stitch.

diagram 2 Steps in sewing together two cast-on or cast-off edges using mattress stitch.

Mattress stitch

Mattress stitch makes a fine seam that is almost undetectable. It is worked on the right side of the knitting, which means that you can easily match stripes, patterns and textures on the back and front of the garment. If you have never tried it, you will be surprised at how easy it is, and how neat the result.

Mattress stitch can be used for sewing together two side edges (see photograph on page 25), sewing a side edge to a cast-off or cast-on edge, or sewing together two cast-off or cast-on edges (see photographs below). It is shown here on stocking stitch, but it can be used on most types of knitted fabric.

Lay the pieces to be joined flat, right sides up and edge to edge. Thread a wool needle with appropriate yarn and fasten the end to one piece at the back. Bring the needle out from back to front between the first stitch and the second stitch in the first row. Insert the needle between the first stitch and the second stitch in the first row of the opposite side. Pass the needle under the strands of one or two rows, then bring it back to the front. Take it down into the hole from which the last stitch exited on the first side and pass it under the strands of one or two stitches, so that it emerges in the same place as on the opposite side. Continue in this zigzag manner, always taking the needle under the strands that correspond exactly with those on the other side. Take care not to miss any rows. After every few stitches, pull up the yarn to close the seam. Don't pull it too tight; it should have the same tension as the rest of the garment. Repeat until all the seam is sewn.

sewing together two side edges Used, for example, to sew up two shoulder seams.

sewing side edge to cast-off or cast-on edge Used, for example, to sew sleeve to garment.

Crocheted details

The crochet stitch known as double crochet (dc; or, in the USA, single crochet/sc) is often used to give a decorative edge to a knitted item, or to join together two pieces, such as the back and front of a cushion. Crochet chains can be used as ties. These simple techniques are employed in several projects in this book.

crochet chain Draw the yarn through the loop on the hook. Continue for desired length.

dc around edge, step two Insert hook through edge of knitting and draw through a loop of yarn.

dc around edge, step two continued Draw the yarn through both loops on the hook.

turning a corner To turn a corner, work 3 dc into the same knit stitch, then proceed as normal.

Crochet chain

1 Make a slipknot (see page 15) and put it on the crochet hook.

2 Holding the hook in your right hand and the yarn in your left, catch the yarn with the hook and draw it through the loop of the slipknot, thus making one chain. Repeat for the required number of chain stitches (the slipknot loop counts as the first chain).

Double crochet

1 To work dc around the edge of a knitted piece, first tie the yarn to the edge of the knitting with a knot. Insert the crochet hook into the knitted piece at the same place where you made the knot, one stitch in from the edge, with RS facing. Draw through a loop of yarn.

2 Insert the hook into the next stitch or row of the knitting and draw through another loop of yarn (making two loops of yarn on the hook). Catch the yarn with the hook and draw through both loops on the hook. You have now made 1 dc. Repeat Step 2 until you have crocheted around the entire edge.

3 To finish, insert the hook into the first stitch of the round and draw through the yarn. Cut yarn, pull the tail through the loop and fasten off.

Using graphs or charts

In a chart or graph, each stitch is represented by a single square, and the symbol within that square indicates what you do with that stitch; for example, knit, purl, increase, decrease or cable.

Some symbols go across more than one square of the chart; for example, an instruction to make a 6-stitch cable may be represented by two diagonal lines each crossing three squares (which represent the three stitches in each 'leg' of the cable).

Charts are read from the bottom up, starting at the first row, and from right to left on odd-numbered (right-side) rows, and from left to right on even-numbered (wrong-side) rows. Charts show the pattern as it appears from the right side of the work, so you need to work out what stitch to make on wrong-side rows to get the correct effect on the right side. For example, a stitch marked as knit on the chart will need to be knitted on a right-side row but purled on a wrong-side row.

This diagram shows a pattern in chart form, followed by the same pattern in written form.

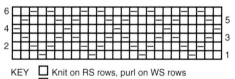

KEY ☐ Knit on RS rows, purl on WS rows
     ⊟ Purl on RS rows, knit on WS rows

Row 1 (RS): k3, p1, (k5, p1) to last 3 sts, k3.
Row 2: p2, k1, p1, k1, (p3, k1, p1, k1) to last 2 sts, p2.
Row 3: k1, p1, (k3, p1, k1, p1) to last 5 sts, k3, p1, k1.
Row 4: k1, (p5, k1) to end.
Row 5: As row 3.
Row 6: as row 2.
Rep these 6 rows.

Working from a pattern

Patterns come in both written and chart (or graph) formats. When starting out, you will probably find it easiest to work from a written pattern, but once you come to attempt more complicated patterns, you may prefer to work from charts. One advantage of a chart is that it is a visual representation of the pattern, so it will give you an idea of how the pattern will look in a way that written instructions cannot.

It's a good idea to make a photocopy of the pattern on which you can mark off every row as you finish it. This way, if you have to put the knitting away, you are less likely to lose your place in the pattern. On this copy also write any changes you've made to the pattern, and any notes of things you need to remember. If the pattern gives instructions for several different sizes, you will find it useful to circle or highlight the instructions pertaining to the size you are making.

A pattern should give the finished size of the item; if for a sweater, it should give measurements for the chest, length and sleeve seams. If the pattern has both imperial and metric measurements, use one or the other; never mix them up. Many patterns are written for several sizes. Instructions for the smallest size are given first, then for the remaining sizes in parentheses. If only one instruction or figure is given, it pertains to all the sizes. The pattern should also tell you the equipment and amounts of yarn required and the tension (gauge) (see page 30).

Knitting instructions are generally given in abbreviated form to save space. The pattern will explain what each abbrevation means and, where appropriate, how you make that stitch or perform that technique.

When a sequence of stitches is repeated, this is indicated with asterisks or parentheses. For example, '*p3, k3, rep from * to end' means to purl three stitches, then knit three stitches, then repeat that sequence to the end of the row. This instruction could also be written '(p3, k3), rep to end'.

When there are decreases or increases, a figure or figures will often be given in square brackets — for example [56 sts] — to indicate how many stitches you should have at the end of that row or section of knitting.

Before beginning, read the pattern completely, to make sure you understand all the abbreviations. Look up any unfamiliar terms or stitches. If attempting a stitch pattern for the first time, work a sample swatch to familiarize yourself with the sequence before beginning the garment itself. It is less frustrating to have to re-do a small swatch than part of a large garment. If you cannot understand part of a pattern, don't assume that the pattern is wrong or that you are stupid; some sections of a pattern may only become clear once you are actually knitting them.

Abbreviations

The following are the most common abbreviations used in this book. Abbreviations that are specific to a particular pattern are explained on the pattern page.

alt alternate

beg begin/beginning

C1, C2, C3 etc contrast colour 1, 2, 3 etc (when there are several contrast colours)

C4B make 4-stitch right-twisting cable: slip 2 sts onto cable needle, hold cable needle at back of work, k2 from left needle, k2 from cable needle

C4F make 4-stitch left-twisting cable: slip 2 sts onto cable needle, hold cable needle at front of work, k2 from left needle, k2 from cable needle

C6B make 6-stitch right-twisting cable: slip 3 sts onto cable needle, hold cable needle at back of work, k3 from left needle, k3 from cable needle

C6F make 6-stitch left-twisting cable: slip 3 sts onto cable needle, hold cable needle at front of work, k3 from left needle, k3 from cable needle

CC contrast colour (when there is only one contrast colour)

CO cast on (see also 'end cast-on')

col(s) colour(s)

cont continue

dec decrease/decreasing

double rib 1 row of knit 2, purl 2, alternating with 1 row of purl 2, knit 2, continued to form pattern

dpn(s) double-pointed needle(s)

end cast-on a cast-on performed in the middle of a row: wrap the yarn around your left thumb, then insert the tip of the right needle into the thumb loop and transfer it to the right needle. This casts on one stitch. Rep as needed.

foll follows/following

garter st garter stitch

in inch(es)

inc increase/increasing; or, increase by working into the front and back of the same stitch

k knit

kfb increase by one stitch, by knitting into front and back of same stitch

knitwise inserting needle into next stitch as for a knit stitch (that is, from left to right and front to back)

k1b knit into the next stitch one row below, slipping st above off left needle (to create fisherman's rib pattern)

k2tog knit 2 stitches together to decrease number of stitches by one

k3tog knit 3 stitches together to decrease number of stitches by two

L work loop stitch: see explanation and photographs on pages 78–79

m1 make one (increase) by picking up the loop between two stitches and working into the back of it

MC Main Colour

p purl

patt pattern

pfb increase by one stitch, by purling into front and back of same stitch

prev previous

psso pass slipped stitch over previous stitch

purlwise inserting needle into next stitch as for a purl stitch (that is, from right to left and back to front)

rem remain(s)/remaining

rep repeat(ed)

rev St st reverse stocking stitch: one row knit, one row purl, as for stocking stitch, but with the reverse (purl) side of the fabric used as the right side of the work

RS right side(s)

sl 1 slip 1 stitch onto other needle without working it

st(s) stitch(es)

st holder stitch holder

St st stocking stitch/stockinette: one row knit, one row purl, continued to form pattern

tbl through back loop

tog together

WS wrong side(s)

yrn take yarn around needle to create new stitch

Crochet abbreviations

ch chain

dc double crochet (US single crochet/sc)

sl st slip stitch

Tension (gauge)

Tension, or gauge, refers to the number of stitches and rows per 2.5 cm (1 in) of the knitted fabric. Every knitting pattern will tell you what gauge should be used; it is vital to pay attention to this, as the gauge determines what size the finished garment will be. Every knitter knits at a different tension; some people knit loosely and others tightly. A slight difference in tension may not be crucial in an item such as a scarf, but it can ruin a garment such as a sweater that needs to fit precisely.

As well as determining the fit of a garment, an even tension produces a neat, even fabric. If you are a beginner, you may find that your tension varies from stitch to stitch and row to row at first. This is frustrating, but persevere; as you grow accustomed to the feel of the needles and yarn, and develop a smooth, rhythmic action, the fabric that you produce will become neater and more even.

Even if you think that you knit at a standard tension, always check your tension before beginning a garment. The half-hour or so that this takes is a worthwhile investment of time, as it will prevent the disappointment, and the waste of time and money, of a garment that does not fit.

The two tension swatches pictured opposite were knitted by the same person from the same wool, one of them on 4 mm (US 6/UK 8) needles and the other on 5 mm (US 8/UK 6) needles. The difference in needle size results in a noticeable variation in the size of the swatches.

Knitting a tension square

Before you being to knit a garment, you will need to check your tension by knitting a tension square. To do this, cast on using the size of needles specified and the yarn that you intend to use, whether the specified yarn or a substitute. Cast on until you have enough stitches so that they measure about 15 cm (6 in) when spread, without stretching, along the needle. Work in stocking stitch, or the stitch specified in the pattern, for at least 15 cm (6 in).

Cast off and (if appropriate for the yarn) lightly press the tension square. Insert a pin a few stitches in (do not measure from the sides, as the side edge is always slightly distorted). Measure precisely 10 cm (4 in) from the pin and place another pin at that point as a marker. Do the same vertically, placing the first pin a few rows in from the cast-on or cast-off edge. Count how many stitches and rows there are between the pins; this is your tension.

Hint

Save your tension square; it may come in handy later for testing how well the yarn washes, and whether it can tolerate being pressed. It is better to risk ruining a tension square than a finished garment.

Pin the ball band to the tension square so that you have a reference of the yarn used and how it knits up.

If the counts are correct, go ahead and start knitting the garment. If you have more stitches than the specified tension, you are knitting too tightly, and your garment will be too short and too narrow. Make another tension square with slightly larger needles, and measure again. If you have fewer stitches than specified, you are knitting too loosely, and your garment will be too long and too wide. Make another tension square with slightly smaller needles, and measure again.

If necessary, repeat this process more than once, until the tension is correct. This may seem tedious, but it will save disappointment, time and money in the long run.

Substituting yarns

In general, it is best to buy the exact yarn specified in the pattern, as the pattern has been designed for that yarn and other yarns may give different results. However, if you can't find (or don't like) the specified yarn, you will need to find another yarn of similar composition, properties and texture to the specified yarn. Check the thickness; the substitute yarn should be the same thickness as the specified yarn so that it will knit up to the same gauge. You can check the required gauge by looking at the ball band.

To work out how many balls to buy, it is more accurate to go by the length of yarn in the ball than by the ball's weight. For example, if the pattern specifies 13 balls of a yarn that contains 120 metres or yards per ball, you require 1560 metres or yards of yarn. If your intended substitute yarn measures 95 metres or yards per ball, divide 1560 by 95; the result is 16.4, meaning you will need to buy 17 balls of the substitute yarn.

Whether you are using the specified yarn or a substitute, it is always advisable to buy an extra ball just in case, as quantities of yarn used will vary between knitters. Always knit a tension swatch before starting your garment, so that you can adjust the needle size if necessary.

Note that even when you find a substitute yarn that knits up to the same tension, the knitted fabric that it produces may not have the same appearance as that of the recommended yarn. This is due to differences in, for example, the way the yarn is spun or finished. If possible, buy just one ball of the substitute yarn to start with and knit a sample swatch to see if you are happy with the look of the yarn.

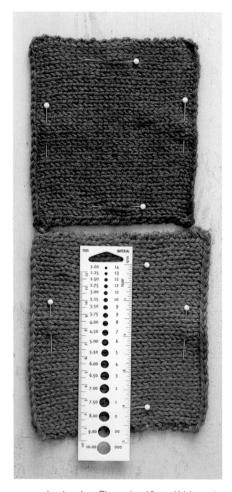

measuring tension Place pins 10 cm (4 in) apart and count the stitches and rows between them.

Casual bag

This stylish casual bag uses a lovely Japanese silk-mix yarn with gradual colour changes that give the effect of soft stripes. Bands of eyelets on one side provide textural variation. Lining the bag is optional, but will add strength and prevent the knitted fabric from stretching too much or becoming misshapen. Choose a lining colour that contrasts with the yarn and looks good when showing through the eyelets. If you don't want to line the whole bag, at least line the strap with ribbon to prevent it from stretching.

The back of this bag is plain, but you could easily work it in a pattern or a textured stitch to make the bag reversible. In this case, omit the button and button closure and instead make two lengths of knitted cord (see page 35) at least 15 cm (6 in) long, attach one to the centre of each top edge, and tie to fasten.

Materials
Three 50 g (1¾ oz) balls Noro Silk Garden, Col 208
If lining the whole bag: 35 cm (14 in) of a densely woven fabric such as quilters' cotton, 115 cm (45 in) wide
If lining the strap only: 90 cm (35 in) petersham or grosgrain ribbon, 4 cm (1½ in) wide
1 button or toggle, 5–6 cm (2–2½ in) long

Tools
4 mm (US 6/UK 8) needles
1 set 4 mm (US 6/UK 8) double-pointed needles
(or sizes required to give correct tension)
4 mm (US 6/UK 8) crochet hook
Wool needle

Size
Bag approx 30 cm (12 in) square; strap approx 85 cm (33 in) long

Tension (gauge)
17 sts and 26 rows to 10 cm (4 in) over St st using 4 mm (US 6/UK 8) needles, or size required to give this tension

yrn (yarn round needle) Take the yarn around the needle to create an extra stitch.

row 14 Purl into the right-hand leg of the stitch made by the yrn in the previous row.

Hint

To avoid sudden colour changes when joining in a new ball of this yarn, unwind the new ball to a section that is the same colour as the last row knitted with the previous ball, and make the join at that point.

CO 55 sts. Work in St st until work measures 30 cm (12 in), ending with RS row.
Next row (WS) Knit. This row marks the fold line for the bottom of the bag.

Work second side of bag:
Rows 1–12 Work in St st, beg with a knit row.
Row 13 (RS) Begin to make eyelets: k2, *yrn, k2tog*, rep from * to * until 1 st rem, k1. (See photograph.)
Row 14 Purl. (This row completes the eyelets; see photograph.)
Rows 15–18 Cont in St st.
Rep rows 13–18 four more times. This completes the pattern repeats.

Cont in St st for 35 rows, or until work measures same length as first side of bag, ending with WS row. Cast off loosely on RS.

Fold bag in half along fold line, with RS tog, and sew up using backstitch. Turn bag to RS. Using crochet hook and with RS facing, crochet in dc (US sc) around top, starting at a side seam and working 1 dc into each cast-off or cast-on stitch.

To make strap, with RS facing, pick up 9 sts with knitting needle, centring them over side seam. Work in St st, beg with a purl row, until strap measures 85 cm (33 in) or length desired. Cast off. Sew cast-off end

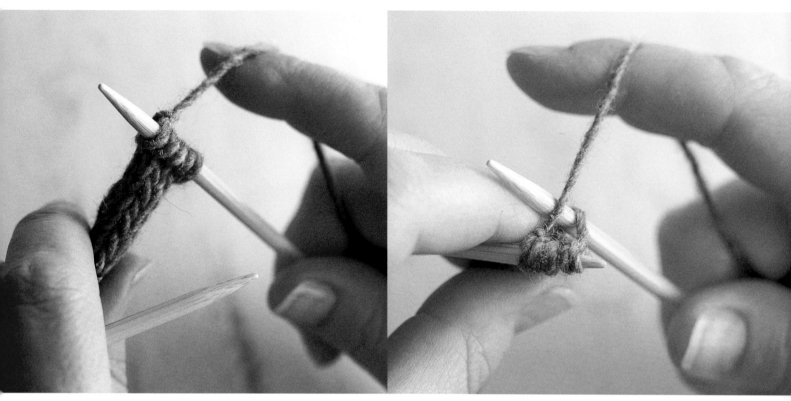

knitted cord At the end of the row, slide the work from the left-hand to the right-hand end of the needle.

starting a new row The ball end of the yarn will be at the left of the work.

of strap to other side seam of bag, centring strap over side seam.

LINING AND FINISHING

If lining bag, measure height and width of both bag and strap. Cut a piece of lining fabric 1 cm (⅜ in) larger all round than size of bag. Cut another piece the same width as strap but 2 cm (¾ in) longer. Fold bag lining in half widthways, with RS tog and raw edges even, and sew 1 cm (⅜ in) seam down each side. Fold sides of strap lining under 1 cm (⅜ in) on WS and press. With RS tog and matching raw edges, pin ends of strap lining to bag lining, centring strap lining over side seam of bag lining, and sew

1 cm (⅜ in) seam for width of strap lining. Fold top edge of bag lining under 1 cm (⅜ in) on WS and press. Turn lining to RS. Insert lining into bag, WS tog, and slip-stitch folded edges of top of lining about 1 cm (⅜ in) from top edge of bag, using matching thread. Slip-stitch strap lining to underside of strap.

To finish bag, using dpns, CO 4 sts and make about 12 cm (5 in) of knitted cord (see right). Sew both ends to centre of top edge of back of bag. Fold loop over to front of bag, keeping top edges of bag even, and mark position of button. Sew on button using strong thread. Sew in all loose ends.

Making knitted cord

Using two double-pointed needles, cast on 4 or 5 stitches and knit 1 row. Do not turn the work; instead, slide the stitches along the needle from the left to the right tip. Transfer this needle to your left hand; the ball end of the yarn will be coming from the left of the row of stitches. Knit the next row, pulling the yarn firmly across the back of the stitches as you do so. Repeat until the cord is the desired length. Cut yarn, thread through all the stitches and tie off firmly.

Felted bag and hat

The fibres of untreated wool have a natural
tendency to shrink and mat when washed
incorrectly or rubbed. Normally you wouldn't
want to encourage this, but this trait can be
exploited to produce lovely felted fabrics and
garments such as this hat and bag. The items
are knitted first, then machine-washed in hot
water; the agitation of the wash cycle combined
with the hot water causes the wool to shrink and
felt. You can easily do this at home, but you need
to keep an eye on the items so that they don't
shrink beyond the required size. It's a good idea
to knit a small swatch and then wash it as
instructed so that you can check the shrinkage
rate and see how long it takes to felt.

Materials for bag
Mollydale Hand-dyed Wool 8 ply (DK): 300 g
(10½ oz) of each of Lime Green for Main
Colour (MC) and Marine Blue for Contrast
Colour (CC) (these yarns are available from
www.mollydale.com.au)

Tools
7 mm (US 10½/UK 2) circular needles
(60 or 80 cm/24 or 32 in long)
7 mm (US 10½/UK 2) double-pointed needles
(or sizes required to give correct tension)
Wool needle
Large button or toggle

Size
Body of bag: width 34 cm (13½ in) at base,
54 cm (21 in) at top; height of sides 24 cm
(9½ in). Straps: 80 cm (32 in) long

Tension (gauge)
13 sts and 17 rows to 10 cm (4 in) over St st
using 7 mm needles and two strands
of wool held together

Felted bag

A double strand of 8-ply (DK) wool is used throughout. The finished knitted bag is large and loose but the felting process will result in a firm fabric. Garter st is used for the base. Stocking st is used for the body of the bag. The straps and button loop are knitted separately. The sides of the bag are knitted with the wrong side (WS) facing, so the purl side is the right side (RS). The bag is turned inside out and the top border, straps and button loop are all sewn into place before the bag is felted. The button is added after felting.

BASE OF BAG

With circular needles and 2 strands of CC held together, CO 48 sts.
Knit 48 rows.
Leaving sts on the needle, rotate work and pick up and k 24 sts (1 st for each ridge) on the side edge, 48 sts from the cast-on edge and 24 sts from the other short side [144 sts]. Place a marker at beg of round.
Change to MC and cont knitting with circular needles until yarn is almost finished, ending at start of round where marker was placed.
To make top border, change to CC and cont for a further 10 cm (4 in).
Cast off loosely. Cut yarn, leaving approx 3 m (3 yd) for sewing top border. Fold the top border in half to the inside of bag (RS) and slip-stitch cast-off edge to bag.

STRAPS

Using 2 strands of CC and dpns, CO 2 sts.
Rows 1 & 3 Knit.
Row 2 Inc in each st [4 sts].

Row 4 Inc in 1st st, k to last st, inc in last st [6 sts].
Row 5 & 6 Rep rows 3 and 4 [8 sts].
Knit 5 more rows without further inc. Do not turn work after last row.
Begin making knitted cord (as explained on page 35) for strap: slide stitches to other end of needle, take yarn across back of work, and keeping a firm tension on the yarn, k8. Do not turn work, but continue in this manner until work measures 100 cm (39½ in) from cast-on.
Turn work and k 5 rows.
Now start the dec for the last 6 rows.
6th-last row k2tog, k to last 2 st, k2tog [6 sts].
5th-last row Knit.
4th-last & 3rd-last rows Rep last 2 rows (4 sts).
2nd-last row k2tog, k2tog [2 sts].
Cast off last 2 sts.

BUTTON LOOP

Using 2 strands of CC, CO 35 sts.
Next row Cast off 35 sts.

MAKING UP

With RS facing, pin straps to outside of bag on both sides, taking care that they are placed evenly. Measure distance between the handles of one side and pin the button loop in the middle of this space. Slip-stitch the straps and button loop securely onto the bag. Sew in any loose ends.

FELTING THE BAG

Place the bag in a zippered mesh laundry bag or a pillowcase tied at the neck. Half fill a top-loading washing machine with hot water and add a generous amount of wool-approved detergent. The water level

Joining yarns by splicing

When joining yarn that has not been treated to make it machine-washable, you can splice the ends together. Splicing exploits the tendency of untreated wool to mat and felt. To splice, unravel one end of the wool and tear off about 7 cm (3 in) of one strand of the wool. Do the same to the yarn to be joined. Wet both ends with warm water and overlap them on the palm of your hand. Rub very vigorously to create heat, while also moving the join up and down your palm until both ends have felted together.

For other yarns, you will need to tie the ends together using a reef knot (see diagram on page 49). Where possible, make the knot at the side of the work, not in the middle of a row. Using a wool needle, weave the tails of the knot along the seams or edges of the work.

should be high enough to allow the bag free movement during the felting process.

Start the machine and check the bag every few minutes. You may need to wash the bag 2 or 3 times before it reaches the desired size. Start the wash again before the machine finishes its cycle and begins to empty the water.

Once the bag has felted to a firm fabric, remove the bag and rinse it in warm water. Spin the rinse water out on a gentle spin cycle. Stretch the bag and the straps into shape and allow to dry in the shade. Once dry, sew button to centre of bag on opposite side to loop.

To care for your bag, gently hand-wash, reshape and dry in the shade. Use a warm iron if you wish.

Felted broad-brimmed hat

Using 7 mm straight needles and mohair and wool in MC held together, CO 91 sts.
Work 2 rows in garter st.
Row 3 (k8, inc in next st), rep to end.
Row 4 (k9, inc in next st), rep to end [110 sts].
Row 5 to 14 Cont in garter st.
Row 15 (k9, k2tog), rep to end.
Row 16 (k8, k2tog), rep to end.
Row 17 (k7, k2tog), rep to end.
Row 18 (k6, k2tog), rep to end.
Change to 7 mm circular needles and CC. Cont with circular needles until work measures 20 cm (8 in) from where you began knitting with the circular needles.

SHAPE CROWN

Change to MC. Place marker at beg of row.
Row 1 (k5, k2tog), rep to end of round.
Row 2 Knit.
Row 3 (k5, k2tog), rep to end of round.
Row 4 Knit.
Row 5 (k2, k2tog), rep to end of round.
Row 6 Knit.
Row 7 (k1, k2tog), rep to end of round.
Row 8 (k2 tog), rep until 4 sts rem.
Cut yarn and sew through rem sts to secure. Using a flat seam, sew up bottom seam on the garter st brim and darn in any loose ends. Your hat is now ready to felt.

FELTING

Put a top-loading washing machine on the small load setting and fill it with hot water. Add a generous amount of wool-approved detergent. Set the machine on a normal cycle, keeping watch and checking the hat frequently. You may need to stop the machine and start a second or third cycle to achieve the desired effect. Keeping watch on the felting process will ensure the hat felts to the required size. (It's very easy to end up with a doll-sized hat.)

When the hat is sufficiently felted, rinse it in warm water, spin out the excess rinse water and place the hat onto a hat block or wig stand. Allow to dry in the shade.

CARE

Using wool-approved detergent, gently hand-wash and rinse in warm water. Spin out the rinse water on spin cycle in washing machine. Reshape, place on a hat block or wig stand (a pudding bowl will also do the trick) and dry in the shade.

Materials for hat

Main Colour (MC): 100 g (3½ oz) Mollydale Mohair 8-ply (DK) in Lime Green; 100 g (3½ oz) Mollydale Hand-dyed Wool 8-ply (DK) in Lime Green

Contrast Colour (CC): 100 g (3½ oz) Mollydale Mohair 8-ply (DK) in Marine Blue; 100 g (3½ oz) Mollydale Hand-dyed Wool 8-ply (DK) in Marine Blue (yarns are available from www.mollydale.com.au; if substituting yarns, note that the actual amounts used for hat are: brim and top, 50 g/1¾ oz each of mohair and wool in MC; body of hat, 50 g/1¾ oz each of mohair and wool in CC)

Tools

7 mm (US 10½/UK 2) needles
7 mm (US 10½/UK 2) circular needles, 40 cm (16 in) long
(or sizes required to give correct tension)
Hat block or wig stand

Size

To fit average-sized woman's head (approx 56 cm/22 in)

Tension (gauge)

12 sts and 18 rows to 10 cm (4 in) over St st on 7 mm needles using wool and mohair yarns held together

Two-toned ruched scarf

Simple decreases and increases give a ruched effect in this simple and stylish scarf. Big needles and loose tension give the desired airy effect.

Materials

Main Colour (MC): Two 50 g
(1¾ oz) balls Cleckheaton
Mohair 12 ply, Col 260
Contrast Colour (CC): One
50 g (1¾ oz) ball Jo Sharp
Silkroad Aran Tweed,
Col 139 Spring

Tools

9 mm (US 13/UK 00) needles
6.5 mm (US 10½/UK 3)
needles
(or sizes required to give
correct tension)
Wool needle

Size

Approx 190 x 15 cm
(75 x 6 in)

Tension (gauge)

10 sts and 12 rows to 10 cm
(4 in) over St st using
Cleckheaton Mohair and
9 mm needles, or size
required to give this tension

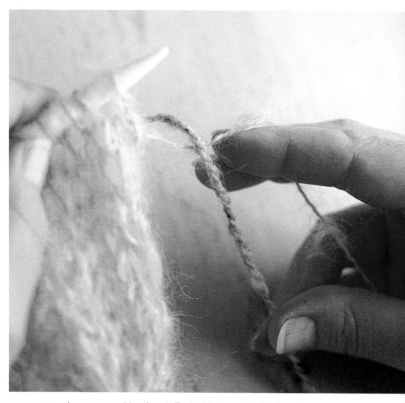

carrying yarn up side of work To do this, loosely twist the colour not being used once around the one in use, then continue knitting.

Using 9 mm needles, MC and cable cast-on, CO 30 sts.

Row 1 Knit.
Row 2 Purl.
Rows 3–16 Cont in St st.
*Change to 6.5 mm needles and CC.
Row 17 (RS) (k2tog), rep to end [15 sts].
Rows 18–22 Cont in garter st.
Change to 9 mm needles and MC.
Row 23 (RS) (kfb), rep to end [30 sts].
Row 24 Purl.
Rows 25–38 Cont in St st.*
Rep from * to * 11 times, or until scarf is desired length. Cast off loosely.
Sew in loose ends. Do not press or block; damp finish if desired (see page 25).

Hints

When choosing yarns for this scarf, you will get a particularly pleasing effect if you choose one yarn that is mottled or variegated and the other plain.

Be sure to maintain a loose tension throughout, especially when increasing; tight tension here will make it more difficult to knit into both the front and back of the same stitch as required.

When changing colours, do not cut the yarn, but carry it loosely up the sides of the work (see photograph above). The natural curl of the edge of the stocking stitch fabric will serve to conceal the different yarns.

Men's sweater

This simple, chunky, no-frills men's sweater has crew-neck and polo-neck variations. Knitted in pure wool, it will give many years of sturdy service and comfortable wear. The sweater pictured has a polo neck; instructions for a round-neck variation are given on page 45.

The plainness of a garment such as this makes it a great template for experimenting with stitch textures and patterns. You could add columns of cables, make it entirely in moss stitch, or add an intricate aran panel up the centre of the front and sleeves. If you're planning any embellishment of the basic pattern, always remember to knit a tension square and make any necessary adjustments to your tension.

Materials

15 (15, 16, 17) 50 g (1¾ oz) balls Nundle
    Woollen Mill Pure New Wool 12 ply in Olive

Tools

6 mm (US 10/UK 4) needles
5.5 mm (US 9/UK 5) needles
(or sizes required to achieve correct tension)
4 stitch holders
Wool needle

Size

	S	M	L	XL
Length from shoulder to hem				
	75 cm	77 cm	79 cm	80 cm
	(29½ in)	(30 in)	(31 in)	(31½ in)
Chest				
	105 cm	110 cm	115 cm	120 cm
	(41 in)	(43 in)	(45 in)	(47 in)
Sleeve seam				
	45 cm	46 cm	47 cm	48 cm
	(17½ in)	(18 in)	(18½ in)	(19 in)

Tension (gauge)

15 sts and 20 rows to 10 cm (4 in) over St st on 6 mm (US 10/UK 4) needles, or size required to give this tension

preparing to knit the collar The seams have been joined, with the back left raglan seam left open to allow the neck-edge stitches to be picked up for the collar.

picking up stitches for collar Starting at left back shoulder, pick up specified number of stitches evenly around neck edge, including stitches from holders.

Working with multi-size patterns

When a pattern, such as this one, is written for more than one size, the first figure given in any part of the instructions is for the smallest size. Figures for larger sizes are given in parentheses. Instructions that apply to all sizes are given as a single figure. To make it easier to work with the right set of figures, read through the whole pattern before you begin knitting and highlight all the numbers for the relevant size.

BACK

With smaller needles, CO 80 (84, 88, 92) sts. Work 10 rows in double rib. Change to larger needles and work in St st until piece measures 51 (52, 53, 54) cm (20, 20½, 20¾, 21¼ in), or length desired, from beg, ending with a purl row.

Shape raglan armholes: cast off 4 sts at beg of next 2 rows [72, 76, 80, 84 sts].
Next row sl 1, k1, psso, k to end.
Next row sl 1, p1, psso, p to end.
Rep prev 2 rows until 30 (32, 32, 34) sts rem. Work 1 row. Slip sts onto st holder.

FRONT

Work as for back until piece is 11 cm (4¼ in) shorter than back, ending on a purl row. Shape neck as foll: sl 1, k1, psso, k18 (18, 18, 19) sts. Slip rem sts onto st holder. Return to sts on needle and cont to dec 1 st at neck edge in next 2 rows, while at the same time dec, as before, at armhole edge at beg of knit rows. Then dec at neck edge in every 4th row 4 (4, 5, 5) times, at the same time dec at armhole edge at beg of all knit rows [2 sts]. Work 2 rows. K2 tog. Fasten off. Return to sts on holder. Put centre 14 (14, 16, 18) sts onto another st holder. Put rem sts onto needle. Cont, to correspond with first side, reversing shaping.

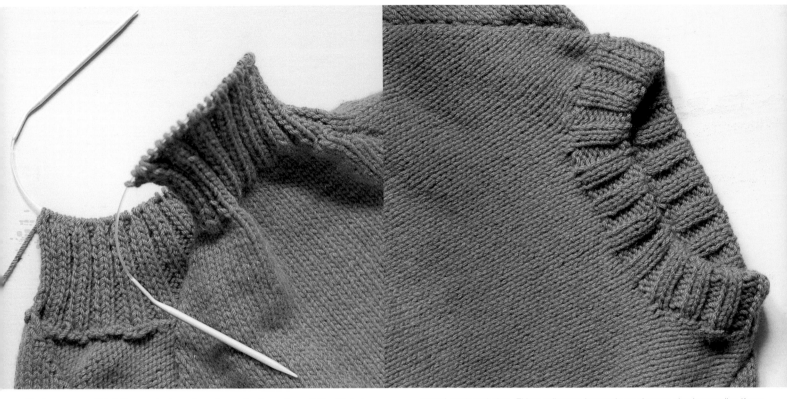

collar in progress Work the required number of rows for the collar variation that you are making, then cast off loosely and make up as instructed.

round-neck variation Either collar can be made on dpns or circular needles if you wish; first sew the entire back left raglan seam before picking up the stitches.

SLEEVES (MAKE TWO ALIKE)

With smaller needles, cast on 40 (44, 44, 48) sts. Work 10 rows in double rib. Change to larger needles and work in St st, inc at each end of every 8th row until there are 56 (60, 60, 64) sts.

Cont until piece measures 45 (46, 47, 48) cm (17¾, 18, 18½, 18¾ in), or length desired, from beg, ending with a purl row.

Shape raglan sleeve: cast off 4 sts at beg of next 2 rows [48, 52, 52, 56 sts].

Next row sl 1, k1, psso, k to end.

Next row sl 1, p1, psso, p to end [46, 50, 50, 54 sts].

Rep prev 2 rows until 8 (8, 6, 6) sts rem. Work 1 row and leave on st holder.

POLO NECK

With a damp cloth, press pieces (except for ribbed sections) lightly on WS. Unless otherwise stated, sew seams with back stitch. Join raglan seams, leaving left back raglan seam open. With RS facing and smaller needles, evenly pick up 80 (84, 88, 88) stitches around neck, 1 st in from edge, including sts from holders. Work 20 rows in double rib and cast off loosely in double rib.

MAKING UP

Join left back raglan seam, side and sleeve seams using backstitch. With flat seam, join collar, reversing seam halfway where collar folds to front. Sew in all loose ends.

Round-neck variation

Make as for polo-neck sweater up to and including picking up 80 (84, 88, 88) sts around neck. Using smaller needles, work in double rib for 7 cm (2¾ in). Change to larger needles and cont in double rib for 7 cm (2¾ in). Cast off loosely in double rib. To make up, join left back raglan seam, side and sleeve seams using back stitch. With flat seam, join collar. Fold collar in half to wrong side and slip-stitch loosely into place. Sew in all loose ends.

Snowflake slippers

These cosy slippers for loafing about the house have a snowflake motif worked in fair isle on the instep. If you like the snowflake design but don't want to attempt it in fair isle, it could be worked in knitting-stitch embroidery instead. This simple technique is explained on page 49.

Materials

For child's size: Nundle Woollen Mill 8 ply (DK) pure new wool, 50 g (1¾ oz): 1 ball Steel Blue for Main Colour (MC), 1 ball Oatmeal for Contrast Colour (CC)

For women's size: Nundle Woollen Mill 8 ply (DK) pure new wool, 50 g (1¾): 2 balls Steel blue for Main Colour (MC), 1 ball Oatmeal for Contrast Colour (CC)

Tools

4 mm (US 6/UK 8) needles (or size required to give correct tension)

Wool needle

Size

These are easy-fitting items; actual length from toe to back of heel is 22 cm (8½ in) for child's size and 26 cm (10¼ in) for women's size. To make smaller slippers, use smaller needles; to make larger slippers, use larger needles

Tension

20 sts to 10 cm (4 in) over St st on 4 mm (US 6/UK 8) needles, or size required to achieve this tension

Abbreviations and explanations

K1b = knit into the next st one row below, slipping st above off left needle (this creates fisherman's rib pattern)

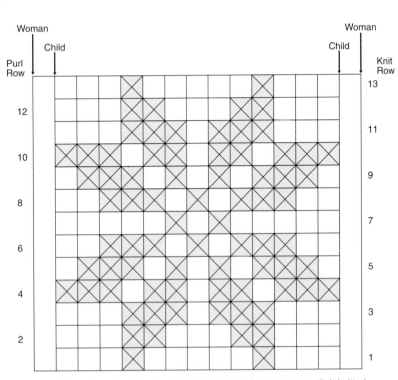

snowflake pattern A shaded square with a cross in it represents a stitch knitted in the contrast colour.

knitting stitch embroidery If you don't want to knit the design in, you can embroid it instead (see instructions for knitting stitch embroidery opposite).

SOLE AND SIDES

With MC, CO 66 (78) sts.

Row 1 Knit.

Row 2 Knit.

Row 3 k1, m1, k30 (36), m1, k4, m1, k30 (36), m1, k1 [70, 82 sts].

Row 4 Knit.

Row 5 k1, m1, k31 (37), m1, k6, m1, k31 (37), m1, k1 [74, 86 sts].

Row 6 Knit.

Row 7 k1, m1, k32 (38), m1, k8, m1, k32 (38), m1, k1 [78, 90 sts].

Rows 8–10 Knit (without further inc).

Row 11 (k1, k1b) until 2 sts rem, k2.

Repeat prev row 5 (9) times.

SHAPING

Note Unless otherwise stated, stitches are slipped knitwise.

Row 1 k46 (54), sl 1, k1, psso, turn.

Row 2 sl 1 purlwise, k13 (15), p2tog, turn.

Row 3 sl 1, k13 (15), sl 1, k1, psso, turn.

Rep Rows 2–3 once, then rep row 2 again.

SNOWFLAKE PATTERN

Note Always carry the contrast shade to the ends of the rows at back of work. The following 13 snowflake rows are in stocking stitch, beginning with a knit row. Follow the chart above for changes of colour; sts to be worked in CC are shaded.

Row 1 sl 1, k13 (15) as per Row 1 of chart, then sl 1, k1, psso.

Row 2 sl 1 purlwise, p13 (15) as per Row 2 of chart, then p2tog.

Row 3 sl 1, k13 (15) as per Row 3 of chart, then sl 1, k1, psso.

Cont in this way, with slipped stitches at beg of rows and decreases at end of rows, while following Rows 4–13 of chart.

Row 14 In MC, sl 1 purlwise, p13 (15), p2tog.

COMPLETE SLIPPER TOP

The rem rows are worked in garter st.

Row 1 sl 1, k13 (15), sl 1, k1, psso, turn.

Row 2 sl 1 purlwise, k13 (15), p2tog, turn.

Rep prev 2 rows 9 (12) times, turn.

Next row Knit to end of row [40, 44 sts].

Next row Knit one row.

Next row Change to CC and knit 2 rows. Cast off loosely.

MAKING UP

Using a flat seam, sew heel and sole of foot. Sew in all loose ends.

KNITTING STITCH EMBROIDERY

Also known as Swiss darning, this simple embroidery stitch imitates the appearance of stocking stitch fabric.

1 Thread a wool needle with a contrast-coloured yarn of the same weight as the main yarn used. To start, weave in the yarn invisibly at the back of the work.

2 Bring the needle out at the base of the first stitch to be covered then take it to the back, under the top of the same stitch, and out again.

3 Insert it at the base of the stitch, at the same point where it first came out. Take it across the back of the work and out at the base of the next stitch to be covered.

Repeat Steps 2–3 until you have embroidered over all stitches to be covered.

This stitch can be worked horizontally or vertically; see the diagrams below.

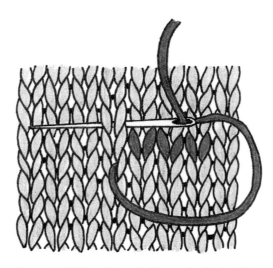

diagram 1 Knitting stitch embroidery worked horizontally

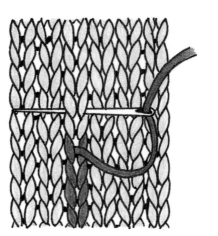

diagram 2 Knitting stitch embroidery worked vertically

Joining in yarn

When you come to the end of a ball of yarn, you will need to join in a new one. Wherever possible, do this at the end of a row, as this will result in a less visible join and the yarn ends can be hidden in the seam.

One method is simply to drop the old yarn, pick up the new one and work a few rows. Then tie a double overhand knot (see Diagram 3), drawing up the yarns so that the stitches around the join have the same tension as the others. When making up the garment, sew the ends into the seam to conceal them.

For knitting in the round, however, and other situations where joining in the middle of a row is unavoidable, use a reef knot (see Diagram 4) and later sew the ends along the rows as neatly as possible.

diagram 3 An overhand knot (a double overhand knot is made by tying a second knot in the same way on top of the first)

diagram 4 Joining two lengths of yarn with a reef knot

Two-toned jacket

This jacket is knitted sideways, from right front to left front, and takes the form of a large rectangle with gaps left for the armholes. The corrugated garter-stitch pattern creates a stretch-rib effect.

The finished garment can be pressed to size, to create a looser fit. A row tension of 36 rows to 10 cm (4 in) in the finished garment can be blocked to 26 rows to 10 cm (4 in). The stitch tension determines the length of the garment and the row tension determines its chest size. The secret of a good fit is to make the back only as wide as you are across the shoulders.

The front edges of the jacket can be folded and pinned in a number of ways to create different collar effects.

Materials
Signatur 8-ply (DK) pure new wool, 50 g (1¾ oz) balls: Main Colour (MC) 11 (12, 13, 14) balls; Contrast Colour (CC) 3 (3, 4, 5) balls

Tools
3.75 mm (US 5/UK 9) needles
4 mm (US 6/UK 8) needles
4.5 mm (US 7/UK 7) needles
(or sizes required to give correct tension)

Size
To fit chest: 81 (94, 104, 117) cm (32, 37, 41, 46 in). Finished garment: chest 92 (102, 114, 125) cm (36¼, 40, 44¾, 49 in); Length 68 (73, 77, 79) cm (26¾, 28¾, 30¼, 32 in)

Tension
For the body: 21½ sts to 10 cm (4 in) over St st on 4.5 mm (US 7/UK 7) needles. For the sleeve, 22½ sts to 10 cm (4 in) on 4 mm (US 6/UK 8) needles, or sizes required to give these tensions

Multicoloured beret

This is a good project for using up odds and ends. Use a mix of plain and fancy yarns, and ensure that yarns A, B, E, F and I are 8-ply (DK) and will knit up to the specified tension.

Materials
Small amounts of 12 different yarns. Yarns A, B, E, F and I should be 8-ply (DK); for the others, use a variety of fancy or textured yarns

Tools
3.75 mm (US 5/UK 9) needles
4 mm (US 6/UK 8) needles (or sizes required to give correct tension)
4 mm (US 6/UK 8) crochet hook
Wool needle

Size
To fit 55 cm (22 in) head. For a larger fit, use 4.5 mm (US 7/UK 7) needles

Tension
20 sts to 10 cm (4 in) in St st using 4 mm needles and 8-ply (DK) yarn, or size required to achieve this tension

Using larger needles and Yarn A, CO 87 sts.
Row 1 Change to smaller needles and Yarn B, (k1, p1) to end.
Row 2 (p1, k1) to end.
Rep rows 1–2 twice, then change to Yarn C and rep rows 1–2 once [8 rows].
Change to larger needles and cont in St st, changing yarns and working as follows:
Row 1 k4, m1, (k3, m1) to last 2 sts, k2 [115 sts].
Row 2 Purl.
Rows 3–4 In Yarn D, work 2 rows.
Row 5 In Yarn E, work 1 row.
Rows 6–8 In Yarn F, work 3 rows.
Rows 9–10 In Yarn G, work 2 rows.
Rows 11–12 In Yarn A, work 2 rows.

SHAPING BERET
Row 13 In Yarn H, k2, m1, (k9, m1) 12 times, k5 [128 sts].
Row 14 In Yarn I, work 1 row.
Row 15 In Yarn J, work 3 rows.
Row 18 In Yarn K, work 4 rows.
Row 22 In Yarn B, work 2 rows.
Row 24 In Yarn L, work 1 row.
Row 25 (Yarn L) k3, k2tog, (k8, k2tog) 12 times, k3 [115 sts].
Row 26 With Yarn A, work 3 rows.

Row 29 In Yarn C, k2, k2tog, (k7, k2tog) 12 times, k3 [102 sts].
Row 30 (Yarn C) work 3 rows.
Row 33 In Yarn D, k2, k3tog, (k12, k3tog) 6 times, k7 [88 sts].
Row 34 (Yarn D) work 1 row.
Row 35 In Yarn E, work 2 rows.
Row 37 (Yarn E) k2, k3tog, (k10, k3tog) 6 times, k5 [74 sts].
Row 38 In Yarn F, work 1 row.
Row 39 In Yarn G, work 2 rows.
Row 41 In Yarn A, k2, k3tog, (k8, k3tog) 6 times, k3 [60 sts].
Row 42 In Yarn I, work 1 row.
Row 43 (Yarn I) k2, k3tog, (k6, k3tog) 6 times, k1 [46 sts].
Row 44 (Yarn I) p1, (p3tog, p4) 6 times, p3 [34 sts].
Row 45 In Yarn J, (k2, k3tog) 6 times, k4 [22 sts].
Row 46 In Yarn K, (p2 tog) to end [11 sts].

MAKING UP
Using crochet hook, thread yarn through rem 11 sts, draw yarn up firmly and fasten off. Sew centre seam using mattress stitch or fine backstitch. Use crochet hook to weave in loose ends.

Tassel hat

This is a fun, bright design for kids — or for a

not-too-serious adult.

peaks When beginning to shape peaks, put the remaining stitches on a stitch holder.

Materials

50 g (1¾ oz) balls Nundle Woollen Mill pure new wool 8 ply (DK): 2 balls Lime for Main Colour (MC); 1 ball Fern for Contrast Colour (CC)

Tools

4 mm (US 6/UK 8) needles (or size required to give correct tension)

Wool needle

4 mm (US 6/UK 8) crochet hook

Size

Finished circumference:

Child 4–8 years: 46 cm (18 in)

Child 8–12 years: 49 cm (19¼ in)

Adult: 52 cm (20½ in)

Tension (gauge)

20 sts to 10 cm (4 in) over St st on 4 mm needles, or size required to give this tension

---

Using St st throughout, make 2 pieces alike.

With MC, CO 44 (47, 50) sts.

Work 24 (24, 26) rows in St st, beg with a knit row.

With CC, work 8 rows.

With MC, work 20 (20, 22) rows.

SHAPE PEAKS

Row 1 k30 (33, 34), k2tog, k to end.

Row 2 p11 (12, 13), p2tog, turn. (Put rest of stitches on stitch holder; see photograph.)

Row 3 k2tog, k to end.

Row 4 p9, p2tog, turn.

Cont to shape peak, dec in this way at inside edge of every row, until 2 sts rem. K2tog. Fasten off.

Rejoin yarn and cast off centre 16 (17, 18) sts. Transfer rem sts from st holder to left-hand needle, p2tog, then p to end.

Next row k11 (12, 13), sl 1, k1, psso.

Next row p2tog, p to end.

Dec in this way at inside edge of every row, until 2 sts rem. P2tog. Fasten off.

MAKING UP

Press pieces lightly on WS. Using a fine backstitch, join along top and down sides, reversing seams where bottom edge rolls. Using double thickness of MC, crochet two chains each of 42 sts. Attach a chain near each side seam. For tassels, cut six 15 cm (6 in) lengths of MC and join to ends of ties.

Plaited chunky velvet scarf

Made in a thick chenille yarn, this scarf is knitted in three strips, which are then plaited together. This design uses a provisional cast-on, a useful technique when you want both ends of an item to be symmetrical — for instance, in a lace-patterned scarf. Once the provisional cast-on is undone, the exposed knit stitches can be picked up and worked as desired. Don't be daunted if you've never tried this technique; it's gratifyingly easy and is explained at right.

Materials
One 100 g (3½ oz) ball Rozetti Dolphin in Green

Tools
8 mm (US 11/UK 0) needles
  (or size required to give correct tension)
2 medium stitch holders
6 mm (US 10/UK 4) crochet hook
3 small stitch holders or large safety pins

Size
Approx 150 x 7.5 cm (60 x 3 in)

Tension (gauge)
9 sts and 13 rows to 10 cm (4 in) over St st
  using 8 mm needles (or size required to give
  this tension)

Explanations
To make a provisional cast-on, with a crochet hook and smooth waste yarn, loosely work a few more crochet chain sts than are needed for the cast-on edge of the knitted piece. Fasten off loosely; you will need to undo the provisional cast-on later. You will notice that the front of each chain forms smooth loops, while the back of each stitch has a distinct 'hump'. With a knitting needle and the main yarn, pick up a stitch through each of these humps until you have cast on as many stitches as are needed. Work the garment as instructed. When you need to undo the provisional cast-on, simply undo the crochet chain from the loosely fastened end to expose the live stitches. Pick up these stitches and continue as instructed.

provisional cast-on Make crochet chain with waste yarn, then using crochet hook and chenille yarn, pick up 15 sts, one through the back of each chain.

plaiting Plait the three knitted strands firmly, making sure they do not twist.

First, cut 6 lengths of yarn, each 25 cm (10 in) long, for the fringe. Set aside.

Using provisional cast-on (see page 58), CO 15 sts. Transfer sts to knitting needle.
Row 1 Knit.
Row 2 Purl.
Row 3 Knit.
Row 4 Purl.
Next row (RS) k5, slip rem sts onto st holder. Working on these 5 sts, cont in St st until work measures approx 155 cm (61 in) or length desired. Transfer sts to small st holder. Cut yarn, leaving a 15 cm (6 in) tail. Join yarn to rem 10 sts. K5 sts off st holder (leaving rem 5 sts on st holder) and cont

in St st until work measures approx the same length as the previous strip. (Don't worry about making the strips exactly the same length, as you will need to adjust their lengths once they are plaited together.) Transfer sts to another small st holder. Cut yarn, leaving a 15 cm (6 in) tail. Join yarn to rem 5 sts and work in St st as before until this strip is approx the same length as the previous two strips. Transfer sts to a third small st holder. Cut yarn, leaving a 15 cm (6 in) tail.

Plaiting Lay work out, RS facing, on a flat surface. Smooth out the cast-on end of the scarf and hold it in place with a heavy

picking up stitches Pick up the stitches in the order in which they occur on the plaited strips.

finishing After undoing the provisional cast-on, draw a length of yarn through all stitches to make the end of the scarf bunch up, then fasten off.

object. Plait firmly, making sure that the strips do not twist, until you reach the end. Even up the strips by removing the st holders and unravelling row(s) until all the strips are even. Pick up the sts on an 8 mm needle in the order in which they fall on the the plaited strips (see photograph).

Join in yarn, leaving a 15 cm (6 in) tail. With RS facing, work 4 rows St st. Do not cast off. Cut yarn, leaving a 15 cm (6 in) tail. Take all sts off the needle. Cut two 30 cm (12 in) lengths of yarn, and using a crochet hook, draw one piece of yarn through all the sts. Draw up the yarn and tie off firmly, so the end of the scarf bunches together.

For the other end of the scarf, undo the provisional cast-on and repeat the same procedure, tying off firmly.

Weave in ends of yarn at the start of the second and third plaited strips. (Use a crochet hook, as this yarn is too thick to be threaded through a needle.)

For the fringe, using a crochet hook and 3 strands of the fringe yarn, make a fringe at each end of the scarf, pulling through from front to back. Also catch in the tied-off ends of the drawing-up yarn and any other tails of yarn. Knot the end of each fringe strand to prevent the yarn from fraying.

Storing knitted items

Always store knitted garments flat; if put on a hanger, the weight of the garment will distort it, or the hanger may poke through the shoulders. If storing the garment for any length of time, wash or dry clean it first. Store in a cloth bag or a pillow-case, not a plastic bag, as this will not allow the knitted fabric to breathe.

Pure silk top and tie-front jacket

The semi-fitted sleeveless top, worked in stocking stitch, has gentle side shaping and a ladder-stitch panel at the front yoke. The jacket features extended fronts that may be tied at centre front, left open or wrapped and fastened. The bottom of the sleeve is gently flared, with a notched detail at the seam. The jacket back is worked in stocking stitch, with the fronts and sleeves in ladder stitch. A picot trim in crochet finishes all edges of both garments.

The ladder-stitch pattern has been devised so that when the designated stitch is dropped, it will ladder down only until it is stopped by a yarn forward of a prior row. The fabric then becomes quite organic as the stitches around the ladder start to move and enlarge as they take up the excess yarn from the ladder.

Materials

Tussah Tape, 100% pure silk, 50 g (1¾oz), in colour Natural: for top, 3 (3, 3) balls; for jacket, 5 (6, 7) balls (available from www.sarahdurrant.com)

Tools

5.5 mm (US 9/UK 5) knitting needles (or size required to give correct tension)
5 mm (US 8/UK 6) crochet hook
Stitch holders
Wool needle

Size

To fit bust size

86–91 cm	97–102 cm	107–112 cm
(34–36 in)	(38–40 in)	(42–44 in)

Top measures at bustline

95 cm	105 cm	116 cm
(37½ in)	(41½ in)	(46 in)

Length of top from shoulder

50 cm	53 cm	56 cm
(19½ in)	(21 in)	(22 in)

Jacket measures at bustline

102 cm	112 cm	121 cm
(40 in)	(44 in)	(47½ in)

Length of jacket from shoulder

55 cm	58 cm	61 cm
(21¾ in)	(23 in)	(24 in)

Jacket sleeve seam

43 cm	43 cm	43 cm
(17 in)	(17 in)	(17 in)

Tension

17 sts and 21 rows to 10 cm (4 in) over St st, and 16 sts and 20 rows to 10 cm (4 in) over ladder st using 5.5 mm (US 9) needles, or size required to give this tension

Hints

All shaping in these garments is worked decoratively, several stitches in from the end of the row. The top is recommended as an intermediate knit, with the jacket being more suited to advanced knitters.

While the pattern positioning is set for each piece, the knitter will have to make judgments concerning patterning within shaped sections; likewise, the shaping for the fronts requires a number of functions to be carried out at the same time.

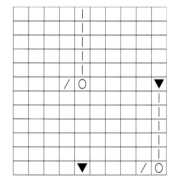

1 patt rep = 10 sts x 12 rows
Odd-numbered rows are RS rows, read right to left
Even-numbered rows are WS rows, read left to right

Pattern notes

Read complete pattern instructions prior to commencing work.

The pattern is positioned by the pattern set-up row in the written instructions. The pattern repeat is as shown in the chart below. To make ladder, slide stitch marked ▼ off needle and allow to ladder until halted by the yfwd of 6 rows below (always check that you are dropping the correct stitch), then replace top ladder bar onto left needle and knit off as normal. When working in ladder stitch pattern, maintain pattern placement as set, but always keep at least 3 sts in St st at edges of work when shaping. Thus it is sometimes necessary to drop a pattern st a row or two before the usual 1st or 7th row, but drop *only* the stitch(es) affected, and complete the remainder of the row as charted.

It is recommended that you use a backward loop or a provisional cast-on (see page 58) for this project.

All decs on both garments are worked on the 4th st in from the edge.

For dec on left-hand edge of work: For RS rows, work to last 5 sts, k2tog tbl, k3. For WS rows: p3, p2tog tbl, work in patt to end.

For dec on right-hand edge of work: For RS rows, K3, k2tog, work in patt to end. For WS rows: work to last 5 sts, p2tog, p3.

	k on RS, p on WS rows
I	worked as above, then unravelled at row 1 or 7
/	k2tog
O	yarn forward
▼	make ladder (see pattern notes, above)

Sleeveless top

FRONT

*Using 5.5 mm needles, CO 81 (89, 99) sts. Beg with a knit row (RS), cont in St st until work measures 9 (10, 11) cm (3½, 4, 4¼ in) from beg, ending after a WS row.
Shape waist as follows:
Next row k3, k2tog, k to last 5 sts, k2tog tbl, k3.
Working decs as set by last row, dec 1 st at each end of every foll 6th row until 75 (83, 93) sts rem.
Work 11 rows straight, ending after a WS row.
Next row k3, m1, k to last 3 sts, m1, k3.
Working incs as set by last row, inc 1 st at each end of every foll 6th row until 81 (89, 99) sts rem. Cont straight until work measures 27 (28, 29) cm (10½, 11, 11½ in), ending after a WS row.
Next row (This row sets up the pattern, and is worked once only, in lieu of row 1 of chart): k5 (4, 4) *yfwd, k2tog, k8; rep from * to last 6 (5, 5) sts, yfwd, k2tog, k4 (3, 3).
Note: the first yfwd corresponds to the first st of row 1 of chart and the edge sts are not shown on chart. Beg with row 2 of chart and cont in ladder st patt as set until work measures 31 (33, 35) cms (12, 13, 13¾ in), ending after a WS row.

SHAPE ARMHOLES

Cast off 3 (4, 4) sts at beg of next 2 rows, then 2 (3, 3) sts at beg of foll 2 rows. Dec 1 st at both ends of foll 4 rows, then 1 st at both ends of foll 2 (2, 4) alt rows. Dec 1 st at both ends of next 4th row [57, 61, 67 sts].** Cont in patt until armhole measures 10 (11, 12) cm (4, 4¼, 4¾ in), ending after a WS row.

SHAPE NECK

Next row Work first 23 (25, 28) sts, turn and place rem sts on a holder.

Complete left front neckline as follows:
Cast off 3 sts at neck edge on next row and foll alt row. Cast off 2 sts at beg of next alt row, and dec 1 st at neck edge at beginning of foll 3 alt rows. Work straight until armhole measures 19 (20, 21) cm (7½, 8, 8¼ in). Cast off remaining 12 (14, 17) sts loosely.

Rejoin yarn to 23 (25, 28) sts on right side of neckline, leaving the 11 sts of centre neck on the holder, and complete to match left side, reversing shapings as necessary.

BACK

Work as front from * to ** but in St st throughout (that is, no patterned yoke). Cont straight until armhole measures 15 (16, 17) cm (6, 6¼, 6¾ in), ending after a WS row.

SHAPE BACK NECK

Next row Work first 20 (22, 25) sts. Turn and place rem sts on a holder. Cast off 3 sts at neck edge at beg of next row and 2 sts at beg of foll alt row. Dec 1 st at neck edge on next 3 rows. Work 1 row, then cast off rem 12 (14, 17) sts loosely. Leaving 17 sts on holder for centre neckline, rejoin yarn and complete second side to match, reversing shapings where necessary.

TO MAKE UP

Carefully block all pieces to size, using a warm steam iron on WS, held above work to avoid flattening fabric. Neatly join shoulder seams. Working from the RS, join side seams using mattress stitch, working 1 st in from side edge and taking care to match decs.

TRIM

From RS, using 5 mm crochet hook, work 1 round of dc (US sc) around lower edge, working 1dc into every st of cast-on row, and joining round with a slip stitch.

Next round (picot edge): 2 ch, *work 1 sl st into each of the next 2 dc, 3 ch, work 1 sl st into next dc**. Rep from * to ** to end of round, joining with a sl st to finish.

Apply these 2 rounds of trim to armhole and neckline, taking live sts off holder as you work and, where necessary, dec sts at inner curves to ensure trim remains firm and flat. Give the trim a final light press.

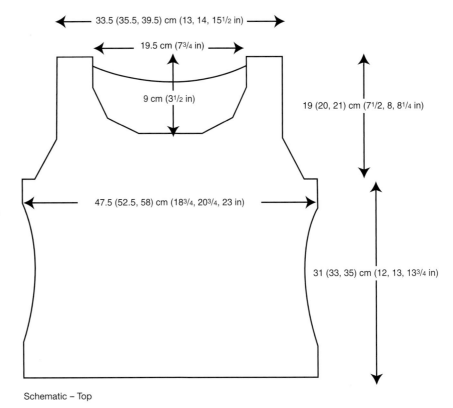

33.5 (35.5, 39.5) cm (13, 14, 15½ in)

19.5 cm (7¾ in)

9 cm (3½ in)

19 (20, 21) cm (7½, 8, 8¼ in)

47.5 (52.5, 58) cm (18¾, 20¾, 23 in)

31 (33, 35) cm (12, 13, 13¾ in)

Schematic – Top

Tie-front jacket

JACKET BACK

Using 5.5 mm needles, CO 87 (95, 103) sts.
It is recommended that you use a backward
loop or a provisional cast-on (see page 58)
for this project.

Beg with a knit row (RS) and working in
St st throughout, cont until work measures
35 (37, 39) cm (13¾ 14½, 15½ in), ending
after a WS row.

SHAPE ARMHOLES

Cast off 4 (4, 5) sts at beg of next 2 rows,
then dec 1 st at each end of next 1 (4, 4)
rows. Then dec 1 st at each end of foll alt
rows 6 (5, 7) times in all [65, 69, 71 sts].

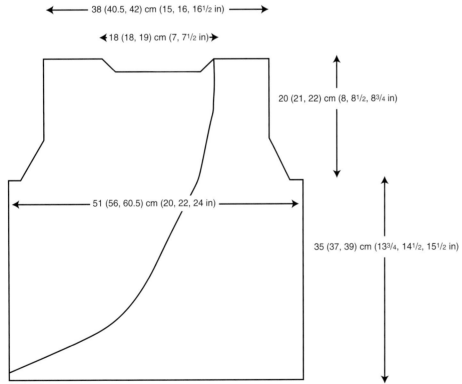

38 (40.5, 42) cm (15, 16, 16½ in)

18 (18, 19) cm (7, 7½ in)

20 (21, 22) cm (8, 8½, 8¾ in)

51 (56, 60.5) cm (20, 22, 24 in)

35 (37, 39) cm (13¾, 14½, 15½ in)

Schematic – Jacket back and one front

Cont straight until armhole measures
18 (19, 20) cm (7, 7½, 8 in), ending after
a WS row.

SHAPE BACK NECK

Next row Work first 20 (22, 22) sts. Turn
and place rem sts on a holder. Dec 1 st at
neck edge on next 3 rows. Work 1 row then
cast off rem 17 (19, 19) sts loosely. Leaving
25 (25, 27) sts on holder for centre neckline,
rejoin yarn and complete second side to
match, reversing shapings where necessary.

JACKET LEFT FRONT

(Worked in ladder st patt.)
CO 85 (93, 101) sts and, beg with a knit row
(RS), work 2 rows St st.

Next row (this is pattern set-up row): k3,
*yfwd, k2tog, k8. Rep from * to last 2 (0, 8)
sts then, for 1st size only, k2. For 3rd size
only, yfwd, k2tog, k6.

Note: the first yfwd corresponds to the first
st of row 1 of chart and the edge sts are not
shown on chart.

Beg with row 2 of chart, cont in ladder st
patt as set, and commence neckline slope
shaping on next row, as follows: dec 1 st at
neck edge on every row 24 (28, 32) times,
then every foll 2nd and 3rd row 11 times
[39, 43, 47 sts]. Then dec 1 st at neck edge
on each alt row 7 times, and 1 st on every
foll 4th row 4 (4, 5) times. *At the same
time*, when work measures 35 (37, 39) cm
(13¾, 14½, 15½ in), work armhole shaping
as for back [17, 19, 19 sts].

Cont in patt until armhole measures same
as for back to shoulder, then cast off all
sts loosely.

RIGHT FRONT

Complete to match left front, reversing shapings, and noting that pattern set-up row will be as follows: k11 (9, 7) sts, *yfwd, k2tog, k8. Rep from * to last 4 sts, yfwd, k2tog, k2.

SLEEVES

Cast on 49 (51, 55) sts and, beg with a knit row (RS), work 2 rows St st.
Next row (pattern set-up row): k4 (5, 7) *yfwd, k2tog, k8. Rep from * to last 5 (6, 8) sts then yfwd, k2tog, k3 (4, 6). Work straight in ladder st patt until sleeve measures 26 (24, 26) cm (10¼, 9½, 10¼ in). Inc 1 st at each end of next row and every foll 6th (7th, 6th) row until 59 (61, 65) sts, then work straight until sleeve measures 43 cm (17 in), or length desired.

SHAPE SLEEVE HEAD

Cast off 4 (4, 5) sts at beg of next 2 rows then dec 1 st at both ends of every foll row 5 (4, 1) times. Dec 1 st at both ends of every foll alt row 7 (9, 12) times and then every row 5 (5, 3) times. Cast off rem 17 (19, 23) sts loosely.

MAKING UP

Carefully block all pieces to size, using a warm steam iron on WS, held above work to avoid flattening fabric. Neatly join shoulder seams. Set in sleeves, easing to fit where necessary. Working from the RS, join side and sleeve seams using mattress stitch, working 1 st in from side edge, and leaving lower 5 cm (2 in) of sleeve seam open.

TRIM

Beg at side seam, and working from RS, crochet the 2-row picot trim (as per instructions for top) around all edges of jacket, ending at the same side seam. Beg at start of sleeve seam (5 cm/2 in above lower edge of sleeve), work trim along the short exposed unseamed edge and around lower sleeve, ending at seam again.
Give the trim a final light press.

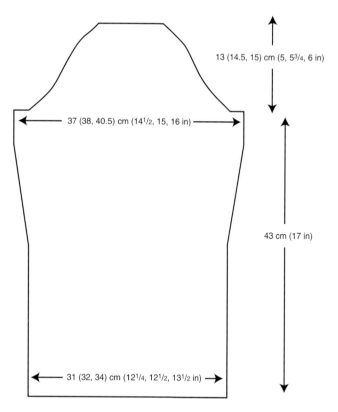

13 (14.5, 15) cm (5, 5¾, 6 in)

37 (38, 40.5) cm (14½, 15, 16 in)

43 cm (17 in)

31 (32, 34) cm (12¼, 12½, 13½ in)

Schematic – Jacket Sleve

Fine lace shawl vest

This shawl–vest hybrid is made of two strips of easy lace joined down the centre with two holes left for the arms. A lace border is then added. Like most lace items, this project must be blocked; when taken straight off the needles, it is crumpled and the lace stitches indistinct. Once correctly blocked, as explained on pages 24 and 70–71, the lace pattern opens up beautifully.

Materials

80 g (3 oz) Artisan NZ Merino Lace Weight (each of the two pieces takes just under 40 g/1½ oz of yarn)

Tools

3.25 mm (US 3/UK 10) needles
3.75 mm (US 5/UK 9) needles
Extra-long knitting needles for blocking
Rustless pins
Safety pins
Sewing needle and polyester thread

Size

After blocking: approximately 160 x 76 cm (65 x 30 in) including border

Tension

Before blocking: 20 sts and 30 rows to 10 cm (4 in) over patt, using 3.25 mm needles
After blocking: 16 sts and 22 rows to 10 cm (4 in) over patt, using 3.25 mm needles

Abbreviations and explanations

k: Knit
k2tog: Knit 2 stitches together
K2Tog: Knit 2 stitches together where first stitch is the last stitch of the border pattern and second stitch is from the shawl
p2tog: Purl 2 stitches together
sPf: Slip-stitch purlwise with yarn in front, then bring yarn to back ready to knit
yf: Yarn forward (bring yarn to front of work)
yrn (yarn round needle): This makes a loop over the right-hand needle when working purl stitches. The purl stitch is worked with the yarn at the front of the work, rather than at the back as is usual. Wind yarn from the front over the right-hand needle and back to the front, ready to work the purl 2 together

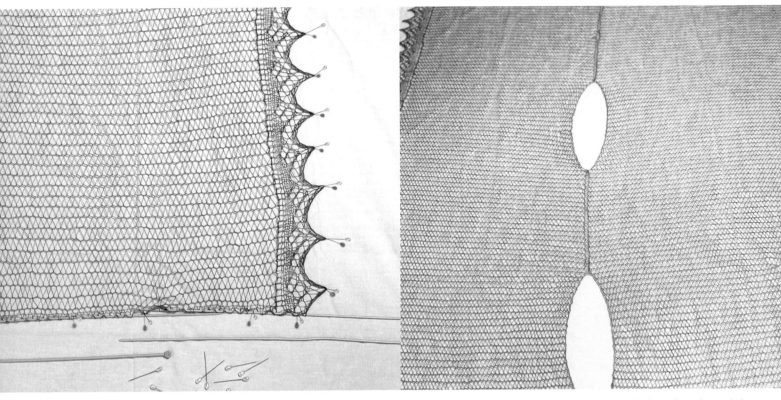

blocking Pin out damp garment to measurements, using long knitting needles threaded through the ends of the pieces then pinned into place.

opening armholes Once the blocked garment is dry, pull out the armhole threads to open up the armholes.

Hints

Form the p2tog very carefully. Make sure the two stitches (the stitch and the loop formed by the yrn) are both slipped off the left-hand needle. The p2tog is always the stitch and the yrn is always the loop. If you find you have a loop left before the next p2tog, lift this loop over the stitch behind it on the left-hand needle.

Alternatively, the shawl can be worked in garter stitch (knit every row) on 3.75 mm needles.

SHAWL VEST

Make 2 pieces the same.

Using 3.25 mm needles, CO 272 sts, leaving a 40 cm (16 in) tail to use for sewing later.

Work every row thus: p2, *yrn, p2tog; rep from * to last 2 sts, p2tog.

When work measures 26 cm (10 in) slightly stretched, or there is 15 g (½ oz) yarn left, whichever comes first, change to 3.75 mm needles and work 1 row thus: p2, * yrn, p2tog; rep from * to last 2 sts, yrn, p2 [273 sts].

Do not break yarn. Cast on 7 sts and using 3.75 mm needles, work lace border as given in graphs and instructions opposite. Cast off loosely. Weave in end of cast-off yarn.

MAKING UP

Lay the 2 pieces flat, placing cast-on edges together. Mark off the measurements for joining seams (see Diagram 1) and sew together as invisibly as possible. Weave in the ends of the thread back along the sewn seam to finish off. Using polyester sewing thread, sew the armholes together, leaving a 15 cm (6 in) tail at either end. Do not secure this sewing; it will be pulled out after blocking to open up the armholes.

BLOCKING

Soak the garment in warm water for 30 minutes. Gently squeeze out excess water and roll up in a clean, colourfast towel to absorb water. Place a clean sheet on a carpeted floor or on a bed.

Thread straight knitting needles through the ends of the garment, overlapping as necessary. Pin out the needles, stretching the work to the finished size. Pin out each lace point, stretching as you go. Keep adjusting the pins to keep the garment straight and stretched. The stretch should be comfortably firm.

Rub your hands gently over the stretched surface. This tangles the small fibres of the wool and helps to hold the pattern in place. Allow to dry completely. Remove the knitting needles and pins, then pull out the armhole threads.

BORDER PATTERN

Cast on 7 sts.

Set-up Row 1 sPf, k2, yf, k3, K2Tog (last st from border and the first st from shawl).

Set-up Row 2 Knit (see Diagram 2 for chart of cast-on and set-up rows).

Begin border pattern (see Diagram 3):

Row 1 sPf, k2, yf, k4, K2Tog.

Row 2 Knit.

Row 3 sPf, k2, yf, k5, K2Tog.

Row 4 Knit.

Row 5 sPf, k2, yf, k2, yf, k2tog, k2, K2Tog.

Row 6 Knit.

Row 7 sPf, k2, yf, k2, [yf, k2tog twice], k1, K2Tog.

Row 8 Knit.

Row 9 sPf, k3, yf, k2tog, k1, yf, k2tog, k2, K2Tog.

Row 10 k10, k2tog.

Row 11 sPf, k3, yf, k2tog, k4, K2Tog.

Row 12 k9, k2tog.

Row 13 sPf, k3, yf, k2tog, k3, K2Tog.

Row 14 k8, k2tog.

Row 15 sPf, k3, yf, k2tog, k2, K2Tog.

Row 16 k7, k2tog.

These last 16 rows form patt. Rep these 16 rows until all the shawl sts have been used up. Cast off and weave in thread.

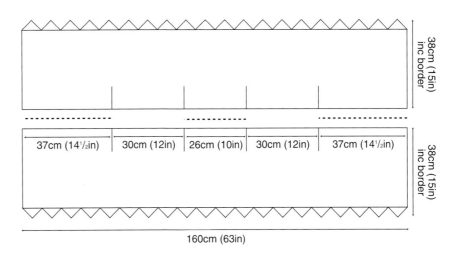

| 37cm (14½in) | 30cm (12in) | 26cm (10in) | 30cm (12in) | 37cm (14½in) |

160cm (63in)

38cm (15in) inc border

38cm (15in) inc border

diagram 1 Sew up as shown.

- - - - - - - - - - - -
Sew up between these points

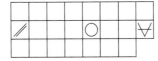

diagram 2 Setting up the stitches for the border pattern: first row is cast-on row, second row is set-uo row 1, third row is set-up row 2.

Chart Symbols

⩊ Slip stitch purlwise with yarn in front, then bring yarn to back ready to knit

◯ Yarn forward

╱ k2tog

▨ K2Tog where first stitch is the last stitch of the lace border pattern and second stitch is the stitch from the shawl

☐ Knit

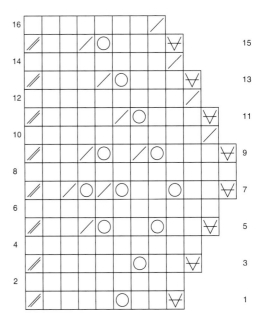

diagram 3 Chart for lace edging; once set-up rows have been established, these 16 rows form patt.

Hot-water bottle cover

Worked in stocking stitch in stripes of three colours, this is a comfortingly old-fashioned accessory to keep you cosy on a cold winter's night. The opening at the back is fastened with ties made of crochet chain; lengths of ribbon could be used instead if you wish.

Materials
Nundle Woollen Mill pure new wool 8 ply (DK), 50 g (1¾ oz) balls: 1 ball Camel, 1 ball Oatmeal, 2 balls Natural

Tools
4 mm (US 6/UK 8) needles (or size required to achieve correct tension)
4 mm (US 6/UK 8) crochet hook
Wool needle

Size
To fit standard hot-water bottle: total length of cover is 34 cm (13½ in), width of body 21 cm (8¼ in), width of neck 11 cm (4½ in)

Tension (gauge)
20 sts to 10 cm (4 in) width in St stitch using 4 mm (US 6/UK 8) needles, or needle size required to achieve this tension

back hems Using a wool needle, slip-stitch hems of both back pieces into place.

beginning ties Using crochet hook, draw the doubled length of yarn from the back through to the front at the edge of one back piece.

FRONT

With Camel, CO 32 sts using cable method.

Row 1 (WS): purl.

Row 2 (RS): k1, M1, k to last 2 sts, M1, k1.

Cont in St st, inc at each end of every row and making every increase 1 st in from edge as for Row 2, until there are 44 sts. Cont in St st, without increasing further, until back measures 9.5 cm (3¾ in) from cast-on edge, ending with a purl row. Join in Oatmeal and work a further 9.5 cm (3¾ in) St st, ending with a purl row. Join in Natural and work a further 6.5 cm (2½ in) St st, ending with a purl row. Then dec 1 st (by k2tog, 1 st in from edge of work) at each end of next and foll

alt rows, then at each end of foll 3 rows [34 sts]. Cast off 5 sts at beg of next 2 rows [24 sts].

Work 8 cm (3 in) St st for neck, ending with a purl row. Cast off.

LOWER BACK

Using Natural, CO 32 sts using cable method. Work in St st throughout, beg with a purl row. Then inc 1 st at each end of every row, in same manner as for front, until there are 44 sts. Cont in St st, without increasing further, until piece measures 20 cm (8 in) from cast-on edge, ending with a purl row. Cast off.

making ties Using the doubled length of yarn, make 25 crochet chain for tie.

back of cover Make four crochet-chain ties, matching positions as shown.

UPPER BACK

Using Natural, CO 44 sts using cable method. Work in St st until piece measures 11 cm (4¼ in) from cast-on edge, ending with a purl row.

Then dec 1 st at each end of next and foll alt rows, in same manner as for front, then at each end of foll 3 rows [34 sts].

Cast off 5 sts at beg of next 2 rows [24 sts]. Work 8 cm (3 in) for neck, ending with a purl row. Cast off.

MAKING UP

Press pieces lightly on wrong side, pressing top edge of lower back and bottom edge of upper back under by 4 rows to form hem.

Using a wool needle, slip-stitch hems of both back pieces into place.

Carefully match upper back piece to front, with WS tog. Using mattress stitch (see page 26), invisibly sew side seams, working from neck down to last 8 rows. Then, ensuring hem edge is in place, sew final rows into place.

Carefully match lower back piece to front, with WS tog, sewing up in the same manner but leaving an 8-st wide opening in the centre of the base of the cover if you intend to use your hot-water bottle's hook hole. Sew in all loose ends along seams.

To finish, attach crochet ties as explained at right. Sew in all loose ends along seams.

Ties for back of cover

Cut four 180 cm (71 in) lengths of Natural for ties. Fold one length to double thickness. Insert a crochet hook through front to back of hem layers of upper back, one third of the way across (see photo). Hook the folded end of the yarn through and bring to front, then work 25 chain and fasten off. Rep on other side of upper back to match, and then make two corresponding ties on lower back. Trim ends of all ties.

Loop-stitch cushion

Stripes of stocking stitch and knitted loops add texture to this two-toned cushion. Make the loops roughly 2.5 cm (1 in) long, but don't worry it they vary a bit in length, as this adds visual interest. Once the cushion is finished, the loops can be cut to form a shag-pile effect (see photo on page 79) or left intact.

The back is made in two pieces and fastened with buttons and simple button loops made of crochet chain. For basic crochet instructions, see page 27.

Materials
Main Colour (MC): Three 50 g (1¾ oz) balls
  Jo Sharp Silkroad Aran Tweed, Col 141 Bark
Contrast Colour (CC): Two 50 g (1¾ oz) balls
  Jo Sharp Silkroad Aran, Col 121 Parchment
3 buttons, 2.5 cm (1 in) diameter
45 x 45 cm (18 x 18 in) cushion insert

Tools
5 mm (US 8/UK 6) needles
4.5 mm (US 7/UK 7) needles
5 mm (US 8/UK 6) crochet hook
Wool needle

Size
Approx 43 x 43 cm (17 x 17 in)

Tension
16 sts and 25 rows to 10 cm (4 in) over St st
  using Jo Sharp Silkroad Aran Tweed and
  5 mm needles

Abbreviations and explanations
L — work loop stitch: see step-by-step
  instructions and photographs overleaf

loop stitch, step 1 Knit a stitch, but do not slip the stitch off the left needle.

loop stitch, step 2 Bring yarn between the needles, around your thumb, and bac[k] between the needles again.

FRONT

Using larger needles, MC and cable method, CO 65 sts.

Work in St st for 14 rows, beg with a knit row. *Change to smaller needles and CC.

Row 15 (RS) k 1, L until 1 st rem, k1.

Row 16 Purl.

Rep these 2 rows twice.

Next row (RS) As for Row 15.

Change to larger needles and MC.

Next row (Row 22) (WS) Purl.

Work 14 more rows St st, ending on a WS row.* Rep from * to * 3 times.

Using larger needles and MC, work 14 rows St st, ending on a WS row.

Cast off loosely.

LOWER BACK

Using larger needles, MC and cable method, CO 65 sts.

Work in St st until piece measures 22 cm (8½ in), ending on a WS row. Cast off loosely.

UPPER BACK

Using larger needles, MC and cable method, CO 65 sts.

Work in St st until piece measures 21 cm (8¼ in), ending on a WS row. Cast off.

Next row (RS) Make button loops: these are worked in crochet chain and dc (US sc) using MC, with RS facing and working 1 dc into each cast-off stitch, as follows:

loop stitch, step 3 Knit again into the same stitch as before on the left needle, then slip the stitch off the left needle.

option If desired, the loops can be cut to give a shag-pile effect.

(10 dc, 10 ch, 22 dc) twice, dc to end. Fasten off.

MAKING UP

With WS tog and matching edges, put front and back pieces together. The lower back and upper back pieces should just meet in the middle of the cushion. Using MC and crochet hook, with RS facing, and working dc (US sc) 1 full stitch in from the edge, crochet the front and back pieces together, making sure you don't catch in the loops. At the cast-on and cast-off edges, work 1 dc into each knit st; on the side edges, skip a row every few sts. This will prevent the edge from buckling.

At the corners, work 3 dc (sc) into the same stitch. When you have crocheted around the whole cushion, join with a slip stitch into the first dc. Fasten off.
Sew buttons onto the upper back section, aligning them with the button loops.
Using a wool needle, sew in loose ends.

Working loop stitch

Step 1 Knit 1 st without slipping original stitch off left needle.
Step 2 Bring the yarn between the needles, clockwise around your thumb, and back between the needles again.
Step 3 Insert tip of right needle into the same loop as before on the left needle and knit a stitch. Slip original stitch off left needle. You will have created two new stitches on the right needle.
Step 4 Slip the second stitch on the right needle over the first to secure the loop. Repeat Steps 1–3 as required.

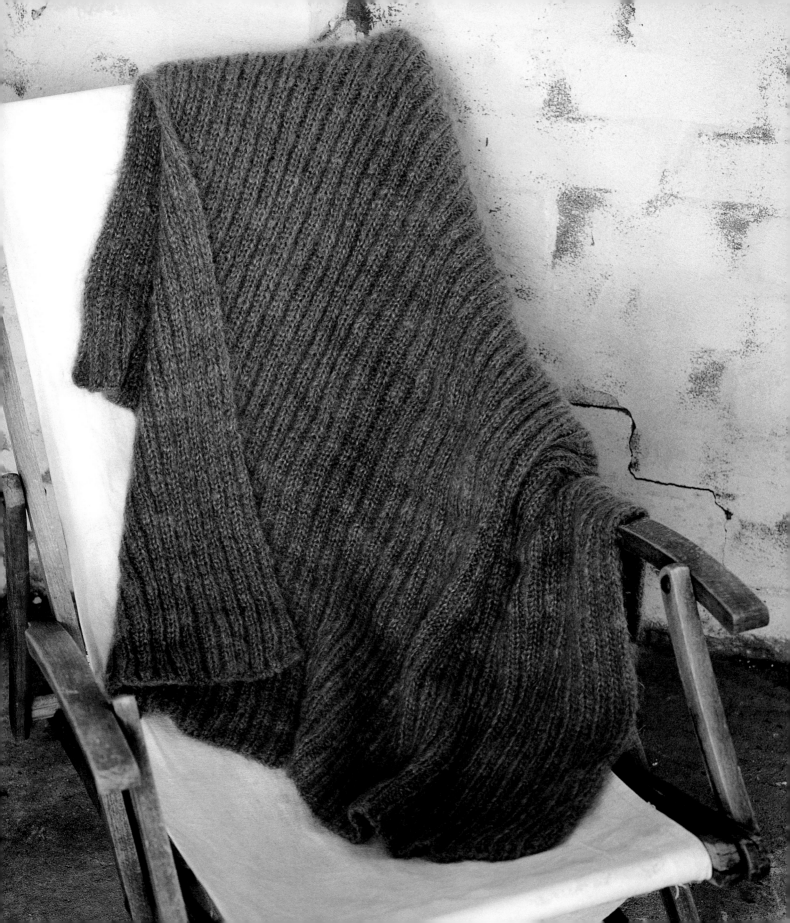

Double-rib mohair rug

This delightfully soft and cosy throw is big

enough for a single bed. This is an easy

project suitable for a beginner, requiring

only a little patience due to its size.

detail The first stitch of every row is slipped to give a neater edge.

Materials

500 g (17½ oz) Mollydale
  Mohair 8-ply (DK) in Grey-
  blue (available from
  www.mollydale.com.au)

Tools

6 mm (US 10/UK 4) circular
  needles, 80 cm (31½ in)
  long (or size required to
  give correct tension)

Size

Approx 150 x 85 cm
  (59 x 33 in)

Tension (gauge)

16 sts and 24 rows to 10 cm
  (4 in) over St st using 6 mm
  needles, or size required to
  give this tension

CO 180 sts.

Every row is knitted in double rib. The first stitch of every row is slipped to create a neater edge.

Row 1: Slip first st knitwise, k1, p2, (k2, p2), rep to end of row.

Row 2: Slip first st purlwise, p1, k2, (p2, k2), rep to end of row.

These 2 rows form double-rib patt. Work in patt until rug measures approx 150 cm (59 in), leaving enough yarn to cast off and, if desired, to oversew the top and bottom edges. (Oversewing gives a neater look to the cast-on and cast-off edges.)

CARING FOR YOUR RUG

Gently hand wash using an approved wool detergent. Rinse in warm water, then place the throw in a pillowcase and spin it in the washing machine on a gentle cycle. Reshape to size and lay flat in the shade to dry.

Chunky cable and check rug

Richly patterned knitted rugs make gorgeous heirlooms, but not everyone has the time, skill or patience to devote to them. This contemporary version knits up quickly in a chunky mohair-mix yarn on large needles. It features vertical panels of alternating moss-stitch and stocking-stitch squares. Each panel of three squares is separated from the next by cables; these twist first to the right then to the left, making the design symmetrical.

The pattern is given in chart form; if you have never worked with charts before, see the explanation on page 28.

Materials
Nine 100 g (3½ oz) balls Cleckheaton Gusto 10, Col 2095 Blue

Tools
9 mm (US 13/UK 00) circular needles, at least 80 cm (32 in) long
Wool needle

Size
Approx 90 x 135 cm (35½ x 53 in)

Tension
8½ sts and 10 rows to 10 cm (4 in) over St st using 9 mm needles

Abbreviations and explanations
C4B: make 4-stitch cable: slip 2 sts onto cable needle, hold cable needle at back of work, k2 from left needle, k2 from cable needle (to produce right-twisting cable)
C4F: make 4-stitch cable: slip 2 sts onto cable needle, hold cable needle at front of work, k2 from left needle, k2 from cable needle (to produce left-twisting cable)

working cable, step 1 For a right-slanting cable (the first and third cables in the design), slip two stitches onto a cable needle and hold at the back of the work.

working cable, step 2 Work the two stitches off the left needle.

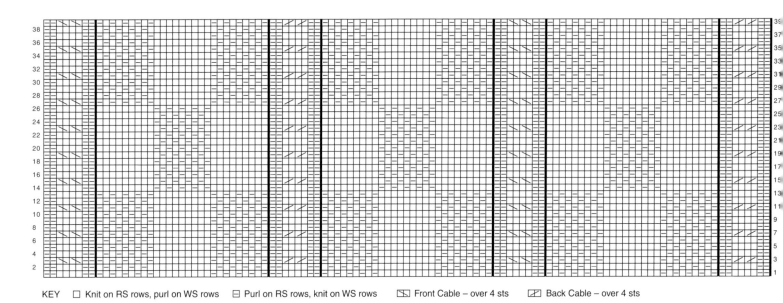

KEY □ Knit on RS rows, purl on WS rows   ⊟ Purl on RS rows, knit on WS rows   ◣ Front Cable – over 4 sts   ◿ Back Cable – over 4 sts

working cable, step 3 Work the two stitches off the cable needle.

left-twisting cable For the second and fourth cables in this design, the cable needle is held at the front of the work, thus changing the direction of the cable's twist.

CO 113 sts, then follow the chart opposite. Work each odd-numbered row as a RS row, reading the chart from right to left; work each even-numbered row as a WS row, reading the chart from left to right.

When following the chart, think of the rug as being constructed in panels; each cable (along with the 2 purl sts on either side) forms one panel, and the three squares of alternating moss stitch and stocking stitch form another panel. Once the design is set up, it will be fairly easy to follow by sight, but keep a record of the number of rows you have made so that you know when to start alternating the squares vertically.

After Row 39 of chart, cont in patt. Exact vertical pattern repeats cannot be given for the overall design, as the cables are worked over a different number of rows from the textured squares; the cables are turned on the 3rd and foll 4th rows and the squares of moss stitch and stocking stitch are worked over 9 sts and 13 rows.

Cont in patt until the rug is 9 squares long, ending on Row 38 (a WS row). For the next (RS) row, cast off loosely in patt.

To finish, sew in ends.

Hints

This rug is unsuitable for babies, as the short fibres of the mohair component shed readily; the rug is also very heavy, and could potentially cause the baby to overheat.

crochet

Types of crochet

Some types of crochet require only a hook and yarn; in others (such as broomstick and hairpin crochet), the yarn is wound around another tool, then the crochet stitches are formed with the hook.

Broomstick crochet (also known as broomstick lace) This technique combines the use of a crochet hook and another long, slender item (traditionally a broomstick, but now more usually a thick knitting needle or a piece of craft dowel). The foundation of the piece is a chain, into which are worked loops that are then transferred to the knitting needle or dowel. Several loops are then crocheted together and slipped off the dowel, creating a soft but stable fabric.

Cro-hook This special double-ended crochet hook is used to make double-sided crochet. The hook has two ends, allowing two colours of yarn to be handled at once and freely interchanged.

Filet crochet A type of crochet consisting of filled and open meshes constructed from chain and treble crochet stitches. The way in which the filled and open meshes are arranged creates an infinity of possible patterns. It is usual for open mesh to form the background and for the pattern to be created in filled mesh. Filet crochet instructions are generally given as charts rather than words.

Hairpin crochet (also known as hairpin lace) In this technique, lace is made using a crochet hook and a small U-shaped metal loom (formerly a hairpin was used, hence the name). Yarn is wrapped around the prongs of the loom, and one crochets into the middle of the loops to create a strip of lace. The strips thus formed can then be joined to create a lightweight fabric.

Irish crochet An intricate and beautiful type of lace in which motifs are crocheted separately, laid out and tacked onto a temporary background fabric, then joined using crochet mesh. Sometimes, parts of the motifs are reinforced with cord to give extra definition. In mid-19th century Ireland, in the wake of the devastating potato famine, the craft was encouraged as a cottage industry to provide income for families that might otherwise have been destitute. Families often had their own carefully guarded designs; a unique pattern was worth more money.

Tunisian crochet (also known as Afghan crochet) In this technique, stitches are formed in two parts. Working from right to left, a loop is picked up in each stitch across the row without being worked off the hook. At the end of the row, and working from left to right, the yarn is drawn through two loops at a time, thus completing each stitch. This technique creates a dense fabric with a definite right and wrong side.

Yarns and threads

Any yarn that is suitable for knitting can be used for crochet. Yarns may be natural, synthetic or a mixture of both. Natural yarns are derived either from animals (including wool, mohair, alpaca and angora), or plants (including hemp, linen, soy silk, corn silk and bamboo). Synthetic yarns include rayon, nylon, acrylic and polyester, and are often combined with natural fibres to enhance their performance or texture. Each fibre has its own inherent characteristics, which the manufacturer may modify in various ways during processing; for example, yarns can be treated and spun to make them fluffier, denser, flatter, shinier or more twisted.

When choosing a yarn, there are several factors to consider. Beginners will find it easier to work with a smooth yarn than a highly textured one. A smooth yarn is also the best choice for an intricate pattern, as a highly textured or novelty yarn will mask the beautiful details of the piece. If you wish to use one of the many interesting textured or 'busy' yarns that are available, choose a simple stitch pattern so that the yarn itself is the focus of the finished article.

Consider also the use to which the finished item will be put. For an easy-care garment, for example, choose a machine-wash yarn; this will ensure that the garment does not felt and shrink when it is washed. Cotton also wears and washes well. Items made of delicate yarns should be gently hand-washed or, in some cases, dry-cleaned only. The ball band — the piece of paper that comes wrapped around the ball of yarn when you buy it — will tell you how the garment should be treated, as well as the composition of the yarn, the weight of the ball and the length of yarn it contains, among other things.

The terms used to describe yarns vary from country to country. The following conversion chart may be useful.

yarns and threads The term 'yarn' usually refers to thicker fibres and 'thread' to thinner ones, although the terms are sometimes interchanged. Clockwise from the top are various yarns: fine mohair, DK-weight mercerized cotton, aran-weight Tencel, aran-weight cotton, cashmere–merino mix, and alpaca. In the centre are two spools of mercerized cotton thread.

Some terms used to describe yarn refer to its content (such as wool, cashmere, cotton) and others (such as bouclé, tweed, aran) to its texture, finish and/or thickness.

Crochet uses about 30 per cent more yarn than knitting.

International yarn equivalents Note that figures given are approximate and will vary between manufacturers and individual crocheters. Tension is expressed as the number of stitches per 10 cm (4 in) over double crochet/dc (US single crochet/sc).

Weight	Australia/NZ	USA	UK and Canada	Tension	Hook
Super-fine	2 or 3-ply	Sock, fingering, baby	Lace weight, sock	21–32 sts	2.25–3.5 mm
Fine	4 or 5-ply	Sport, baby	Sport	16–20 sts	3.5–4.5 mm
Light	8-ply	Double knitting (DK), light worsted	Double knitting (DK)	12–17 sts	4.5–5.5 mm
Medium	10-ply	Worsted weight, afghan, aran	Aran	11–14 sts	5.5–6.5 mm
Bulky	12-ply	Chunky, craft, rug	Chunky	8–11 sts	6.5–9 mm
Super bulky	14-ply plus	Bulky, roving	Super chunky	5–9 sts	9 mm or larger

Hooks

types of hook Fine metal hooks are used with fine cotton threads; aluminium, bamboo or plastic hooks are used with thicker yarns.

Crochet hooks come in various sizes and materials. The thinnest hooks, used with very fine yarns, are made of steel. Larger hooks are made from aluminium, plastic or bamboo. No one material is superior to another; they are simply different, and you should use whichever material suits you better. People with arthritis, for example, may prefer plastic hooks to the colder and slightly heavier metal ones.

Crochet hook sizes are expressed differently from country to country; see the table at left. The patterns in this book give hook sizes in metric (millimetres) followed by the equivalent US and pre-metrification UK/Canadian sizes. Sometimes there will be more than one equivalent for a metric size. The hook size is often printed or stamped onto the flattened part in the middle of the hook's shaft. If not, the shaft of the hook can be inserted into the holes in a knitting-needle gauge to determine the size. Hooks vary slightly in size between manufacturers; always be guided by your tension square rather than the nominal size of the hook.

For any yarn, the size of crochet hook needed will be larger than that of the knitting needle recommended on the ball band; this is because a crochet stitch consists of three threads of fabric, unlike a knitted stitch, which consists of only two.

Other equipment

As well as hooks of various sizes, the following will be useful:

Blunt-ended wool needle Used for darning in ends of yarn and for sewing seams. Choose a needle with an eye large enough to take your chosen yarn.

Dressmaker's pins Glass-headed pins are preferable to plastic-headed ones, as they will not melt if you accidentally press them with an iron.

Knitting needle gauge Useful for measuring crochet hooks that do not have the size printed or stamped on them.

Ruler To obtain an accurate measurement when measuring a tension square, use a ruler (which is inflexible) rather than a tape measure, which may stretch or warp.

Safety pins To hold together two pieces of crochet while joining them.

Scissors A small pair with sharp points is best.

Tape measure Choose a pliable one with both metric and imperial measures.

Metric	UK Yarn	UK Cotton	US Yarn	US Cotton
0.6 mm		7, 7½, 8		14
0.75 mm		6½		13
1 mm		6, 5½		11, 12
1.25 mm		4½, 5		9, 10
1.5 mm		3½, 4		7, 8
1.75 mm		2½, 3		6
2 mm	14	1½, 2		4, 5
2.25 mm	13			
2.5 mm	12	0, 1	0, 1	B, 1, 2, 3
2.75 mm				
3 mm	11	3/0, 2/0	2	C, 0
3.25 mm	10			
3.5 mm	9		3, 4	D, E
3.75 mm	–			
4 mm	8		5	F
4.5 mm	7		6	G
5 mm	6		7	
5.5 mm	5		8	H
6 mm	4		9	I
6.5 mm	3			
7 mm	2		10	J, K
8 mm	0		11, 12	L
9 mm	00		13, 15	M, N
10 mm	000		15	N, P
15 mm				P, Q

Holding the hook and yarn

There is no one 'right' way to hold the hook or yarn; you should do so in any way that is comfortable, lets you obtain an even tension and allows the yarn to flow freely. Aim to hold the hook gently and comfortably, about a third of the way down the shaft, rather than gripping it tightly. Shown below are two common holds.

Holding the yarn

Holding the yarn is also a matter of personal choice and comfort. The yarn needs to flow freely and not be stretched, which may change the gauge to which it works. The way in which you hold the yarn should also be comfortable enough to be sustained through a long crocheting session; if your hands cramp up frequently, try various holds until you find one that suits you better.

Two possible methods of holding the yarn are shown below left. In the first, the yarn is run over the ring finger, under the second finger and over the index finger. In the second, the yarn is run under the middle two fingers and around the little finger.

knife hold One method is to hold the hook as you would a knife.

pen hold Alternatively, hold the hook as you would a pen.

one method of holding the yarn The yarn is laced between the fingers.

alternative method The ball end of the yarn is wound around the little finger.

Hints

When making loops around the hook, do so along the main part of the shaft, rather than close to the head of the hook, where the hook is narrower. If you do the latter, your stitches will be too small.

Unless otherwise instructed, the yarn is always put over the hook before being caught and pulled through. If the yarn is taken under the hook and then caught, the stitch produced will look different from that in the pattern.

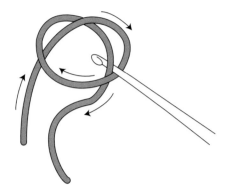

Making a slipknot

Make a loop in a length of yarn. Bring the yarn up from back to front through the loop and pull to tighten. You have now made a slipknot. Place the loop on the crochet hook. You can now begin making a crochet chain. Remember that the slipknot is not included when counting how many chain stitches you have made.

The basic stitches

Crochet can be worked either flat, as shown on the following pages, or in rounds (see page 102). When crochet is worked flat, it is turned at the end of each row; the fabric thus produced is the same or very similar on both front and back. When working in the round, however, the work is not turned; the same side of the work always faces you, and the appearance of back and front will be quite different. Usually, the flatter side is considered the 'right' side, but if you prefer the other side, by all means use that as the front of the work.

Chain

The chain is the basis of all crochet, whether it is worked flat or in the round. The chains worked at the start of a piece of crochet are known as foundation chain.

1 First, make a slipknot (see left) and put it onto the crochet hook.

2 Insert the hook under then over the yarn and draw the yarn through the loop of the slipknot. You have created one chain stitch. Repeat as required.

Note When counting foundation chains, the initial slip stitch is not counted.

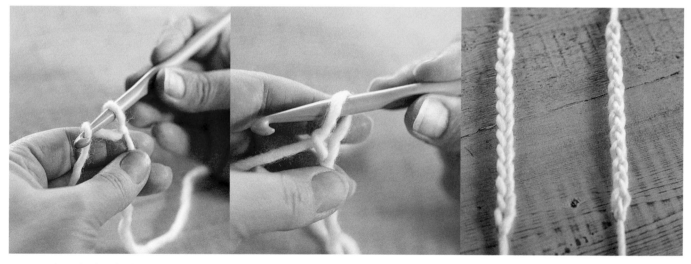

step two Insert hook under then over yarn and draw the yarn through the loop on the hook.

the completed chain stitch Repeat Step 2 until you have the required length of chain.

back and front The front of the chain forms a smooth series of V shapes; the back looks bumpy.

Turning chain

Chains are also used at the beginning of a row or round, to lift the hook up to the same height as the stitches that are to be worked in the next row or round. These are known as turning chain. The various crochet stitches are each of a different height, so the number of turning chain worked depends on the height of the stitch in use. You will generally need to work one chain for double crochet, two chain for half-treble crochet, three chain for treble crochet, and so on. See also Hint at right.

Chain mesh or lace

Chains are also used to make lacy patterns, or to separate one block or group of stitches from another, creating a mesh effect. To produce a series of arches, several chains are worked, then a double crochet or slip stitch is made into the row below; these steps are repeated to the end of the row.

Slip stitch

The slip stitch is essentially a chain that is worked into another stitch or another part of the fabric. It is used to join a round of crochet, and also to move the hook from one position to another, as when making motifs; it forms a barely visible link between one area and the next, particularly useful when creating lacy motifs.

Hint

When working trebles or longer stitches using yarn rather than cotton, you may find that you need one less turning chain than the pattern specifies. Work a small sample first, or experiment with your tension swatch. Should working the specified number of turning chain result in a curved edge or a small hole at the beginning of a row, try working one less turning chain to see if the effect is better.

slip stitch Insert the hook into the fabric, then catch the yarn with the hook.

slip stitch, continued Draw the yarn through both the fabric and the loop on the hook.

slip stitch fabric When worked in rows or rounds, slip stitch creates a very dense fabric.

Double crochet

Double crochet (dc) — known in the United States as single crochet (sc) — produces a fabric that is firm, dense and stable, yet also flexible. When worked in rows, as shown right, a distinct horizontal pattern is created.

When working in double crochet, the number of foundation chain should equal the number of stitches required, plus one for the turning chain. Hold the chain with the smooth side facing you.

1 Insert the hook from front to back through the second chain from the hook, picking up two strands of chain. Wrap the yarn over the hook (yoh).

2 Draw the yarn through the chain to the front; there will be two loops on the hook. Wrap yarn over hook again.

3 Draw the yarn through both loops on the hook. You have now completed one double crochet stitch. One loop will remain on the hook.

4 Repeat Steps 1 to 3 to the end of the row, working one double crochet into each chain. At the end of the row, turn and work 1 turning chain; this counts as one stitch, so the first double crochet of the second row is worked into the second stitch of the previous row.

5 When working back along the row, insert the hook under both loops of each stitch in the previous row.

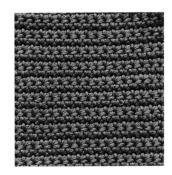

step one Insert the hook into the second chain from the hook, then wrap the yarn over the hook.

step two Draw the yarn through the chain (two loops on hook). Wrap the yarn over the hook again.

start of second row Turn, work 1 turning chain, insert hook in second stitch of previous row.

last stitch of a row This is worked into the turning chain at the start of the previous row.

Half treble crochet

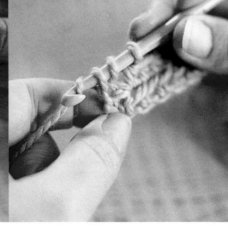

Half treble crochet (htr) — known in the United States as half double crochet (hdc) — produces a fabric that is flexible, yet less dense than double crochet. When working in half treble crochet, the number of foundation chain should equal the number of stitches required, plus two for the turning chain. Hold the chain with the smooth side facing you.

1 Wrap the yarn over the hook and insert the hook into the third chain from the hook, picking up two strands of chain. Wrap the yarn over the hook.

2 Draw the yarn through the chain to the front; there will be three loops on the hook. Wrap the yarn over the hook again.

3 Draw the yarn through all three loops on the hook. You have now completed one half treble crochet. One loop will remain on the hook.

4 Repeat Steps 1 to 3 to the end of the row, working one half treble crochet into each chain. At the end of the row, turn and work two turning chain; these count as one stitch, so the first half treble crochet of the second row is worked into the second stitch of the previous row.

5 When working back along the row, insert the hook under both loops of each stitch in the previous row.

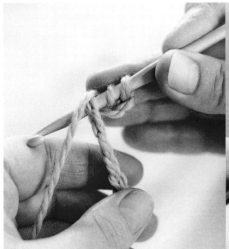

step one Wrap the yarn over the hook and insert it into the third chain from the hook.

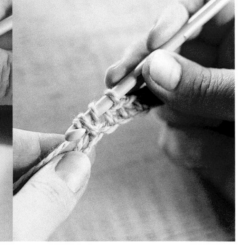

step two Draw yarn through chain (three loops on hook), then wrap the yarn over the hook again.

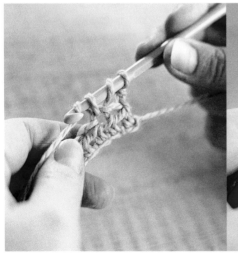

start of second row Work 2 turning chain, yarn over hook, insert hook into second stitch.

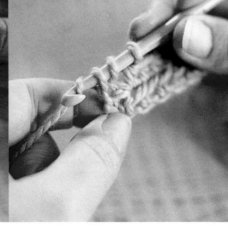

last stitch of a row This is worked into the top of the turning chain at the start of the previous row.

Treble crochet

Treble crochet (tr) —known in the United States as double crochet (dc) — produces a flexible, slightly open fabric. When working in treble crochet, the number of foundation chain should equal the number of stitches required, plus three for the turning chain. Hold the chain with the smooth side facing you.

1 Wrap the yarn over the hook and insert the hook into the fourth chain from the hook, picking up two strands of chain. Wrap the yarn over the hook.

2 Draw the yarn through the chain to the front; there will be three loops on the hook. Wrap the yarn over the hook again.

3 Draw the yarn through two loops on the hook. Wrap the yarn over the hook again and then draw it through two more loops. You have now completed one treble crochet stitch. One loop will remain on the hook.

4 Repeat Steps 1 to 3 to the end of the row, working one treble crochet into each chain. At the end of the row, turn and work three turning chain; these count as one stitch, so the first treble crochet of the second row is worked into the second stitch of the previous row.

5 When working back along the row, insert the hook under both loops of each stitch in the previous row.

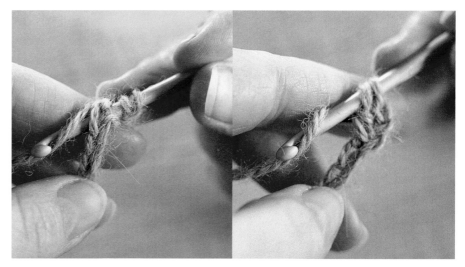

step one Wrap yarn over hook, insert it in third chain from hook, and wrap yarn over hook again.

step two Draw yarn though chain, yarn over hook, draw yarn through two loops on hook, yarn over hook.

end of first row At the end of the row, work three turning chain.

end of subsequent rows Work the last stitch of a row into the top of the turning chain.

Double treble

Double treble crochet (dtr) — known in the United States as treble crochet (tr) — is usually used in combination with other stitches rather than to form a fabric on its own.

When working in double treble crochet, the number of foundation chain should equal the number of stitches required, plus four for the turning chain.

1 Wrap the yarn over the hook twice and insert the hook into the fifth chain from the hook, picking up two strands of chain. Wrap the yarn over the hook.

2 Draw the yarn through the chain to the front; there will be four loops on the hook. Wrap the yarn over the hook again.

3 Draw the yarn through two loops on the hook, *wrap yarn over hook and draw it through two more loops.* Repeat from * to * once. You have now completed one double treble stitch. One loop remains on the hook.

4 Repeat Steps 1 to 3 to the end of the row, working one double treble crochet into each chain. At the end of the row, turn and work four turning chain; these count as one stitch, so the first double treble of the second row is worked into the second stitch of the previous row. Work the last stitch of each row into the the top of the turning chain of the previous row.

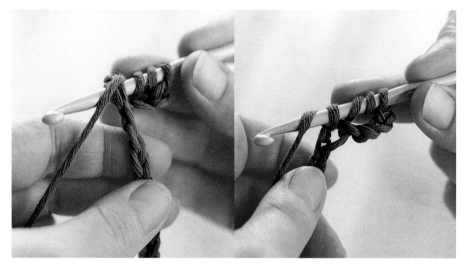

step one Yarn over hook twice, insert hook into fifth chain from hook, yarn over hook.

step two Draw the yarn through the chain to the front. Wrap yarn over hook.

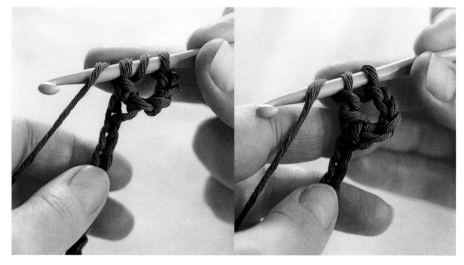

step three Yoh and draw through two loops on hook. Repeat once.

step three, continued Yoh and draw through two loops on hook.

Triple treble

Triple treble crochet (trtr) is known in the United States as double treble crochet (dtr). When working in triple treble crochet, the number of foundation chain should equal the number of stitches required, plus five for the turning chain.

1 Wrap the yarn over the hook three times, then insert the hook into the sixth chain from the hook. Draw the yarn through the chain to the front.

2 *Yarn over hook, draw through two loops on hook*, repeat from * to * until only one loop remains on hook.

3 At the beginning of each row, turn, then work five turning chain. At the end of each row, work the last stitch into the top of the turning chain at the beginning of the previous row.

Quadruple treble

Quadruple treble crochet (qdtr) is known in the United States as triple treble crochet (trtr). When working in quadruple treble crochet, the number of foundation chain should equal the number of stitches required, plus six for the turning chain.

1 Wrap the yarn over the hook four times, then insert the hook into the seventh chain from the hook. Draw the yarn through the chain to the front of the work.

2 *Yarn over hook, draw through two loops on hook*, repeat from * to * until only one loop remains on the hook.

3 At the beginning of each row, turn, then work six turning chain. At the end of each row, work the last stitch into the top of the turning chain at the beginning of the previous row.

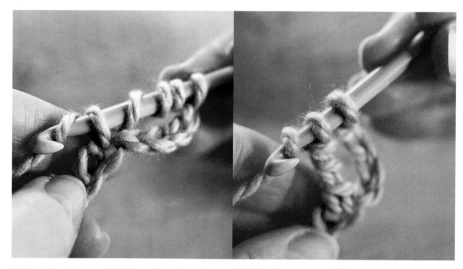

triple treble, step one Yoh three times, insert hook into sixth chain, draw yarn through.

triple treble, step two (Yoh, draw through two loops on hook) until only one loop remains.

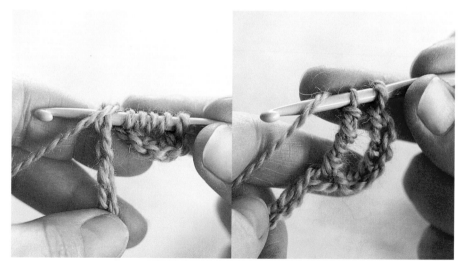

quadruple treble, step one Yoh four times, insert hook into seventh chain, draw yarn through.

quadruple treble, step two (Yoh, draw through two loops on hook) until only one loop remains.

Working groups of stitches

Working a number of stitches together produces a group (also known as a cluster). Groups can be utliized with any of the longer stitches (half treble crochet and up). They can be worked all in one type of stitch, or in a combination.

Each stitch of the group is worked until two loops remain on the hook (rather than the usual one loop). The last step of the last stitch of each group is to draw the yarn through all the loops on the hook, thus gathering the tops of all the stitches together.

Groups can be worked into a chain loop or chain space (as shown in blue yarn in the photographs at left), or into a single stitch. Alternatively, each successive stitch of the group can be worked into a separate stitch of the previous row (as shown in pink yarn). Groups are usually separated from each other with a number of chain, as shown.

1 Using the required stitch type, work a stitch until two loops remain on the hook. Repeat until you have worked the required number of stitches for that group.

At the end of this step, there should be one more loop on the hook than there are stitches in the group (for example, if working a group of four stitches as at left, you will end up with five loops on the hook).

2 Wrap the yarn over the hook and draw the yarn through all the loops on the hook. You have now completed one group.

3 Work the required number of chains to separate the group from the next.

4 Repeat Steps 1 to 3 as required.

working into a chain loop Here, each group consists of four treble crochet stitches.

last step of last stitch Yoh and draw the yarn through all the loops on the hook.

working into successive stitches Work one stitch into each stitch of the previous row.

Increases

To make an internal increase along a row, work to where the increase is required, then work two or more stitches into the same stitch. To shape garment edges neatly, this method is used one stitch in from the edge at the beginning or end of a row. At the beginning of a row, work the first stitch, then work the increase in the next stitch. At the end of the row, work until two stitches remain, work the increase in the second-last stitch, then work the last stitch.

To make an external increase at the start of a row, work the required number of chains at the end of the previous row (remember to include the turning chain), then turn and work along the row as usual. At the end of a row, leave the last few stitches unworked. Remove the hook, join a length of yarn to the last stitch of the row, and work the required number of extra chains (remember to include the turning chain). Fasten off. Insert the hook back into the row, complete the row, then work the extra stitches along the chain.

Shaping techniques

A piece of crochet is shaped by increasing or decreasing. Increases are made by working two or more stitches into the same stitch of the previous row. Decreases are made by skipping stitches, or by working two or more stitches together. These shapings are described as 'internal' when made along a row, and 'external' when made at the beginning or end of a row. Each method produces a different effect.

internal increase along a row Work two or more stitches into the same stitch.

internal increase at edge of crochet Work the increase one stitch in from the edge.

external increase at start of row Work extra chain at end of previous row, turn, then work along row.

external increase at row end, step one Join in yarn and work required number of extra chains.

external increase at row end, step two Reinsert hook into row and work to end of chain.

Decreases

To decrease, skip one or more stitches when working across the previous row (which creates a small hole in the fabric), or work two or more stitches together. To do this, work to where the decrease is required, then work a partial stitch by working it until two loops remain on the hook. Work another partial stitch until a total of three loops remain on the hook. Wrap the yarn over the hook and draw it through all three loops on the hook. You have now decreased one stitch. To decrease two stitches at once, work three partial stitches (four loops will remain on the hook), then wrap the yarn over the hook and draw it through all four loops.

To work an external decrease at the start of a row, simply slip-stitch across the number of stitches to be decreased. Work the turning chain, then continue across the row. For an external decrease at the end of a row, stop several stitches before the end of the row, then turn, work the turning chain and continue back across the row.

internal decrease along a row, method one
Skip one or more stitches in the previous row.

internal decrease along a row, method two
Work two or more stitches together.

external decrease at start of row Slip stitch across the required number of stitches.

external decrease at start of row, step two Work the turning chain, then continue across the row.

external decrease at end of row Stop several stitches before end of previous row, then turn.

Making and working into a ring

To make a ring, work the specified number of chain, then insert the hook into the first chain that you made and join with a slip stitch. Wrap the yarn over the hook and draw it through both the chain and the loop on the hook. You have now created a ring of chains. This becomes the centre of your crochet and is what you will work into to create the first round.

To commence the first round, make the appropriate number of turning chain. Insert the hook from front to back into the ring (not into the chain) and work the number of stitches specified in the pattern. At the end of the round, join the round by working a slip stitch into the top of the starting chain that you made at the beginning of the round.

At the end of the last row of the shape or motif, join the round with a slip stitch. Cut the yarn, leaving a tail, then draw the tail of yarn through the loop left on the hook. Pull the yarn firmly to fasten off.

Working in rounds

Crochet can easily be worked in the round to create many different shapes and motifs, both simple and elaborate. All pieces worked in the round begin with a short length of chain joined to form a ring. Successive rounds are formed from combinations of stitches and chain spaces or chain loops. The piece is worked in rounds rather than back-and-forth rows, and is never turned; the right side always faces you.

joining chain to form a ring Make a slip stitch into the first chain that you made.

working first round Work all the stitches of the first round into the centre of the ring.

end of first round Join round with a slip stitch into top of first stitch (or into the turning chain).

second round Chain loops form the foundation for the third and final round.

finished motif A simple but effective openwork flower in crisp aran-weight cotton.

Measuring tension (gauge)

Tension, or gauge, refers to the number of stitches and rows to 2.5 cm (1 in) over the crocheted fabric. Every crochet pattern will specify a gauge; always pay attention to this, as the gauge determines the size of the finished item. Every person crochets at a different tension; some people crochet loosely and others tightly. Tension may not be crucial in, say, a scarf or cushion, but it is crucial in a garment that is meant to fit precisely. It is vital to check your tension before beginning a garment. In your eagerness to get started on a project, it is tempting to skip this step, but crocheting a tension swatch may prevent the disappointment, and the waste of time and money, of a garment that does not fit.

Crocheting a tension square

The first step in every crochet project should be a tension square. Use the specified hook size and the yarn that you intend to use, whether it is the yarn recommended in the pattern or a replacement. Make a crochet chain about 15 cm (6 in) long, then work in the specified stitch until the piece is at least 15 cm (6 in) long. If the pattern is constructed from motifs, you will need to make one whole motif as instructed, then measure its diameter.

Fasten off the yarn and, if appropriate, block (see page 107) or lightly press the tension square. Insert a pin a few stitches in (do not measure from the sides, as the side edge is always slightly distorted). Avoid stretching the tension square. Measure precisely 10 cm (4 in) from the pin and place another pin at that point as a marker. Do the same vertically, placing the first pin a few rows in from the edge. Count how many stitches and rows there are between the pins; this is your tension.

If the counts are correct, go ahead and start crocheting the item. If you have more stitches than the specified tension, you are working too tightly, and your garment will be too short and too narrow. Make another tension square with a slightly larger hook, and measure again. If you have fewer stitches than specified, you are working too loosely, and your garment will be too long and too wide. Make another tension square with a slightly smaller hook, and measure again. If necessary, repeat this process more than once, until the tension is correct.

Save your tension square and use it to test how well the yarn washes and whether it can be pressed. Pin the ball band to the square, and note on the ball band if you changed the hook size to obtain the correct tension. You now have a reference for the yarn used, and for how the crocheted fabric looks and feels.

tension squares These two tension squares were crocheted by the same person, in the same 8-ply (DK) yarn, but with different-sized crochet hooks. The purple square was made using a 4.5 mm crochet hook and the blue one with a 5 mm hook. The size difference is clear even over such a small sample; over a large item or a garment, the consequences of using the incorrect tension can be ruinous.

measuring a tension square Using pins, and an inflexible ruler rather than a tape measure, mark two points precisely 10 cm (4 in) apart and count the number of stitches between the pins.

Reading diagrams

The written pattern for the motif shown below reads as follows:

Make 5ch, join with ss to form a ring.

Round 1: 1ch, 8dc into ring, ss into ch at beg of rnd.

Round 2: 3ch, (ss into next dc, 3ch), rep to end, ss into 1st ch sp at beg of rnd.

Round 3: 2ch (counts as 1htr), (2tr, 1htr) into same ch sp as ss, *(1htr, 2tr, 1htr) into next ch sp*, rep from * to * to end, ss into base of 2ch at beg of rnd.

Floral motif This motif can be made by following either the instructions above or the diagram below.

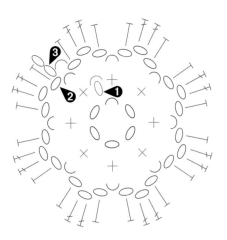

diagram of motif See opposite for a key to the symbols used.

Working from a pattern

Crochet patterns can be either written in words or represented by symbols. A beginner may feel safer using a written pattern. However, as you become more adept at crochet, or when tackling large or complicated motifs, working from a diagram may be preferable. A diagram is a visual representation of the motif or pattern, with the symbols used replicating the stitches; as such, the diagram will show how the motif or pattern should look in a way that words cannot.

The pattern will tell you which yarn and hook size to use, the tension required and the size of the finished item. For a garment with more than one size, instructions for the smallest size are given first and those for larger sizes in parentheses.

Before you begin crocheting, it is vital to work a tension square (see page 103). You should also read through the pattern and make sure you understand all the abbreviations used. If the pattern uses an unfamiliar stitch, practise the stitch on a small test swatch first; it is less time consuming and frustrating to have to pull back and redo a small piece than a large one. If using a multi-size pattern, read right through the pattern and highlight the figures that relate to the size you are making.

Differences in terminology

Different regions use different terms for crochet; confusingly, sometimes the same term is used for a different stitch. The following chart may help. When choosing a pattern, first determine where it was published (this will be stated on the pattern) and then adjust the instructions if needed. Any differences in terminology will be of little concern if you are working from a diagram rather than a written pattern.

Australia/New Zealand/UK	United States
slip stitch	slip stitch
double crochet (dc)	single crochet (sc)
half treble (htr)	half double crochet (hdc)
treble (tr)	double crochet (dc)
double treble crochet (dtr)	treble crochet (tr)
triple treble crochet (trtr)	double treble crochet (dtr)
quadruple treble (qdtr)	treble treble (trtr) or long treble (ltr)
tension	gauge

Symbols

⬭	chain
⌢	slip stitch
+	double crochet
T	half treble
⊤	treble
⫟	double treble
⫟	triple treble
⫟	quadruple treble
⋀	tr2tog
⋀	tr3tog
⋁	inc 1tr
⋀	2 half-treble group
⋀	3 half-treble group
⋀	4 half-treble group
⋔	3 treble group
⋔	3 double-treble group
⋔	3 triple-treble group
⋔	3 quadruple-treble group
●	bead
●	beaded chain
●	beaded double crochet
○	bouclé loop stitch
○	solomon's knot
◢2	number of row/round showing direction in which you work from one row or round to the next

Abbreviations

Abbreviations are used extensively in crochet patterns to save space. Not all publications will use the same abbreviation for the same term, so read through the pattern to familiarize yourself with what each abbreviation means. Be aware that terminology differs between regions; for example, what is known as dc (double crochet) in Australia, New Zealand and the United Kingdom is called sc (single crochet) in the United States. This book uses the Australian, New Zealand and United Kingdom terminology. See opposite for some common US equivalents.

3tr group three-treble group (three incomplete treble stitches worked into one stitch before the yarn is drawn through all remaining loops on hook)

4tr group four-treble group (four incomplete treble stitches worked into one stitch before the yarn is drawn through all remaining loops on hook)

alt alternate
b/ch beaded chain
b/dc beaded double crochet
beg begin/beginning
bet between
blk block
ch chain
ch loop chain loop
ch sp chain space
cl cluster
cm centimetre(s)
col(s) colour(s)
cont continue
dc double crochet (US single crochet/sc)
dc2tog decrease 1 dc over 2 sts
dc3tog decrease 1 dc over 3 sts
dec decrease/decreasing
DK double knitting
dtr double treble
dtr group double treble group
g gram(s)
gr group

htr half treble
htr group half treble group
in inch(es)
inc increase/increasing
include include/including
lp(s) loop(s)
MC Main Colour
mm millimetre
pc picot
patt pattern
prev previous
qdtr quadruple treble
qdtr group quadruple treble group
rem remain(s)/remaining
rep repeat(s)/repeated
rnd round
RS right side(s) of work
sp(s) spaces(s)
ss slip stitch
st(s) stitch(es)
tog together
tr treble
tr group treble group
tr2tog decrease 1 tr over 2 sts
tr3tog decrease 1 tr over 3 sts
trtr triple treble
WS wrong side(s) of work
yoh yarn over hook

Finishing techniques

Crocheted pieces may be joined with sewn or crocheted seams. Each has its advantages and disadvantages, so choose the most appropriate seam for the item you are making. The pattern will generally tell you which type of seam is preferred. Sewn seams are less visible than crocheted seams, but they stretch more; they are generally best avoided in any crocheted piece that has a tendency to drop.

Oversewn seam

This method produces a very flat seam. Place the two pieces to be joined on a flat surface, with right sides up and edges aligned. Insert a large, blunt-ended needle through corresponding stitches in both pieces. The seam can be sewn through both loops of the stitch, or the back loop only.

Backstitch seam

This method produces a strong but non-elastic seam. Hold the two pieces to be joined with right sides facing. Using a large blunt-ended needle, secure the yarn by passing it around the end of the seam twice. On the next stitch, pass the needle around the back of the work and through the second stitch to the front. Pass the needle one stitch to the right, then through the fabric from the front to the back. Bring it out two stitches along and repeat for the length of the seam. (Note that stitches on the back of the fabric travel forwards and those on the front of the fabric travel backwards.)

Woven seam

Lay the pieces flat, right sides up and edges aligned. Start at the bottom and work in a ladder fashion (first from left to right, then right to left), passing the yarn through the loops of corresponding stitches. Pull the yarn tight every 2.5 cm (1 in) or so.

oversewn seam, step one Sew through loops of corresponding stitches on each piece.

oversewn seam, step two The finished seam is flat but slightly visible.

backstitch seam A backstitch seam is very sturdy, but less flexible than a crocheted seam.

woven seam When stitched in the same colour as the garment, a woven seam is almost invisible.

Crocheted seams

A crocheted seam is more visible than a sewn one, but will have a similar degree of elasticity to the rest of the item.

Crocheted seams can be worked with the right sides or the wrong sides of the pieces together, depending on the effect you wish to create. If worked with the wrong sides together, the finished seam will be visible on the right side of the item. A visible seam can be a feature on, for example, a cushion or rug (especially if worked in a contrasting colour), but may be undesirable on the outside of a garment. If in doubt, try out both methods to see which you prefer.

Double crochet seam

Hold the pieces together, having the edges even. Join in the yarn. Inserting the hook through both loops of both corresponding stitches on each side, work in double crochet for the length of the seam. If joining rows of motifs, as for a rug, join all the motifs in one direction first, then work the seam in the other direction.

Slip stitch seam

For a slightly less raised seam (not pictured), join the two pieces with slip stitch rather than double crochet.

Blocking and pressing

Blocking and pressing are methods of shaping a finished piece of crochet. They are not always necessary; check the pattern instructions, and also the yarn's ball band. Blocking and pressing are often required for crocheted lace or motifs, as they improve stitch definition and give a better shape. The extra effort required to block and press a piece is small, and will give your work a professional-looking finish.

Blocking should be done before sewing seams. To block, lay a clean, colourfast towel or sheet on a padded surface such as carpet. Lay the item to be blocked on top of this and pin it out to size, easing and gently stretching where necessary and making sure the sides and ends are completely straight.

For natural fibres such as wool or cotton, set the iron on a steam setting and hold the iron about 2.5 cm (1 in) above the fabric and allow the steam to penetrate for several seconds. Work in sections, without allowing the iron to touch the crochet. Allow to dry before removing the pins.

Pieces made from synthetic yarns should not be pressed; they will go limp, or in some cases melt. Instead, pin as described above, then spray lightly with cold water and leave to dry completely before removing the pins.

When the pins are removed, a blocked piece should be flat, be the correct size, and have clearly defined stitches.

double crochet seam, step one Work double crochet through both loops of each stitch.

double crochet seam Double crochet produces a strong, visible, raised seam.

Table runner

Give a table or dresser a retro look with this table runner. With its hippie-style bobbles draped over the edge, it will add groove to your table setting.

Double-knit cotton yarn is practical and hard-wearing, and washable in case of spills and drips.

Materials
100 g (3½ oz) Rowan Handknit Cotton double-knit (8-ply) yarn in each of Colour 1 and Colour 2
Small bag of polyester fibrefill

Tools
3 mm (US 2/UK 11) crochet hook

Size
Approximately 100 x 20 cm (39 x 8 in), not including bobble fringe

Tension
20 sts and 11 rows over pattern = 10 cm (4 in)

Abbreviations
ch: chain
dc: double crochet
dtr: double treble
qtr: quadruple treble
ss: slip stitch
tr: treble

runner Two colours are alternated throughout the piece.

RUNNER

Using Colour 1, make 202ch, turn.

Row 1 Miss 1ch, 1dc into each ch to end, turn.

Row 2 6ch, miss 1dc, *1qdtr into next st, 1ch, miss 1st*, rep from * to * to end, 1qdtr into last st, turn.

Row 3 1ch, 1dc into each st to end, turn.

Row 4 As for Row 3.

Row 5 Using Colour 2, as for Row 3.

Row 6 3ch, 1tr into each st to end, turn.

Row 7 1ch, 1dc into each st to end, turn.

Rows 8–9 Using Colour 1, as for Row 3.

Row 10 Using Colour 2, as for Row 3.

Row 11 3ch, miss 1dc, *1dtr into next st, 1ch, miss 1st*, rep from * to * to end, 1 dtr

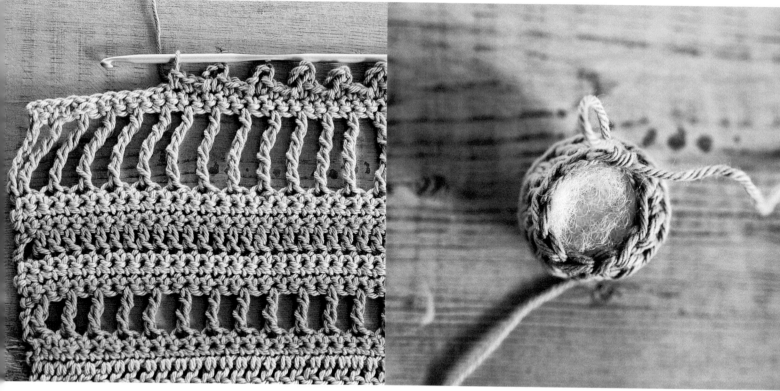

picot edge Work at each side of the runner in Colour 2.

bobble 1, round 5 Insert a small amount of fibrefill into the bobble.

into last st, turn.

Row 12 Make 1ch, 1dc into each st to end, turn.

Using Colour 1, rep Row 3, then Row 6.

Using Colour 2, rep Row 7, then Row 2, then Row 3.

Using Colour 1, rep Row 3, then Row 6.

Using Colour 2, rep Row 7, then Row 11, then Row 12.

Using Colour 1, rep Row 3 twice.

Using Colour 2, rep Row 3, then row 6, then row 7.

Using Colour 1, rep Row 3 twice, then Row 2, then Row 3.

Fasten off and finish ends into the piece.

PICOT EDGE

1 With the right side of the work facing, join Colour 2 to the right-hand edge of the end of the piece.

2 1ch, 1dc into each of first 2dc, *4ch, 1ss into same st as prev dc (to make 4-ch picot), 1dc into each of next 3dc*, rep from * to * to end. Fasten off, finish ends into piece.

3 Repeat Steps 1 and 2 for the other edge of the piece.

BOBBLE 1 Make 16 (8 of Colour 1, 8 of Colour 2)

Round 1 Make 2ch, 7dc into 1st ch to make a small disc.

Round 2 2ch into each dc to end.

tails, step 1 Work in double crochet back down the length of the chain.

tails, step 2 Attach one large and one small bobble to each tail.

Round 3 1ss into each st to end.

Round 4 1dc into each st to end.

Round 5 1dc into each st to end.

Fill bobble with a small amount of polyester fibrefill.

Round 6 1ss into next dc, *skip 1dc, 1ss into next dc (to decrease)*, rep from * to * to end.

Round 7 As for Round 6.

Feed end of yarn through ch at top of bobble, pull tight and fasten off. Finish ends into bobble.

BOBBLE 2 Make 16 (8 of Colour 1, 8 of Colour 2)

Round 1 2ch, 5dc into 1st ch to make a small disc.

Round 2 2ss into each st to end.

Round 3 1ss into each st to end.

Round 4 1dc into each st to end.

Fill bobble with a small amount of polyester fibrefill.

Round 5 1ss into next dc, *skip 1dc, 1ss into next dc (to decrease)*, rep from * to * to end.

Round 6 As for Round 5.

Feed end of yarn through ch at top of bobble, pull tight and fasten off. Finish ends into bobble.

tails, step 3 When attaching bobbles, match the bobble colour to that of the tail.

TAILS

1 Using Colour 2, make 70ch. Make 2dc through the end of the runner at the short edge, make 1dc into each of the next 50ch (working back down the tail), make 10ch, fasten off.

2 Using the end of yarn on the longer end of the tail, stitch a large bobble onto the tail. Using the other end of yarn at the shorter end of the tail, stitch on a smaller bobble.

3 Create eight tails of varying lengths along either end of the runner, matching the colours to those of the runner at the point where you attach the tails. Work tails of 70ch, 60ch, 50ch and 40ch, working back

50ch, 40ch, 30ch, 20ch respectively, and finishing each tail with 10ch as in Step 1. Repeat Step 2 to attach two bobbles to each tail.

Hint

For placemats to match, crochet the same repeat on a shorter base of 50ch, working the picot edge all the way around and not adding bobbles.

Beaded door curtain

Light plays on the beads that serve both practical and decorative purposes for this shimmering item of décor. As a pretty cover-up for a doorway, this curtain will add a touch of fantasy to a room's entrance, while the movement of the beads will also serve to keep insects out.

Glass beads of various sizes work as weights to keep the crocheted strands from tangling together in the breeze. At the top, the strings of beads are attached to a length of dowel using a fabric pocket. The dowel can be suspended via cup hooks or other means over the doorway.

Materials
5 large spools Coats Buttonhole (bonded nylon) thread
4000 assorted medium-sized beads (the beads should be a mixture of materials, such as glass and plastic, to reduce the weight of the curtain)
10 x 84 cm (4 x 33 in) piece satin fabric
80 cm (31½ in) length of dowel

Tools
1 mm (US 11 or 12/UK 5½ or 6) crochet hook

Size
To fit standard doorway, but can be customized

Tension
Tension is not crucial for this project

Abbreviations
ch: chain
b/ch: beaded chain

beaded chains Thread a selection of beads onto the bonded nylon yarn.

step 1 Slide a bead up the yarn and work over it to create the beaded chain stitch.

BEADED CHAINS

1 String 50 beads onto the yarn. Make 2ch; (1b/ch, 4ch) five times; (1b/ch, 5ch) five times; (1b/ch, 6ch) five times; (1b/ch, 7ch) five times; (1b/ch, 8ch) five times; (1b/ch, 9ch) five times; (1b/ch, 10ch) five times; (1b/ch, 11ch) five times; (1b/ch, 12ch) five times; (1b/ch, 13ch) five times.

Work a further 200ch, or until total length measures height of door, allowing for weight of beads to cause the chain length to drop slightly; see Hint opposite. Break off yarn.

2 Repeat Step 1 another 79 times, to give 80 chains of beads.

rod pocket Make a tube of satin fabric to hold the dowel.

JOINING CHAIN LENGTHS

Make 3ch, *1ss through the top (unbeaded) end of a chain length, 3ch*, rep until all chain lengths are incorporated (the width should be 80 cm/31½ in, which is an average door width).

CREATING ROD POCKET

1 Overlock the edges of the satin fabric and press a small hem allowance on all sides. Sew the strip of chain joining all of the lengths (step 3) to the right side of one edge of the satin fabric, inside the hem allowance.

2 Fold the satin strip in half lengthwise (wrong sides together) and stitch the long edges together to form a tube. Sew one end of the tube closed, insert the dowel and close the other end.

Hang the beaded curtain from cup hooks or similar hooks fixed above the doorway.

Hints

An assortment of bead sizes will give slightly different chain lengths, which creates a more random appearance.

Fewer beads per chain will give a simpler look.

The chains may increase in length once hung for a time, so it is a good idea to hang each chain from a hook as it is completed, to allow some of the length to drop.

Glass beads are heavier and can help the chains swing better, but be careful not to use too many as this can make the whole curtain very heavy.

As alternatives to beads you could use such objects as sequins, shells or even buttons, which will give a unique style.

Smaller versions of this curtain could be made for windows.

Chunky bolster, cushion and throw

Cuddle up on the lounge with cushions and

covers in a soft, chunky yarn. It's meant to be

comfortable, not chic, so go for faded colours

and stippled yarns to bring out the classic

cottony texture. This project uses several

strands of yarn crocheted together to enhance

the chunky, country-style look.

Materials

Bolster: 400 g (14 oz) Jaeger Trinity double-
knit silk/cotton blend yarn
35 x 70 cm (14 x 28 in) soft pillow
Cushion: 250 g (9 oz) Jaeger Trinity double-
knit silk/cotton blend yarn
40 cm (16 in) square cushion insert
Throw: 600 g (1 lb 5 oz) Jaeger Trinity double-
knit silk/cotton blend yarn; use a mixture of
colours for a patchwork effect

Tools

9 mm (US 13 or 15/UK 00) crochet hook
(bolster and cushion)
5 mm (US 7/UK 6) crochet hook (throw)
Darning needle

Size

Bolster: 70 x 35 cm (27½ x 13½ in)
Cushion: 40 cm (16 in) square
Throw: 100 x 85 cm (39½ x 33½ in)

Tension

Bolster and cushion: 11½ sts and 11 rows
over patt using 9 mm (US 13 or 15/UK 00)
crochet hook and 4 ends of yarn together
Throw: tension is not crucial for this project;
1 motif = approximately 17 cm (6½ in)
square, using 5 mm (US 7/UK 6) crochet
hook and 2 ends of yarn held together

Abbreviations

ch: chain
dc: double crochet
dtr: double treble
tr: treble

bolster or cushion, row 3 Work a treble stitch into each stitch of the previous row.

bolster or cushion assembly Stitch up the open edges using blanket stitch.

Hints

The bolster and cushion are made using four ends of yarn held together to give a chunky texture. Both covers are made in one piece.

For extra depth of colour, use a contrast-coloured cushion under the cover, as it will show through between the stitches.

For extra interest, try weaving ribbon through the rows of treble stitches (see photograph on page 123).

Bolster

COVER

Make 36ch, turn.

Row 1 1ss into each ch to end, turn.

Row 2 1ch, miss 1 st, 1ss into each ch to end, turn.

Row 3 3ch, miss 1 st, 1 tr into each st to end, turn.

Row 4 1ch, miss 1 st, 1ss into each st to end, turn.

Rows 5 and 6 As for Row 2.

Repeat Rows 3 to 6 until work measures 150 cm (59 in) (approximately 34 repeats), finishing on Row 4. Fasten off and finish ends into piece.

cushion or bolster assembly Allow a 10 cm (4 in) overlap in the middle of one side, through which the cushion or bolster will be inserted.

ASSEMBLY

Fold widthwise, wrong sides together, allowing 10 cm (4 in) overlap at the centre of one side; the total folded size should be 35 x 70 cm (13½ x 27½ in). Sew up both open edges using blanket stitch. Insert the pillow.

Cushion

COVER

Make 41ch, turn.
Row 1 1ss into each ch to end, turn.
Row 2 1ch, miss 1 st, 1ss into each st to end, turn.

Row 3 3ch, miss 1 st, 1tr into each st to end, turn.
Row 4 1ch, miss 1 st, 1ss into each st to end, turn.
Rows 5 and 6 As for Row 2.
Repeat Rows 3 to 6 until work measures 90 cm (35½ in) (approximately 19 repeats), finishing on Row 4. Fasten off and finish ends into piece.

ASSEMBLY

Fold widthwise, wrong sides together, allowing 10 cm (4 in) overlap at the centre of one side; the total folded size should be 40 cm (16 in) square). Sew up both open edges using blanket stitch. Insert cushion.

Substituting yarns

Where possible, you should use the yarn specified in the pattern, as the pattern has been designed specifically for that yarn; other yarns may give different results. However, this is not always possible; the yarn may be discontinued, too expensive or otherwise unavailable. In this case, you will need to find another yarn of similar composition, texture, properties and — most importantly — thickness.

The substitute yarn should crochet to the same tension (see page 103) as the specified yarn, or your finished item will differ in size to the pattern. It is vital to check your tension; even if the specified yarn and the substitute are both labelled as DK, for example, they may differ in thickness.

Be aware that even when the substitute yarn works up to the same tension as the specified yarn, it may give a quite different finished effect. This can be due to various factors, including the yarn's composition and the way it has been treated by the manufacturer. Another reason to do a tension swatch is so you can check you are happy with the look and feel of the fabric that the substitute yarn produces.

throw The throw is worked in different-coloured squares that are then sewn together in an offset fashion, with each at a 90-degree angle to the previous.

square blocks for throw, row 4 The squares are worked in double treble and double crochet.

Throw

SQUARE BLOCKS Make 30

Using two ends of yarn, make 21ch, turn.

Row 1 1dc into each ch to end, turn.

Row 2 1ch, miss 1 st, 1dc into each st to end, turn.

Row 3 As for Row 2.

Row 4 3ch, miss 1 st, 1dtr into each st to end, turn.

Row 5 1ch, miss 1 st, 1dc into each st to end, turn.

Rows 6–7 As for Row 2.

Repeat Rows 4 to 7 another three times. Fasten off. Finish ends into piece. Block each square to shape using a cool iron.

throw assembly Sew the squares together, offsetting each square to the previous at right angles.

variation Weave ribbon through the rows of double treble.

ASSEMBLY

Arrange the squares into a random pattern of colour, offsetting each square by 90 degrees. Using an oversewn seam or blanket stitch, sew together into strips of five squares and then sew the six strips together to create the throw.

If desired, thread lengths of ribbon through some or all of the double-treble rows before sewing up the blocks, to create a contrasting effect.

Hints

The squares are made using three colours of yarn; make squares in two ends of the same colour, or combine two ends each in a different colour to create variegated shades.

For extra depth of colour, back the throw using a complementary coloured fabric, which will show through between the stitches.

Bathmat and mitt

The bathroom is the one room of the house where luxury is a necessity. With a mat to keep your wet feet off the cold floor, and a soft scrubbing mitt to buff your skin to a healthy shine, you'll never want to leave.

Cotton yarn is absorbent, washable, and soft to the touch, so it's perfect for use on bare skin. Cotton also becomes softer the more it is washed, so the more you use it, the nicer it becomes.

The pictured examples use five different shades to give graduated stripes.

Materials

Jo Sharp Soho Summer double-knit cotton yarn:
  300 g (10½ oz) for Mat; 100 g (3½ oz) for Mitt

Tools

Mat: 5 mm (US 7/UK 6) crochet hook
Mitt: 4 mm (US 5/UK 8)crochet hook

Size

Mat: 48 x 35 cm (19 x 14 in)
Mitt: 18 x 13 cm (7 x 5 in)

Tension

Mat: 13½ sts and 8 rows = 10 cm (4 in) in bouclé
  loop crochet using 5 mm crochet hook and
  2 ends of yarn held together
Mitt: 20 sts and 13 rows over 10 cm (4 in) in
  double crochet using 4 mm crochet hook and
  one end of yarn

Abbreviations

ch: chain
dc: double crochet
blc: bouclé loop crochet (see below)

Bouclé loop crochet

Bouclé loop stitch is worked on a base of double crochet (US single crochet). The following instructions are for right-handed crocheters: Hold yarn with left hand and, with right hand, wrap yarn clockwise around left index finger to make a loop. Insert the hook into the stitch so there are two loops on the hook. Pass the hook *over* the yarn (not under, as usual). Catch both strands of yarn with the hook, and pull them both through the stitch. You should now have 3 loops on the hook. Wrap the yarn over the hook and draw the yarn through all loops on the hook. You have now completed one bouclé loop stitch. Repeat as required.

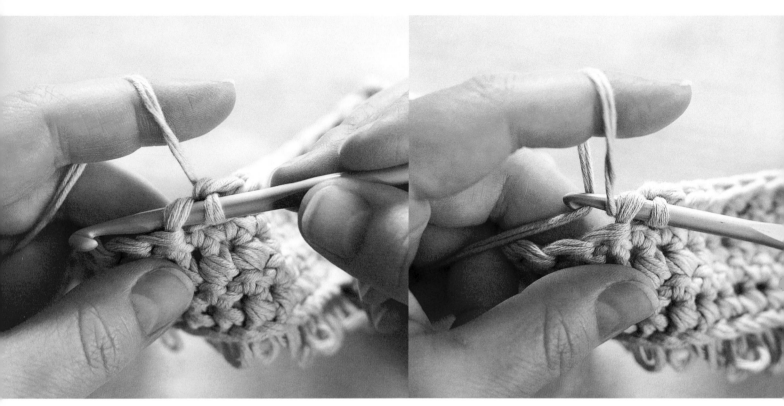

bouclé loop crochet Insert hook in next stitch and wrap yarn anticlockwise around index finger of left hand.

bouclé loop crochet, continued Pass hook over yarn (not under it, as is usual) and draw both strands through to front of work.

Mat hint

To achieve a graduated stripe effect in the mat, simply use two strands of yarn together, each of a different colour, and change the colour combination every couple of rows. The sequence for this piece is: shade 1 + 1, shades 1 + 2, shades 2 + 2, shades 2 + 3, shades 3 + 3, shades 3 + 4, shades 4 + 4, shades 4 + 5, shades 5 + 5, shades 5 + 4, shades 4 + 4, shades 4 + 3, shades 3 + 3, shades 3 + 2, shades 2 + 2, shades 2 + 1, shade 1 + 1 (working from dark to light and back to dark).

Bathmat

Using two ends of yarn, make 45ch, turn.
Row 1 1blc into each ch to end, turn.
Row 2 1ch, miss 1blc, 1dc into each st to end, turn.
Row 3 1ch, miss 1dc, 1blc into each st to end, turn.
Repeat Rows 2 and 3 another 33 times, changing colours every 4 rows in the order suggested in the Hints, at left, or at random. Fasten off; finish ends into piece.

bouclé loop crochet, continued Pass yarn under hook again and draw through all loops on hook. Hold the loop with your finger until the stitch is complete.

Bath mitt

PLAIN SIDE

Make 31ch, turn.

Row 1 1ss into each ch to end, turn.

Row 2 1ch, miss 1 st, 1ss into each st to end, turn.

Rows 3–17 As for Row 2.

Row 18 1ch, 1ss into each of first 3sts, 1dc into each of next 24sts, 1ss into each of last 3sts, turn.

Row 19 As for Row 18.

Rows 20–23 As for Row 2.

Row 24 1ch, 1ss into each of first 3sts, 1dc into each of next 24sts, 1ss into each of the last 3sts, turn.

Row 25 As for Row 2.

Repeat Row 18 six times; rep Rows 24 and 25; rep from * to * again.

Repeat Rows 18 and 19.

Row 42 1ch, 1ss into each of first 2 sts, 1ss into next 2 sts together (to decrease), 1dc into each of the next 23 sts, 1ss into each of last 3 sts, turn.

Row 43 1ch, 1ss into each of first 2 sts, 1ss into next 2 sts together (to decrease), 1dc into each of the next 22 sts, 1ss into each of the last 3 sts, turn.

Continue in this manner, decreasing 1 st at beginning of each row, until 18 sts remain. Fasten off and finish ends into piece.

Mitt hint

Like the mat, the mitt is worked in stripes, with the colours changing every couple of rows. Work from dark to light and back to dark for a graduated effect, or mix the colours up at random.

mitt Use five graduating shades of colour for a subtle stripe effect.

plain side The mitt has one plain side and one bouclé loop side.

BOUCLÉ LOOP SIDE

Make 31ch, turn.

Row 1 1ss into each ch to end.

Row 2 1ch, miss 1 st, 1ss into each st to end.

Repeat Row 2 another 15 times.

Row 18 (WS) 1ch, miss 1 st, 1ss into each of next 3 sts, 1blc into each st until 3 sts rem, 1ss into each of final 3 sts, turn.

Row 19 1ch, 1ss into first 3 sts, 1dc into each of the next 24 sts, 1ss into final 3 sts, turn.

Row 20 As for Row 18.

Repeat Rows 19 and 20 another seven times.

Repeat Row 19 again.

Row 36 1ch, 1ss into each of the first 2ch, 1ss into next 2 sts together (to decrease), 1blc into each of the next 23 sts, 1ss into each of the last 3 sts, turn.

bouclé loop side, odd rows Work double crochet every second row.

finishing Crochet the two sides of the mitt together around the edges, with wrong sides together.

Row 37 1ch, 1ss into first 2 sts, 1ch into next 2 sts together (to decrease), 1dc into each of the next 22 sts, 1ss into each of the last 3 sts, turn.

Continue in this manner, decreasing 1 st at the beginning of each row, until 18 sts remain.

Fasten off and finish ends into work.

FINISHING

Hold the two mitt pieces with the right sides out (the loopy side of one and the slightly more textured side of the other), crochet together around the edges, using ss. Fasten off and finish ends into the piece.

Vest

Soft, silky yarn drapes nicely over the body in this pretty starburst design for a feminine singlet top. Select a yarn with a sheen in a subtle colour to make a fashion statement that will never go out of style.

Materials
150 g (5½ oz) Debbie Bliss Pure Silk

Tools
3 mm (US 2/UK 11) crochet hook

Size
To fit sizes S (80 cm/31½ inch chest), M (90 cm/35½ inch chest), L (100 cm/ 39½ inch chest)

Tension
2 rows of pattern = 14 cm wide x 7 cm high (5½ in wide x 2¾ in high)

Abbreviations
ch: chain
dc: double crochet
dtr: double treble
qdtr: quadruple treble
tr: treble
trtr: triple treble

BACK Sizes S (M, L)

Make 96 (112, 128)ch, turn.

Row 1 Miss 1ch, 1dc into each ch to end, turn.

Row 2 Make 3ch, *miss 1dc, 1dtr into next dc, 1ch, miss 1dc, 1trtr into next dc, 1ch, miss 1dc, 1qdtr into next dc, 1ch, miss 1dc, 1qdtr into next dc, 1ch, miss 1dc, 1trtr into next dc, 1ch, miss 1dc, 1dtr into next dc, 1ch, miss 1dc, 1tr into next dc, 1ch, miss 1dc, 1tr into next dc, 1ch*, rep from * to * to end, turn.

Row 3 Make 6ch. Working into each of the first 4 ch spaces, make a 4qdtr group; *7ch, 1dc into next ch space, 7ch; working into each of the next 7ch spaces, make a 7qdtr group*, rep from * to * another 4 (5, 6) times, 7ch, 1dc into next ch space, 7ch; working into each of the last 4ch spaces, make a 4qdtr group, turn.

Row 4 Make 6ch, 1qdtr into top of 1st qdtr group, (1ch, 1qdtr into top of same qdtr group) 4 times, *1qdtr into top of next qdtr group, 1ch, 1 qdtr into top of same qdtr group) 8 times*. Repeat from * to * another 4 (5, 6) times. 1qdtr into top of last qdtr group, (1ch, 1qdtr into top of same qdtr group) 4 times, turn.

Row 5 Make 3ch, miss 1 qdtr, *1dtr into next ch space, 1ch, 1trtr into next ch space, 1ch, 1qdtr into next ch space, 1ch, miss the ch space between the two qdtr groups, 1qdtr into next ch space, 1ch, 1trtr into next ch space, 1ch, 1dtr into next ch space, 1ch, 1tr into next ch space*, rep from * to * to end.

Repeat Rows 3–5 another 4 (5, 6) times, or until work is length desired.

Row 18 (21, 24): Shape armhole 1ss into each st until you reach the ch space between the first qdtr of the previous row, 1dc into next ch space, *7ch, 1qdtr into each of next 7ch spaces (making a 7qdtr group), 7ch, 1dc into next ch space*, rep from * to * another 4 (5, 6) times, turn.

Row 19 (22, 25) Make 6ch, 1qdtr into top of 1st qdtr group, (1ch, 1qdtr into top of same group) 4 times, *1qdtr into top of next qdtr group, (1ch, 1 qdtr into top of same group) 8 times*. Repeat from * to * another 3 (4, 5) times. 1qdtr into top of last qdtr group, (1ch, 1qdtr into top of same qdtr group) 4 times, turn.

Row 20 (23, 26) 3ch, *1dtr into next ch space, 1ch, 1trtr into next ch space, 1ch, 1qdtr into next ch space, 1ch, 1qdtr into next ch space, 1ch, 1trtr into next ch space, 1ch, 1dtr, 1ch, 1tr into next ch space, 1ch, 1tr into next ch space, 1ch*, rep from * to * to end.

Row 21 (24, 27) Make 6ch. Working into each of the next 3ch spaces, make a 3qdtr group, *7ch, 1dc into next ch space (between the 2 qdtrs), 7ch, 1qdtr into each of the next 7ch spaces (making a qdtr group)*, rep from * to * 3 (4, 5) times, 1qdtr into each of the last 4ch spaces (making a 4qdtr group), turn.

Repeat Rows 19 and 20.

Row 24 (27, 30): create strap Make 6ch. Working into each of the next 3ch spaces, make a 3qdtr group, 7ch, 1dc into next ch space, 7ch; working into the next 4ch spaces, work a qdtr group. Turn.

Row 25 (28, 31) Make 6ch, 1qdtr into top of 1st qdtr group, (1ch, 1qdtr into top of same qdtr group) 4 times. 1qdtr into top of next qdtr group, (1ch, 1qdtr into top of same qdtr group) 4 times, turn.

Row 26 (29, 34) Make 3ch, miss 1qdtr, 1dtr into next ch space, 1ch, 1trtr into next ch space, 1ch, 1qdtr into next ch space (miss 2qdtr), 1qdtr into next ch space (miss 1qdtr), 1ch, 1trtr into next ch space (miss 1qdtr), 1ch, 1tr into next ch space (miss 1qdtr). Fasten off and finish ends into piece.

Repeat the last three rows on the other edge to create the other strap.

FRONT

Make as for back until you reach Row 18.

Row 18 (21, 24): Shape armhole 1ss into each of next 8sts, 18ch, *1qdtr into next 7ch spaces (making a 7qdtr group), 7ch, 1dc into next ch space, 7ch*, repeat from * to * another 4 (5, 6) times, 1qdtr into each of last 8ch spaces, turn.

Row 19 (22, 25) Make 18ch, 1dc through ch space next to end of last row, 1ch into last 10ch, 1ch, 1qdtr into top of qdtr group, (1ch, 1qdtr into top of 1qdtr group) 8 times. Repeat qdtr group another 4 (5, 6) times. Turn.

finishing If desired, work a picot edge around the lower, neck and armhole edges of the garment.

Row 20 (23, 26) Make 6ch, *miss 1dc, 1qdtr into next dc, 1ch, miss 1dc), 1trtr into next dc, 1ch, miss 1dc), 1dtr into next dc, 1ch, miss 1dc, 1tr into next dc, 1ch, miss 1dc, 1tr into next dc, 1ch, miss 1dc, 1dtr into next dc, 1ch, miss 1dc, 1trtr into next dc, 1ch, miss 1dc, 1qdtr into next dc, 1ch*, repeat from * to * to end, turn.

Row 21 (24, 27): Create strap Make 18ch, 1qdtr into each of the next 7ch spaces (making a qdtr group), 7ch, 1dc into next ch space, turn.

Row 22 (25, 28) Make 18ch, 1dc through ch space next to end of last row, 1ss into each of next 10ch, 1ch, 1qdtr into top of 1qdtr group, (1ch, 1qdtr into top of 1qdtr group) 8 times, turn.

Row 23 (26, 29) Make 6ch, miss 1dc, 1qdtr into next dc, 1ch, miss 1dc, 1trtr into next dc, 1ch, miss 1dc, 1dtr into next dc, 1ch, miss 1dc, 1tr into next dc, 1ch, miss 1dc, 1tr

into next dc, 1ch, miss 1dc, 1dtr into next dc, 1ch, miss 1dc, 1trtr into next dc, 1ch, miss 1dc, 1qdtr into next dc, 1ch, turn.
Repeat the last three rows once.

Repeat the last six rows at the opposite end of the work for the other strap. Fasten off and finish the ends into piece.

ASSEMBLY
Stitch the two pieces together at the shoulders and side seams. Finish yarn ends into the piece.

PICOT EDGING (OPTIONAL)
Join the yarn to the edge of the garment, With right side facing, work edging thus: (1dc into each of next 3 sts, 3ch, 1dc into same st as previous dc), rep to end.

Lace hat and scarf

Lacy loops of soft mohair yarn in wintry blues and greys make a feminine ensemble. Settled on the head and shoulders like a light snowfall, these pretty accessories will keep the seasonal chill away.

The narrow scarf is long enough to wrap snugly around any neck, while the cosy hat can be made in three sizes.

Materials
Artyarn Kid Mohair (70% mohair, 30% silk); 50 g (1¾ oz) ball for each of hat and scarf

Tools
4 mm (US 5/UK 8) crochet hook

Size
Hat instructions are given for three sizes.
  S: to fit head circumference approximately 50 cm (20 in)
  M: to fit head circumference approximately 55 cm (22 in)
  L: to fit head circumference approximately 60 cm (24 in)
The scarf is one size fits all, and measures approximately 100 x 16 cm (39½ x 6¼ in)

Tension
For the scarf, tension is not crucial.
For the hat, 17 sts and 8 rows over pattern = 10 cm (4 in)

Abbreviations
ch: chain
dc: double crochet
dtr: double treble
ss: slip stitch

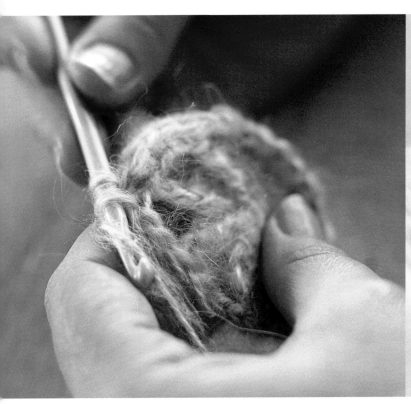

hat, round 2 Work in a circle for the crown.

hat, round 4 Work lacy loops around the crown.

Hint

Tie a coloured thread onto one side of the crown of the hat, so that you can easily see which is the inside and which direction you are working in.

Hat

Make 5 (6, 7)ch, join with ss to form a ring.

Round 1 Make 6ch (counts as 1dtr and 3ch), *1dtr into ring, 3ch*, rep from * to * to end [6 (7, 8) sts]. Join with ss into 3rd of 6ch at beg of rnd.

Round 2 Make 1ch, *1dc in next ch, 3ch*, rep from * to* another 7 (8, 9) times [8, (9, 10) loops]. Join with ss into beg of rnd.

Round 3 *8ch, 1ss into next ch loop*, rep from * to * another 7 (8, 9) times [8 (9, 10) loops].

Round 4 Slip-stitch across to middle of next ch loop (4ss), *8ch, 1ss into next ch loop*, rep from * to * another 7 (8, 9) times [8 (9, 10) loops].

Repeat Round 4 for size L only.

Round 5 (5, 6) Slip-stitch across to middle of next ch loop (4ss), *5ch, 1ss into next ch loop*, rep from * to * to end, 1ss into ss at beg of round [48 (54, 60) ch].

Round 6 (6, 7) As for Round 2 [48 (54, 60) dc].

Round 7 (7, 8) As for Round 3 [16 (18, 20) loops].

Round 8 (8, 9) As for Round 4.

Round 9 (9, 10) As for Round 4 [16 (18, 20) loops].

Round 10 (10, 11) As for Round 5 [(96, 108, 120) ch].

scarf, row 1 The scarf begins with a row of double crochet.

scarf, step 2–6 The fabric is formed from rows of lacy loops separated by a row of double crochet.

Rounds 11 (11, 12)–14 (14, 15) Repeat Rounds 7 (7, 8)–10 (10, 11).

Round 15 (15, 16) Slip-stitch across to middle of next ch loop (4ss), *4ch, 1ss into next ch loop*, rep from * to * to end, 1ss into top of 4ch at beg of rnd [80, (90, 100) ch]. Finish ends into work.

Scarf

Make 28ch, turn.

Row 1 Miss 1ch, 1dc in each ch to end, turn.

Row 2 Make 7ch, 1ss into 3rd dc, *8ch, miss 5dc, 1ss into next dc*, rep from * to * to end, turn.

Row 3 Make 7ch, 1ss into top of next ch loop, *8ch, 1ss into top of next ch loop*, rep from * to * to end, turn.

Row 4 As for Row 3.

Row 5 Make 5ch, 1ss into top of first ch loop, *5ch, 1ss into top of next ch loop*, rep from * to * to end, turn.

Row 6 Make 1ch, skip 1st ch, 1dc in each dc to end, turn.

Repeat Rows 2 to 6 another 17 times. Finish ends into work.

Concealing yarn ends

The term 'finish ends into work' means to hide the tails of yarn at the beginning and end of the work, or at the point where new yarn has been joined in, by darning them into the crocheted fabric. To do this, thread a blunt-ended needle with the tail of yarn and weave it through a few stitches on the wrong side of the work, then cut off the rest of the tail close to the surface of the fabric.

Lace skirt

This pretty skirt incorporates flower and

snowflake motifs linked by loops of lacy chain

in rich yarn colours, making this the perfect

trans-seasonal garment.

Choose a sumptuous, shiny fabric for the

underskirt to add a touch of glamour.

Materials
Rowan Soft 100 per cent merino 4-ply yarn:
  100 g (3½ oz) each of Colour 1 and Colour 2
Coloured slip or underskirt

Tools
3 mm (US 2/UK 11) crochet hook

Size
To fit waist size:
  S: 74 cm (29 in)
  M: 81 cm (32 in)
  L: 88 cm (34½ in)
Length approximately 70 cm (27½ in)
To make larger sizes, see Hint, page 141.

Tension (after blocking)
Small 5-petal flower = 6 cm (2½ in) diameter
Medium 5-petal flower = 8 cm (3¼ in) diameter
Large 8-petal flower = 10 cm (4 in) diameter
Snowflake = 14 cm (5½ in) from picot to picot

Abbreviations
ch: chain
dc: double crochet
qdtr: quadruple treble
ss: slip stitch
tr: treble
trtr: triple treble

snowflake Work in Colour 1.

small five-petal flower Work in Colour 1.

SNOWFLAKE Make 10 (11, 12)

Using Colour 1, make 9ch, join with ss to form a ring.

Round 1 Make 8ch, *3tr into ring, 5ch*, rep from * to * 4 times, 2tr into ring, 1ss into 3rd of 8ch at beg of rnd.

Round 2 1ss into 1st ch, 7ch, 4tr into ch loop, *miss 3tr, 1ch, 4tr into ch loop, 4ch, 4tr into ch loop*, rep from * to * 4 times, 1ch, 3tr into ch loop, 1ss into 3rd of 7ch at beg of rnd.

Round 3 1ss into each of next 2ch, 6ch, 3tr into ch loop (miss 4tr, 1ch, 4tr), *3ch, 3tr into ch loop, 3ch, 3tr into ch loop*, rep from * to * 4 times, 3ch, 2tr into ch loop, 1ss into 3rd of 6ch at beg of rnd.

Round 4 1ss into each of next 2ch, 8ch, 1ss into same place as previous ss (making a 4-ch picot), 1ch, 2tr into ch loop, (miss 3tr, 1ch), *5ch, 1dc around 1ch, (miss 1ch, 3tr), 5ch, 2tr into ch loop, 5ch, 1ss into 4ch, 1ch, 2tr into ch loop*, rep from * to * 4 times, (miss 3tr, 1ch), 5ch, 1dc around 1ch (miss 1ch, 3tr), 5ch, 1tr into ch loop, 1ss into 3rd of 8ch at beg of rnd. Fasten off.

SMALL FIVE-PETAL FLOWER Make 10 (11, 12)

Using Colour 1, make 4ch, join with ss to form a ring.

Round 1 5ch, *1tr into ring, 2ch*, rep from * to * 3 times, 1ss into 3rd of 5ch at beg of rnd.

medium five-petal flower Work in Colour 1.

large eight-petal flower Work in Colour 1.

Round 2 *5ch, 3trtr group into ch space, 5ch, 1dc into next tr*, rep from * to * four times. Fasten off.

MEDIUM FIVE-PETAL FLOWER
Make 10 (11, 12) Using Colour 1, make 4ch, join with ss to form a ring.

Round 1 Make 5ch, *1tr into ring, 2ch*, rep from * to * 3 times, 1ss into 3rd of 5ch at beg of rnd.

Round 2 1ch, 1dc into each st to end, 1ss into 1st ch of rnd.

Round 3 *Make 7ch. Working into each of the next 3 sts, make a 3qdtr group, 7ch, 1dc into same st as last qdtr of group*, rep from * to * four times. Fasten off.

LARGE EIGHT-PETAL FLOWER
Make 10 (11, 12)

Using Colour 1, make 6ch, join with ss to form a ring.

Round 1 Make 1ch, 12dc into ring.

Round 2 Make 2ch, 2tr into each dc to end, 1ss into top of 2ch at beg of rnd.

Round 3 *Make 7ch. Working into each of the next 3 sts, make a 3qdtr group, 7ch, 1dc into same st as last qdtr of group*, rep from * to * seven times. Fasten off.

Finish yarn ends into all motifs. Press all of the flowers and snowflakes to size, taking care not to distort their shape.

Hint

Make this skirt in larger sizes by increasing the waistband in 7 cm (2¾ in) increments. Make one extra of each motif for each 7 cm (2¾ in) increase.

WAISTBAND

Using Colour 2, make 6ch, turn.

Round 1 Make 1ch, miss 1st ch, 1dc into each ch to end, turn.

Round 2 Make 1ch, miss 1st ch, 1dc into each dc to end, turn.

Repeat Row 2 until waistband measures 77 (84, 91) cm (30¼, 33, 35¾, or length required if making a larger size (see Hint, page 141). Stitch the two ends together to make a loop, being careful not to twist the waistband.

ASSEMBLING THE MOTIFS

Join Colour 2 to waistband. Working in rounds, complete the skirt from the top down to the bottom.

Round 1 *Make 8ch, 1dc into top edge of small flower side petal, 8ch, 1dc into waistband (2.5cm/1 in along waistband), 5ch, 1dc into top of next petal, 5ch, 1dc into waistband (2.5cm/1 in along waistband), 8ch, 1dc into top edge of next side petal, 8ch, 1dc into waistband (2.5cm/1 in along waistband)*, rep from * to * to join all of the small flowers to the skirt.

Round 2 Make 33ch, 1dc into bottom petal on small flower, 7ch, 1dc into last petal, 15ch*, rep from * to * to end, 7ch, 1ss through 26th ch on 1st loop.

Round 3 1dc into each st until 1 st rem, miss last st, 1ss into 1st dc of rnd.

Round 4 Make 17ch, miss 14dc, *1dc into next dc (to align between two lower petals of small flower above), 17ch, miss 14dc, 1dc into next dc (to align between two small flowers above)*, rep from * to * to end, 1ss through base of 17ch at beg of rnd.

Round 5 1ss into each of next 8ch, *17ch, 1dc into next ch loop*, rep from * to * to end, 1ss into ch above 8th ss at beg of rnd.

Round 6 1ss into each of next 8ch, *10ch, 1dc into next ch loop*, rep from * to * to end, join with ss to beg of rnd.

Round 7 1ch, 1dc into each ch to end, join with ss to beg of round.

Round 8 *10ch, 1dc into top edge of medium flower side petal; 10ch, miss 7dc, 1dc into next dc, 7ch, 1dc into top of next petal, 7ch, miss 6dc, 1dc into next dc, 10ch, 1dc into top edge of next side petal; 10ch, miss 7dc, 1dc into next dc*, rep from * to * to join all of the medium flowers around the skirt. Join with ss to 1st ch of rnd.

Round 9 45ch, *1dc into bottom petal of medium flower, 20ch, 1dc into last petal, 20ch*, rep from * to * to end, 10ch, join with ss into 35th ch at beg of rnd.

Round 10 1ch, 1dc into each ch to end, join with ss into 1st ch of rnd.

Round 11 *20ch, miss 19dc, 1dc into next dc (to align between lower two petals of flower above)*, rep from * to * to end, join with ss into 1st ch of rnd.

Round 12 1ss into each of next 10ch, *20ch, miss 19ch, 1dc into next dc*, rep from * to * to end, 1ss into ch above the last ss at beg of rnd.

Round 13 1ss into each of next 10ch, *12ch, 1dc into next ch loop*, rep from * to * to end, 1ss into 1st ss of rnd.

Round 14 1ch, 1dc into each ch to end, 1ss into 1st ch of rnd.

Round 15 *Make 15ch, 1dc into the top edge of large flower side petal, 15ch, miss 5dc, 1dc into next dc, 10ch, 1dc into the top of next petal, 10ch, miss 5dc, 1dc into next dc, 10dc, 1dc into the top of next petal, 10ch, miss 5dc, 1dc into next dc, 15ch, 1dc into the edge of next side petal, 15ch, miss 5dc, 1dc into next dc*, rep from * to * to join all of the large flowers.

waistband Work in double crochet in Colour 2 until the required length is reached.

assembly, round 19 Join the motifs in rounds using chain stitch filigree and bands of double crochet in Colour 2.

Round 16 Make 55ch, *1dc into bottom edge of side petal on large flower, 25ch, 1dc into bottom of next petal, 20ch, 1dc into bottom of next petal, 25ch, 1dc into bottom edge of next side petal, 30ch*, rep from * to * to end, 15ch, join with ss into 40th of 50ch at beg of rnd.

Round 17 *Make 6ch, 1dc into next ch loop,* rep from * to * to end, join with ss into 1st ch of rnd.

Round 18 1ch, 1dc into each ch to end, 1ss into 1st ch of rnd.

Round 19 Working backwards along previous round, make 1ss into each of first 3dc. Then, moving forward, *make 25ch, 1dc through side picot of two snowflakes together, 25ch, miss 2dc, 1dc into next dc, 3dc, 10ch, 1dc through next picot on snowflake, 10ch, miss 6dc, 1dc into next dc, 12ch; miss 2tr and 5ch on snowflake, 1dc into central dc on side of snowflake, 12ch, miss 6dc, 1dc into next dc, 10ch, 1dc into next picot on snowflake, 10ch, miss 6dc, 1dc into next dc, 25ch, 1dc through next picot on this snowflake and side picot on next snowflake together*, rep from * to * to join all of the snowflakes to the skirt. Fasten off and finish yarn ends into piece.

Hint

Rather than stitch the silky lining slip to the skirt, choose or make a selection of coloured slips to give your crochet work different flavours for your various moods.

Openwork stole

This lacy stole, with its motifs of snowflakes and swirls, is designed to wrap around the shoulders, with both cuffs being worn on the same arm for a snug fit.

The yarn — a hand-dyed blend of silk, mohair and wool — will be surprisingly cosy despite the open pattern of the crochet work.

Materials
150 g (5½ oz) Noro Silk Garden

Tools
5 mm (US 7/UK 6) crochet hook

Size
Approximate widths: Size S, 130 cm (52 in) from cuff to cuff; Size M 150 cm (59 in); Size L 170 cm (66 in)

Tension
Snowflake motif = 22 cm (8½ in) diameter after pressing
Swirl motif = 20 cm (8 in) diameter after pressing

Abbreviations
ch: chain
dc: double crochet
dtr: double treble
qdtr: quadruple treble
ss: slip stitch
tr: treble

snowflake, round 3 Work groups of three treble stitches into the points.

snowflake, round 4 Work picots on the points of the outer row.

SNOWFLAKE Make 5 (6, 7)

Make 9ch, join with ss to form a ring.

Round 1 8ch, *3tr into ring, 5ch*, rep from * to * another four times, 2tr into ring, 1ss into 3rd of 8ch at beg of rnd.

Round 2 1ss into next ch, 7ch, 4tr into 1st 4-ch loop, *1ch, 4tr into next 4-ch loop, 4ch, 4tr into same 4-ch loop*, rep from * to * another four times, 1ch, 3tr into 1st ch loop of rnd, 1ch into 3rd ch at beg of rnd.

Round 3 1ss into next ch, 6ch, 3tr into first ch loop, *3ch, 3tr into 4-ch loop, 3ch, 3tr into 4-ch loop*, rep from * to * another four times, 3ch, 2tr into ch loop at beg of rnd, 1ch into next ch of ch loop.

Round 4 1ss into each of next 2ch, 8ch, 1ss into 4th ch just made (making a 4-ch picot), 1ch, 2tr into 1st ch loop, *5ch, 1dc into 3-ch loop, 5ch, 2tr into next 3-ch loop, 5ch, 1ss into 1st ch just made, 1ch, 2tr into same 3-ch loop*, rep from * to * another four times, 5ch, 1dc into 3-ch loop, 5ch, 1tr into ch loop at beg of rnd, 1ss into 3rd ch at beg of rnd. Fasten off. Finish ends into piece.

SWIRL Make 4 (5, 6)

Make 9ch, join with ss to form a ring.

Round 1 3ch, *1tr into ring, 2ch*, rep from * to * another six times, 1tr into 1st ch loop at beg of rnd.

Round 2 4ch, 1dtr into next ch space, *4ch, 1dtr into next tr, 4ch, 1dtr into next

swirl, round 4 A round of triple treble is worked after a round of double treble.

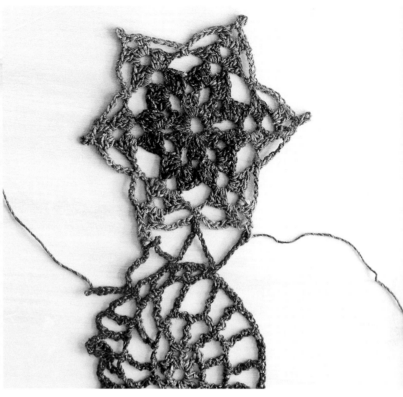

linking the motifs A network of chain stitch joins the snowflakes and swirls; see Diagram 1, on page 148.

ch space, 4ch, 1dtr into next ch space, 4ch, 1dtr into next ch space*, rep from * to * again.

Round 3 4ch, 1trtr into next ch space, 4ch, 1trtr into next dtr, 4ch, 1trtr into next ch space, 4ch, 1trtr into next dtr, *4ch, 1trtr into next ch space, 4ch, 1trtr into next ch space, 4ch, 1trtr into next dtr*, rep from * to * twice.

Round 4 *4ch, 1dtr into next ch space, 4ch, 1dtr into next dtr*, rep from * to * another three times, 4ch, 1tr into next ch space, 3ch, 1tr into next trtr, 3ch, 1tr into next ch space, 2ch, 1tr into next trtr, 2ch, 1dc into next ch space, 1ch into next ch. Fasten off. Finish ends into the piece.

LINKING THE MOTIFS

Press all of the snowflakes and swirls, without distorting their shape (see Hint).

Row 1 Make 1ch through 1st picot on first snowflake, 5ch, 1dc through dc at beginning of first swirl, 8ch, (miss 1ch, 2tr, 5ch), 1dc through dc on snowflake. Make 6ch, (miss 2ch, 1tr, 2ch), 1dc through tr on swirl. Make 8ch (miss 5ch, 2tr, 1ch), 1dc through picot on snowflake. Make 7dc, (miss 3ch, 1tr, 3ch), 1dc through tr on swirl.

Row 2 7ch, 1dc through picot on second snowflake, 5ch, (miss 4ch, 1dtr, 4ch), 1dc through dtr on 1st swirl, 8ch, (miss 1ch, 2tr, 5ch), 1dc into dc on snowflake, make 8ch, (miss 4ch), 1dc through dtr on swirl, make

Hint

Use a warm iron and pressing cloth to press the motifs. The pressing cloth will prevent the motion of the iron from pulling and distorting the shapes.

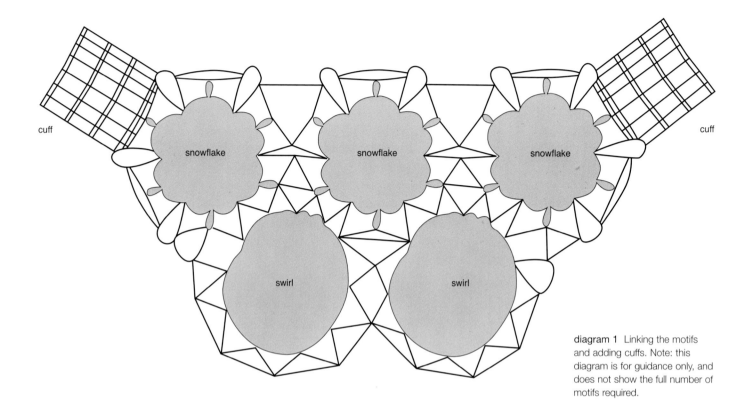

cuff

snowflake

snowflake

snowflake

swirl

swirl

cuff

diagram 1 Linking the motifs and adding cuffs. Note: this diagram is for guidance only, and does not show the full number of motifs required.

Hint

The correct way to wear the stole is with the snowflakes at the top. Both cuffs should be pushed up on one arm with the stole draped over the opposite shoulder. However, if you intend always to wear it in the conventional way, as a draped wrap, omit the cuffs.

8ch, (miss 5ch, 2tr, 1ch), 1dc through picot on snowflake.

Repeat Rows 1 and 2 until all snowflakes and swirls have been incorporated. Fasten off and finish ends into piece.

Row 3 1dc through picot adjacent to picot on first snowflake, *make 14ch, (miss 1ch, 2tr, 5ch), 1 dc through dc, make 14ch, (miss 5ch, 2tr, 1ch), 1dc through picot*. Repeat from * to * another three times. **Make 8ch, 1dc through picot on next snowflake, 7ch, 1dc though 14-ch loop on previous snowflake, 7ch, (miss 1ch, 2tr, 5ch), 1dc through dc on second snowflake. Make 7ch, 1dc through next 14-ch loop on first snowflake, make 7ch (miss 5ch, 2tr, 1ch),

1dc through next picot on second snowflake, *make 14ch, (miss 1ch, 2tr, 5ch), 1dc through dc, make 14ch (miss 5ch, 2tr, 1ch), 1dc through picot*, rep from * to * twice.** Repeat from ** to ** until you reach the end of the snowflakes. Make 14ch, (miss 1dc, 8ch, 4ch, 1dtr, 4ch), 1dc into dtr at the end of fourth swirl. *Make 14ch, (miss 4ch, 1dtr, 4ch), 1dc through dtr*, rep from * to * around fourth swirl. **Make 8ch, 1dc through dc on previous swirl, make 7ch, 1dc though 14-ch loop on previous swirl, make 7ch, (miss 4ch, 1trtr, 4ch), 1dc through trtr on second swirl. Make 7ch, 1dc through next 14-ch loop on first swirl, make 7ch, (miss 4ch, 1trtr, 4ch), 1dc through next trtr on

cuffs Work in rows of quadruple treble alternating with double crochet.

cuffs Wear both cuffs on the same arm, or omit the cuffs to give a draped wrap that can be worn in the conventional way.

second swirl, *make 14ch (miss 4ch, 1trtr, 4ch), 1 dc through trtr*, rep from * to * another four times.** Repeat from ** to ** twice (until you reach the end of the swirls). Make 14ch, 1dc into 1st picot on first snowflake, make 14ch, (miss 1ch, 2tr, 5ch), 1dc into dc, make 14ch (miss 5ch, 2tr, 1ch), 1dc into picot, fasten off and finish the ends into the piece.

Row 4 Make 1dc through first loop on first snowflake, *make 8ch, 1dc through next loop*, rep from * to * the entire way round the stole, fasten off and finish the ends into the piece.

CUFFS

Row 1 Join yarn through point at far end of the stole, 1dc into each of the next 16ch, turn.

Row 2 Make 6ch, *1qdtr into next st, 1ch, miss 1dc*, rep from * to * to end, 1qdtr into last st.

Row 3 Make 1ch, *1dc into each st to end. Repeat Rows 2 and 3 twice, fasten off and finish ends into the piece. Stitch the end of the cuff onto the back of the snowflake to create the cuff loop.

Repeat at other end to create another cuff.

Beaded lace bag

A lacy, crocheted overlay scattered with beads turns a simple bag into something special. Crushed velvet makes the handbag suitable for stylish day or glamorous evening wear.

Beads are easily incorporated into crocheted fabric. First, thread all of the beads onto the yarn or thread, or — if the yarn or thread is too thick to pass through the holes of the beads — onto a piece of nylon filament (invisible thread). This is the method used in this project. The filament is then crocheted alongside the main yarn. As you reach the stitch where a bead is required, slide a bead up the yarn or filament and hold it in place while you form the stitch around it.

Materials
100 g (3½ oz) Rowan Soft 100 per cent
   merino 4-ply yarn
1 spool filament yarn (invisible thread)
200 assorted small to medium beads
30 cm (12 in) velvet or satin fabric
40 cm (16 in) polyester boning

Tools
3 mm (US 2/UK 11) crochet hook

Size
Approximately 25 cm (10 in) long x 22 cm
   (9 in) wide, not including handles

Tension
Tension is not crucial for this item

Abbreviations
b/ch: beaded chain
ch: chain
dc: double crochet
dtr: double treble
ss: slip stitch
tr: treble

Filigree drawstring bag

Silky yarn worked in an open design weaves a

shining web around a simple taffeta pouch.

Solomon's knot is a stitch for more competent

crocheters: it's worth taking the time to practise

as it creates such a beautiful lattice of stitches.

The length of the stitch is controlled by how long

you make the loops; for this project, make them

about 3 cm (1¼ in).

Materials
50 g (1¾ oz) ball Debbie Bliss Spun Silk 3-ply
  yarn
50 cm (20 in) taffeta fabric

Tools
3 mm (US 2/UK 11) crochet hook

Size
Circumference 64 cm (25 in); height
  20 cm (8 in)

Tension
The loops of each Solomon's knot should be
  about 3 cm (1¼ in) long to achieve the size
  stated above

Abbreviations
ch: chain
dc: double crochet
sk: Solomon's knot
ss: slip stitch

Solomon's knot
Starting with one loop on hook, draw this loop
  out to desired length. (Using a finger, thumb
  or thick knitting needle will give regular-sized
  loops.) Wrap yarn over hook and draw
  through (as though making an ordinary chain
  stitch), but with single back thread kept the
  same length as first long loop, and keeping
  single back thread of long chain separate
  from two front threads. Insert hook under
  this single back thread. Wrap thread over
  hook again and draw a loop through. Wrap
  yarn over hook again and draw through both
  loops on hook. You have now completed
  one Solomon's knot. Repeat as instructed.

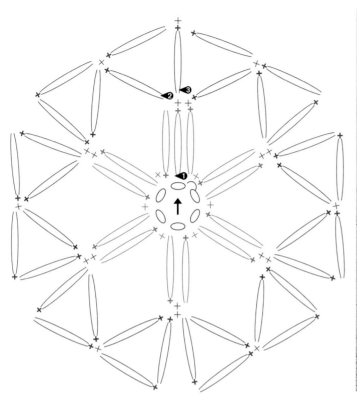

Centre bottom of bag This diagram shows the construction of the first three rounds of the bag. Round 3 is the increasing round; from here on, the bag is worked straight, with no further increases.

round 4 Make a lattice of Solomon's knots.

Hint

To keep track of the rounds, you may find it helpful to put a marker (such as a piece of contrast yarn) at the beginning of each round.

BAG

See page 155 for instructions on working Solomon's knot stitch.

Make 6 ch, join with ss to form a ring.

Round 1 *2sk, 1dc into ring*, rep from * to * five times [six loops], 1sk, 1dc into end of 1st sk at beg of rnd.

Round 2 *2sk, 1dc into centre of next loop*, rep from * to * five times [six loops], 1dc into end of 1st sk at beg of rnd.

Round 3 *2sk, 1dc into end of next sk, rep from * to * to end [12 loops].

Round 4 *2sk, 1dc into centre of next loop*, rep from * to * end [12 loops].

Rounds 5–11 As for Round 4.

Round 12 1sk, 1dc into end of next sk,
5ch, 1dc into centre of next loop, rep from * to * to end, 1ss into dc at beg of rnd.

Round 13 1ch, 1dc into each st to end, 1ss into 1st ch of rnd.

Round 14 1ch, *1dc into each of next 2dc, 2ch, miss 2 sts, 1 dc into each of next 3dc*, rep from * to * to end, 1ss into 1st ch of rnd.

Round 15 1ch, *1ss into each of next 5ch, 4ch, 1ss into same place as last ss just made (creating picot)*, rep from * to * to end, 1ss into 1st ch at beg of rnd. Cut yarn; finish ends into work.

LINING

1 Cut a 26 x 69 cm (10½ x 27 in) rectangle and a 24 cm (9½ in) circle from the fabric.

round 15 Make picots and holes for the drawstring.

drawstring A twisted cord is threaded through the band for closure.

Overlock or hem the two pieces, and stitch the rectangle into a tube by sewing the ends together along the shorter sides. Turn right side out and stitch along the seam again, concealing the raw edges inside a French seam; see Hint, at right. (The wrong side of the fabric now becomes the outside of the tube.)

2 Pin the circle to the end of the tube (wrong sides together), and stitch. Turn the bag inside out and restitch the bottom seam as a French seam.

3 Fold the top edge over twice and stitch flat. Pleat the top of the lining bag so it measures the same width as the crochet bag. Turn the lining with the right side on the outside and put it inside the crochet bag. Pin the two bags together and stitch around the top edge.

DRAWSTRING

Cut two lengths of yarn each 2 m (2 yards) long and knot together at either end. Secure one end and twist the other end until the yarns are tightly twisted (about 100 twists). Fold them in half and allow them to twist up on themselves, making a rope. Use a crochet hook to feed the rope in and out of the eyelets in the band around the top of the bag. Tie a knot near the top of the remaining rope and another towards the end. Trim off the ends.

French seams

To make a French seam, join the fabric with wrong sides together, stitching close to the edge (about 6 mm/1/4 in seam allowance). Carefully trim the fabric close to the stitching line, then press the seam flat. Now fold the fabric along the stitching line so that the right sides are together, and press. Stitch the seam along the seam allowance (about 6 mm/1/4 in from the edge). The raw edges of the fabric will be concealed inside the seam allowance.

quilting

Types of batting

Some battings need to be quilted closer together than others to stop them from drifting around within the quilt or fragmenting when washed. Polyester batting requires less quilting than cotton or wool batting. Some polyester battings have a tendency to 'fight' the sewing machine. Wool battings (usually actually a wool/polyester blend) provide more warmth and comfort than polyester battings. However, they require more quilting, and those that are not needle-punched tend to pill. Needle-punched wool/polyester blends are more stable and require less quilting. Traditional cotton battings require a lot of quilting, as much as every ½–3 in (13–75 mm). Needle-punched cotton battings are more stable and can be quilted up to 10 in (25 cm) apart.

giant hexagon quilt This is an alternative colourway of the design on page 208–9.

The parts of a quilt

Most quilts consists of three layers: the quilt top (the decorative part); the batting (the filling that gives the quilt extra warmth and also contributes to its padded look); and the quilt backing. The batting may be omitted if you want a very light quilt for summer, or if the fabrics that you have used in the quilt top and backing are heavy enough on their own. The edges of the quilt are generally finished with binding.

The quilt top

Often, a quilt top will consist of a central design or a series of blocks surrounded by one or more borders. The top of the quilt may be pieced (made of patchwork), appliquéd (with designs sewn onto a background) or whole-cloth (made entirely of one fabric). In whole-cloth quilts, the visual interest is created by the quilting alone, so these quilts are perfect for showing off a beautiful and intricate quilting pattern.

Batting

Also known as wadding, batting is the quilt's filling, or middle layer. It may be made of wool, cotton or polyester; each type has different properties (see left). Cotton and wool are easier to quilt than polyester, but polyester generally gives greater loft (thickness), although not usually greater warmth.

Backing

The quilt backing is usually made of one fabric, but there is nothing to stop you from making it wholly or partly from leftover patchwork blocks or strips of different fabrics. You will normally need to join two lengths of fabric to create a backing wide enough for anything larger than a cot or lap quilt.

Binding

This is a way of finishing the raw edges of all layers of the quilt by enclosing them in a thin strip of fabric. Binding is generally made from a double thickness of fabric for extra durability, as it is the edges of a quilt that will wear most quickly. Binding is usually the last thing to be done, once the quilting is finished.

Fabric for quilts

For most quilts, it is best to use pure cotton fabrics. These wash and iron well, are easy to sew, take a crease well and do not fray excessively. Generally, all fabrics used for a quilt should be of a similar weight and weave. Using fabrics of different weights may result in some areas of the quilt wearing more quickly than others.

It is possible to use other fabrics, such as velvets, silks and satins, for a more luxurious effect. If using such fabrics, do not wash them before use. If they need ironing, do so at a low heat setting on the wrong side of the fabric. Quilts made from such fabrics should be dry cleaned, not washed.

Fabric can be solid (a uniform colour, without a print or pattern); printed; tone-on-tone (having a background printed with a design of the same colour); or checked. Printed fabrics are divided into four categories: small, medium, large and directional. Small prints may look almost like solid fabrics from a distance. Medium prints are more distinct and are often used to add visual texture. Large prints have very distinct patterns that stand out from the background. These are often used in quilts as borders or feature prints. Directional prints have a very distinct pattern that runs in one direction. Large directional prints, such as stripes, can be very effective when used in a border.

When choosing fabrics, give thought to both the balance of prints and plains as well as the tonal values of the fabrics; that is, the mixture of light, medium and dark fabrics. You will also find that the effect of a fabric may change according to the other fabrics surrounding it, with often surprising results. Experimenting with colour, tone and pattern is one of the pleasures of quilting.

Preparing fabrics

Many quilters prefer to wash, dry and iron cotton quilt fabrics before use. Wash each fabric separately in warm water with a scrap of white cotton fabric to test if the colour runs. If it does, the fabric should be discarded or used for another purpose. Otherwise, when the quilt is washed, the colour may run and ruin the quilt.

Washing pre-shrinks fabric and removes all finishes added by the manufacturer. Such finishes can make the fabric stiffer and easier to sew; if you wish to restore the stiffness, spray the fabric lightly with spray starch before sewing.

Before sewing, remove the tightly woven edges (selvedges) from all fabrics; if left on and included in seams, these may cause the fabric to pucker and bunch.

Fabric grain

Fabric has three grains. The lengthwise grain runs the length of the fabric from top to bottom. The cross grain runs the width of the fabric, from selvedge to selvedge. The bias grain runs at a 45-degree angle to the straight of the grain.

Both the lengthwise and cross grains are straight grains. When cutting fabrics, most instructions and templates will tell you to cut on the straight of the grain. For borders, this is usually the lengthwise grain, to allow for greater length. Rotary-cut strips are usually cut on the cross grain. An arrow on the template or pattern piece shows you the direction in which the grain should run when cutting out the fabric.

Cutting fabric on the bias will cause the cut edges to stretch; this is undesirable when piecing but can be useful if you need to make the fabric curve, as when making bindings for a quilt with a curved border or when making bias strips for curved sections of appliqué.

quilting fabrics Pure cottons are best, as they are easy to cut, sew and wash.

Equipment

Not all of the items listed below are essential; some simply make the work easier. The quilts in this book are pieced by machine, but can be adapted for hand-piecing.

Sewing machine and accessories

For the projects in this book, you will need a sewing machine in good working order that is capable of straight stitch. Before you start sewing, clean out the machine's bobbin with a brush or a lint-free cloth, and oil the machine, if it needs it. Insert a new needle; a dull needle can prevent stitches from forming properly.

Sewing machine feet and needles

For piecing, you need a foot that gives you an accurate ¼ in (6 mm) seam. Most patchwork uses the imperial system rather than metric (see page 167), but most sewing machine dealers will be able to provide an accurate ¼ in (6 mm) foot. For older machines, there are feet that can be adapted. If you cannot acquire a ¼ in (6 mm) foot, place a ruler under the machine's needle and mark ¼ in (6 mm) from the needle to the right, then draw a vertical line at this point with a pen or with masking tape. Make sure the seam is accurate by sewing pieces together and then measuring the seam before starting a project.

For machine quilting, you will need a walking foot and a darning foot. A walking foot is used for all straight-line quilting. It allows layers of fabric to move through the machine without shifting. A darning foot is used to do free-motion quilting by dropping the feed dogs so that you can manoeuvre the quilt in any direction.

For general piecing, the best needle sizes to use for cotton fabrics are sizes 70/10 and 80/12. For machine quilting, use a size 75/11 quilting needle for thin and/or natural batting quilts and a size 90/14 quilting needle for quilts with high loft and/or polyester batting.

Sewing machine threads

Match the thread to the fabric when piecing; for example, when using 100 per cent cotton fabric, use 100 per cent cotton thread. If using a multicoloured fabric, use a neutral thread, such as grey or beige, to match the tone of the background. Don't use a polyester thread for a cotton fabric; over time it will cut through the fibres of the cotton. The same rule applies when choosing thread for machine quilting.

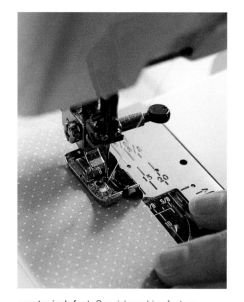

quarter-inch foot Special machine feet are available that give a precise ¼ in (6 mm) seam.

Monofilament thread, which is transparent, is the most appropriate thread for quilt tops, as it takes on the colour of any fabric that it is stitched or quilted over. Although made of nylon, monofilament thread has the elastic quality of cotton. Monofilament thread should be used as the top thread in the machine. A quilting thread that matches the backing fabric should be used in the bobbin. The top tension in the machine should be eased off so that the heavier quilting thread will anchor quilting stitches in the batting, or anchor appliqué stitches to the back.

When machine-piecing, the best stitch length is about 2.0; this should produce 12–14 stitches per inch (2.5 cm). For hand-piecing (see page 170), aim to make 10–12 stitches per inch (2.5 cm).

Rotary cutting

Rotary cutting makes it easy to cut fabrics quickly and accurately. Several layers of fabric can be cut at once.

Rotary cutters

A rotary cutter is a round, razor-sharp blade attached to a handle, protected by a sheath. Many styles of cutter are available. The standard size blade is 1¾ in (45 mm). This is suitable for most cutting tasks, but for cutting templates the most suitable blade size is 1⅛ in (28 mm). For cutting through multiple layers, a 2⅜ in (60 mm) or 2½ in (65 mm) blade gives best results. A cutter with a blade this size is also easier to hold.

Rotary cutters are held in the hand in much the same way as a knife. The handle should rest comfortably in the palm and the index finger should be placed on the top edge of the cutter handle. There is usually a ridged section in this area to help provide grip. The blade side of the cutter should face the body and cuts should be made away from the body, using a smooth, firm motion, to provide control and prevent cuts to the body.

Safety should be a priority when using the rotary cutter. The blade should be exposed only when a cut is to be made (this can be done with the thumb) and the protective sheath should be replaced as soon as the cut is finished to protect you and to prevent the blade from being damaged. Never leave rotary cutters lying about where they can be found by children or pets. A rotary cutter is essentially a circular razor blade, so treat it accordingly.

rotary cutter With blade exposed. Push the blade cover toward the blade to sheath it.

Useful bits and pieces

There are many small accessories to make patchwork and quilting easier, such as:

Erasable pencils: Used for tracing quilting designs onto the quilt top that can later be erased. Some pencils are also water soluble.

Fabric markers: Fine-tipped felt pens with an ink that vanishes automatically over time, or that can be rinsed out in cold water; test them on a scrap of fabric before using.

Quilter's quarter: A perspex rod ¼ in (6 mm) square and about 12 in (30 cm) long, used for tracing precise ¼ in (6 mm) seams along the straight edge of a template.

Seam tracers: Two connected pencils with their tips ¼ in (6 mm) apart; one is held against the edge of a template and the other is used to trace a precise ¼ in (6 mm) seam around the template.

Another type of seam tracer is a small metal disk with a hole in the centre and a groove around the outside. You put a pencil into the hole and the edge of the disk against the edge of the template, and trace around it to produce a precise ¼ in (6 mm) seam. Both types of seam tracer are particularly useful for tracing around curves.

Thimbles: There are two types, leather and metal. Leather ones are used on the fingers of the underneath hand when quilting, to prevent the needle constantly pricking the finger when it is pushed to the underside of the quilt. A metal thimble is used on the middle finger of the upper hand to push the needle through all the layers of the quilt.

Fusible interfacing: Useful for stabilizing fine or slippery fabrics, or those that fray easily, before piecing.

Rotary cutting mats

A cutting mat should be used with a rotary cutter to protect both the blade of the rotary cutter and the work surface. Rotary cutting mats are made from self-healing plastic that allows cuts to mend. The size of the cutting mat depends on the size of the work area, but the mat should be able to accommodate a quarter of the width of the fabric (approximately 11 in/28 cm). The bigger the mat, the longer the cut you will be able to make. Rotary cutting mats should be placed on a firm surface, stored flat and kept away from heat, which causes them to warp.

Rotary cutting rulers

Rotary cutting rulers (sometimes called quilters' rulers) are made of acrylic and are transparent. Designed to be used in conjunction with rotary cutters and mats, they have markings at ⅛ in (3 mm) intervals. To make the quilts in this book, you will need a 6½ x 24 in (16.5 x 60 cm) and a 6½ x 12 in (16.5 x 30 cm) ruler. The first ruler is for squaring up the fabric and cutting long lengths of fabric for borders. The smaller ruler is for cutting smaller strips of fabric.

Always measure and cut using the lines on the ruler rather than those on the cutting mat; if you cut too many times along the same lines on the mat, you will both damage the mat and erase or blur the lines, making them inaccurate.

Square rulers, which come in various sizes, are handy but not essential. The larger sizes make it possible to cut large squares in one movement. The smaller square rulers are good for cutting small pieces of fabric and for trimming up.

Accessories

Various types of pins, scissors and other accessories will make your quilt-making easier and more efficient.

Pins

Long, fine pins with heads that lie flat against the fabric are recommended, as they will go through layers of fabric easily, and allow you to sew up to and over them without the stitching puckering. Fine pins are preferable, as thick, large pins cause the fabric to bunch up and the piecing to be inaccurate. Pins should be placed at right angles to seams. For appliqué, special appliqué and sequin pins are available; they are very short (½ in/8 mm) to prevent the thread becoming caught around the appliqué pieces as you sew them down.

Scissors

You will need three types of scissors for quilt-making: a pair of fabric shears or a large pair of scissors to use exclusively to cut fabric; a pair of thread clips or small scissors to clip threads when sewing; and a pair of scissors to cut templates from plastic and paper. Don't use the same scissors for fabric and paper, as the paper will make them too blunt to cut fabric easily.

Templates and template plastic

Transparent template plastic is used to trace shapes onto fabric in much the same way as cardboard templates. The advantage of template plastic is that it is much more durable than cardboard, so it can be drawn around numerous times without the shape becoming distorted. It comes in a plain version (for freeform shapes) and a grid version (for geometric shapes).

To use template plastic to create a fabric block, trace the block template onto the plastic then, using a craft knife or paper scissors, cut it out. Template plastic can also be used for appliqué.

Commercial templates are also available. These are made of rigid plastic and come in various shapes and sizes. Their advantages are that they are durable, so they can be used over and over again, and very precisely cut for greater accuracy.

for cutting and marking Templates, template plastic, rulers, pencils and markers, craft knife.

for measuring and cutting Rotary cutter, cutting mat, quilters' rulers, scissors, pins.

for binding and quilting Markers, binding clips, thimbles, appliqué pins, safety pins, needles.

Cutting fabric

When cutting fabric, accuracy is essential so that the individual components will align exactly and the finished quilt will be the correct size. Rotary cutting is suitable for geometric shapes; curved shapes will need to be cut by hand.

Rotary-cutting strips

To prepare fabric for cutting strips using a rotary cutter, first iron the fabric flat. Fold the fabric in half along its length, and do this again, so that you have four layers. Make sure you fold on the warp threads (the threads that run down the fabric, parallel to the selvedges). This may mean that the selvedges do not align. Lay the folded fabric on a rotary cutter mat with the raw edge to the right if you are right-handed, to the left if you are left-handed. The folds will now be at a horizontal position. Place a quilter's ruler over the fabric, at right angles to the folds, hold it firmly in place, and trim the raw edges with a rotary cutter. Unfold the piece you have cut off and check the angle of the cut; it must be dead straight, with no kinks at the folds. If not, refold the fabric and try again until the cut is straight.

Leaving the fabric and ruler on the mat, rotate the mat 180 degrees, so that the newly trimmed edge is to the left if you are right-handed or to the right if you are left-handed. Pick up the ruler, being careful not to move the fabric. Using the vertical measurement marks on the ruler, align the required measurement with the

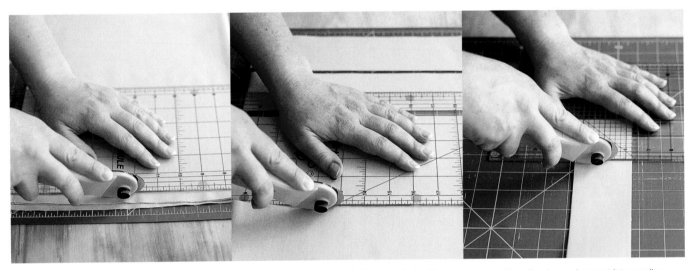

the first cut With the bulk of fabric to your left, square up the end of the fabric.

cutting strips Measure by aligning the fabric with the marks on the ruler, not those on the mat.

cross-cutting A strip can be recut into smaller units such as rectangles or setting squares.

trimmed edge of the fabric. Check the measurement by placing the horizontal indicators on the ruler on the fold and the double fold. When you are sure the measurement is correct, begin cutting strips. Cut strips in batches of three or four, then turn the cutting board around to align and re-trim the cut edge of the fabric.

Rotary-cutting shapes

To save time and increase accuracy, shapes can be cut from strips. The seam allowance will need to be calculated in your measurements.

To calculate the measurement for a square, add ½ in (12 mm) for the seam allowance to the finished size of the square. To cut a square from a strip, open the strip to a double thickness only. Trim the selvedge edge. Cut to the same measurement that you used to cut the strip. To check that the measurement is correct, align the 45-degree mark on the quilters' ruler with the corner edge of the strip. If it runs through the opposite diagonal corner, it is correct. Every third or fourth cut, re-align the cut edge.

To cut a rectangle from a strip, repeat the procedure for a square, remembering to add ½ in (12 mm) to the finished measurement for the seam allowance.

To cut half-square triangles from a strip, calculate the finished size of the block required and add a ⅞ inch (22 mm) seam allowance. Cut strips and then squares to this measurement. Cut once on the diagonal from corner to corner. Each square will yield 2 triangles.

A note on measurements

Measurements for patchwork and quilting are traditionally given in imperial units. This is still generally the case even in countries that have long used the metric system. Many quilting accessories, such as rotary cutting mats and quilter's rulers, give measurements only in imperial. For the quilts in this book, both metric and imperial measurements are given. When cutting, sewing and assembling the quilt, it is vital that you work in only one system of measurement. Choose metric or imperial and then stick to it; if you mix the two, your quilt will not be accurate.

half-square triangles Cut across one diagonal of a square to give half-square triangles.

quarter-square triangles Cut across both diagonals of a square to give quarter-square triangles.

To cut quarter-square triangles from a strip, calculate the finished size of the block required, and add a 1¼ inch (32 mm) seam allowance. Cut strips and then squares to this measurement. Cut twice on the diagonal from corner to corner. Each square will yield 4 triangles.

Cutting shapes by hand

Shapes can be cut by hand using plastic or paper templates. This method is the most practical for curved shapes, and is also the traditional way of cutting hexagons, as shown in the photographs below.

When cutting fabric using templates, the template is made to its finished size, that is, *without* seam allowances; these are added when cutting the fabric. Commercially produced plastic templates are available in various shapes and sizes, or you can make your own templates from thin cardboard or template plastic (available from craft stores).

If making a design from templates provided in a magazine or book, photocopy the template, paste it onto thin cardboard and cut it out. Always check the template's dimensions for accuracy and adjust if need be before using it to cut fabric.

Place the template on the wrong side of the fabric and trace around it. Use a sharp pencil or fine marker to give the finest line and thus the most accurate seam. This tracing line will become the seam line.

English paper piecing

This traditional English method of hand-piecing uses pieces of fabric tacked over a template of paper or thin cardboard. The pieces are then sewn together with a small whip stitch, after which the tacking stitches are cut and the paper templates removed. The templates can be re-used, but should be replaced once their edges become worn or their points lose their sharpness.

If using commercial templates with cut-out centres, as pictured at right, trace around the inner edge of the template to mark the seam line, and trace around the outer edge to mark the cutting line.

When using the English paper piecing method, mark the fabric on the right side of the fabric and sew with the right sides facing out. For all other hand-piecing, mark on the wrong side of the fabric and sew with the right sides together.

English paper piecing, step one Trace around the template onto cardboard.

English paper piecing, step two Sew tacked hexagons together to form a rosette shape.

Piecing

'Piecing' is the name given to sewing together all the separate components of a quilt. It can be done by hand or machine. To keep track of the various components, especially if making complicated blocks with many pieces, put each type of piece in its own lock-seal plastic bag and label the bag.

Machine-piecing techniques

Piecing by machine requires accurate and precise seams (see page 162). The standard seam allowance is ¼ in (6 mm). If you plan to do a lot of machine piecing, a ¼ inch sewing-machine foot will be a good invesment.

Machine-piecing is by its very nature much faster than hand-piecing, but by employing a technique called chain-piecing, you can make it even faster. To chain-piece, do not lift the presser foot and cut the thread each time you finish a seam. Instead, once you finish the seam on one unit (such as a pair of squares, as shown below), sew a little beyond the end of the seam. The reel and bobbin threads will entwine to make a 'chain'. Put another unit under the presser foot and repeat the process until you have sewn all the units. Cut the chains between each unit and join the units to other components. Many parts of a quilt can be chain-pieced in this manner, saving both time and thread.

chain-piecing Here, pairs of squares have been chain-pieced together.

machine-piecing Machine-pieced units with seams pressed toward the darker fabric.

four-patch squares Two pairs of squares are joined to form a four-patch square.

forming rows Four-patch squares are joined to plain squares to form rows.

Fussy cutting

Sometimes you may wish to centre or make a feature of a motif. This is known as 'fussy cutting'. Use a commercial template with a cut-out centre, as pictured below, or make your own from template plastic, which is transparent. Centre the template over the motif, trace around it then cut out the shape, leaving a good ¼ in (6 mm) seam allowance.

If you want the motif to appear in exactly the same place in each fussy-cut piece, mark the edges of the template to show where they overlap with particular elements in the design, then line up these marks with the relevant parts of the printed design each time you cut a new piece of fabric.

Each block is built up unit by unit. In the example pictured on page 169, pairs of squares are first chain-pieced, then the chains are cut. Each unit is pressed with the seam toward the darker piece, then two units are sewn together to give a four-patch square. These squares are then joined to plain squares to form rows, then the rows are joined to form the quilt top. Borders may then be added.

Hand-piecing

Because it can be done much more quickly, machine-piecing has generally replaced hand-piecing. Sometimes, however — such as when sewing small hexagons or other pieces with set-in seams — hand-piecing is still the easiest way. The advantage of hand-piecing is that it is portable, so it can be done, for example, on public transport or taken on holiday with you.

If sewing using the English paper piecing method, the pieces are joined with a small whip stitch on the right side (see page 168). Otherwise, the pieces are put together with right sides facing and seam lines (not raw edges) even. Use a short, fine needle and a matching sewing thread. Begin sewing with a small backstitch, then sew along the seam line using a small running stitch. End with another small backstitch, then fasten off.

'fussy cutting' Position the template over a motif and trace around the outer edge.

seam lines The pencil lines indicate the seam lines along which the shapes are joined.

piecing Using a running stitch, join the pieces accurately along the marked lines.

Quilt layout

The quilt layout diagram provided in the pattern will show you how the various components are assembled. There are numerous ways of laying out a quilt. Blocks within a quilt top may be set square (parallel with the sides and top of the quilt) or on point (at a 45-degree angle to the tops and sides of the quilt). Blocks may be joined so that they abut one another, or be separated with sashing strips. The illustrations at right show two basic but versatile ways of laying out a quilt.

Medallion quilts have as their focal point a central panel (often elaborately pieced or appliquéd, or consisting of a feature fabric), around which there are usually several borders. These may be pieced, plain or appliquéd.

Borders may be added for decorative effect, or to increase the quilt's size, or both. Borders may have squared-off or mitred corners (see page 172).

Always refer to the layout diagram for the quilt you are making, rather than relying on a photograph. Many quilt designs, especially complex ones using more than one type of block, feature optical illusions caused by the way in which the various components are combined. Sometimes the logic of the quilt's construction will not become clear until you look at the layout diagram.

blocks on point This layout features blocks set on point (that is, on the diagonal). Setting triangles have been added to the end of each row, and corner triangles to each corner, to make the sides of the quilt square. The borders can then be added. These borders are squared off; that is, their corners are not mitred.

block rows and sashing rows This layout comprises blocks that are joined to narrow strips of fabric (known as sashing strips) on either side. The rows thus formed are known as block rows. They alternate with sashing rows, comprising sashing strips interposed with small squares known as setting squares. When all the rows have been joined, squared-off borders are added.

The hand-quilting action

With your dominant hand above the quilt and the other beneath, take several running stitches at a time, making them as small and as even as you can. Push the needle through all the layers with the middle finger of your dominant hand (use a metal thimble to make this easier) and use the index finger of the underneath hand to push the needle back up to the top. Protect this finger with a leather thimble. Gently pull the stitches to indent the stitch line evenly.

To move a short distance from one part of the quilting design to another, push the tip of the needle through the batting and up at the new starting point.

When you come to the edge of the hoop, leave the thead dangling so that you can pick it up and continue working with it once you have repositioned the hoop. Work all the quilting design within the hoop before repositioning the hoop and beginning to quilt another area. If you need to quilt right up to the border edge, baste lengths of spare cotton fabric to the edge of the quilt, thus giving you enough fabric area to position the edges of the quilt under the quilting hoop.

To fasten off a length of quilting thread, make a small backstitch, splitting the thread of the previous stitch. Insert the needle into the batting and run it through the batting for about 1 in (2.5 cm). Bring the needle up to the top of the quilt and cut the thread close to the surface.

Traditionally, the best hand-quilting was considered to be that with the tiniest, most even stitches. However, longer stitches can give an attractively casual, rustic look.

Hand-quilting

Quilting by hand produces a softer line than machine-quilting, and will give an heirloom quality to quilts, especially those employing traditional designs. To quilt by hand, the fabric needs to be held in a frame (also known as a quilting hoop). Free-standing frames are available, but hand-held ones are cheaper, more portable and just as effective. One edge of a hand-held frame can be leaned against a table or bench to enable you to keep both hands free.

Hand-quilting, like machine-quilting, should commence in the centre of the quilt and proceed outwards. To commence hand-quilting, place the plain (inner) ring of the frame under the centre of the quilt. Position the other ring, with the screw, over the top of the quilt to align with the inner ring. Tighten the screw so that the fabric in the frame becomes firm, but not drum-tight.

Choose the smallest needle that you feel comfortable with and thread it with 18 in (45 cm) of matching or toning quilting thread. Knot the end of the thread and take the needle down through the quilt top into the batting, a short distance from where you want to start quilting. Tug the thread slightly so that the knot pulls through into the wadding and makes the starting point invisible. Proceed as described at left.

If you are new to hand-quilting, practise on a sample piece of quilt 'sandwich' until your action is smooth and rhythmic and produces small, even stitches. Then move on to the actual quilt.

marking the design Here, a pencil and commercial quilting stencil are being used.

hand-quilting With the fabric in a hoop, take several small running stitches at a time.

Binding

From the width of the binding fabric, cut enough 2½ in (6 cm) strips of fabric to equal the outside edge of your quilt, plus about 6 in (15 cm) to allow for mitred corners and for the ends to be folded under. Seam the strips into a continuous length, making the joins at 45-degree angles. Fold under one end of the binding strip at a 45-degree angle and press. Press the strip in half along its length.

Trim the backing and the batting so that they are even with the quilt top. Beginning at the folded end of the binding strip, pin the binding to one edge of the quilt, starting about 4 in (10 cm) in from a corner and having raw edges even. Machine-sew in place through all the layers of the quilt, using a ¼ in (6 mm) seam allowance and mitring the corners.

To mitre corners, end the seam ¼ in (6 mm) from the corner and fasten off. Fold the binding fabric up at a 45-degree angle, then fold it down so that the fold is level with the edge of the binding just sewn. Begin the next seam at the edge of the quilt and proceed as before. Repeat this process to mitre all the corners. See the diagrams at right.

When you approach the point at which the binding started, trim the excess, tuck the end of the binding under itself and stitch the rest of the seam.

Press the binding away from the quilt. Turn the binding to the back of the quilt and blind hem stitch in place by hand to finish.

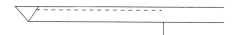

diagram 1 Attach the binding, ending the first seam ¼ in (6 mm) in from the corner.

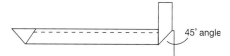

diagram 2 Fold the binding up at a 45-degree angle as shown.

diagram 3 Fold the binding down again so that the fold is level with the edge just sewn.

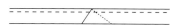

diagram 4 To end, trim excess binding, fold end under itself, and stitch the rest of the seam.

diagram 5 Fold the binding over to the back of the quilt and blind hem stitch in place by hand.

binding Fold the binding over to the back of the quilt and hold in place with binding clips.

finishing Attach the binding on the back of the quilt with small blind hem stitches.

Silk and velvet log cabin quilt

Log cabin is a classic quilt pattern that has been

a favourite for generations due to its ease

of construction and the great variety of patterns

into which its blocks can be arranged. The log

cabin block in this version begins with a 4½ in

(11 cm) centre square to which light and dark

strips — the 'logs' — are added in a spiral

fashion. This striking and luxurious interpretation

uses silks, velvets and brocade to make a very

special bedcover. No batting is used, as the

fabrics alone provide sufficient weight.

Keep in mind that using a silky or satiny fabric

for the backing will make the quilt tend to slip off

the bed; velvet or velveteen will give a backing

with more grip.

Materials
All fabrics are 45 in (112 cm) wide.
For the log cabin blocks:
  20 in (50 cm) gold brocade
  26 in (65 cm) pale pink silk
  30 in (75 cm) pale blue embroidered silk
  45 in (115 cm) mid pink velvet
  50 in (125 cm) mid blue velvet
  60 in (150 cm) burgundy silk dupion
  70 in (170 cm) navy silk dupion
  6.6 yd (6 m) fusible interfacing
For the backing and binding: 4.5 yd (4.1 m)
  mulberry heavy polyester satin
Batting at least 94 x 94 in (235 x 235 cm)
Matching sewing and quilting threads

Tools
Rotary cutter, ruler and mat
Sewing machine

Size
Approx. 85 x 85 in (215 x 215 cm)

Preparation
To make these fabrics easier to handle and
  sew, fusible interfacing is applied to the
  wrong side of each to stabilize them. The
  silk dupions fray very easily; using fusible
  interfacing also helps to prevent this

Cutting instructions
All strips for the blocks are cut across the
  width of the fabric, from selvedge to
  selvedge, *except* for the navy silk dupion,
  which is cut along the length of the fabric to
  give greater economy

Seam allowance
Quarter-inch (6 mm) seam allowances are
  used throughout

preparation Iron fusible interfacing to the wrong side of each fabric.

step two Cut the end of the pale pink silk strip even with the edge of the gold brocade square.

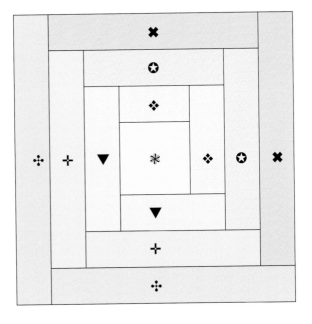

✳	gold brocade
❖	pale pink silk
▼	pale blue embroidered silk
✪	mid pink velvet
✛	mid blue velvet
✖	burgundy silk
✤	navy silk

diagram 1 block construction

CONSTRUCTION

1 From the gold brocade, cut strips 4½ in (12 cm) wide across the width of the fabric, then cross-cut to make 4½ in (12 cm) squares. From the remaining fabrics, except for the navy silk, cut 2½ in (6 cm) strips across the width of the fabric. For the navy silk, cut 2½ in (6 cm) strips down the length of the fabric.

2 With right sides facing, sew the centre square to a 2½ in (6 cm) strip of pale pink silk. Using a rotary cutter, cut the strip even with the edge of the square. Press the seam towards the pink strip.

1930s scrap quilt

'Waste not, want not', a motto appropriate to the Depression-era 1930s, is the inspiration for this scrap quilt. It uses a mix of jaunty reproduction 1930s and 40s print fabrics, but is suited to any small scraps of fabric. Mix them up as you please for a fun, easy quilt.

This quilt comprises two different blocks; one with a four-patch centre and the other with a novelty-print centre.

Materials

All fabrics are 100% cotton, 45 in (112 cm) wide
For the blocks: a total of 2¾ yd (2.4 m) 1930s/
   40s reproduction prints (equivalent to approx
   9 fat quarters or 18 fat eighths)
   8 in (20 cm) feature print fabric
For the sashing and border 1: 36 in (90 cm)
For border 2: 40 in (100 cm)
For the binding: 20 in (50 cm)
For the backing: 3.5 yd (3.2 m)
Matching thread
Batting 78 x 67 in (200 x 170 cm)
22 assorted buttons (optional)

Tools

Rotary cutter, ruler and mat
Sewing machine

Size

Approx. 70 x 59 in (180 x 150 cm)

Cutting directions

From the 1930s/40s reproduction fabrics:
   Cut 120 rectangular strips 2 x 7 in
     (5 x 17.5 cm) for Blocks A and B
   Cut 88 squares 3 x 3 in (7.5 x 7.5 cm)
     for Block B
   Cut 20 squares 2 x 2 in (5 x 5 cm) for
     the setting squares
From the feature print, cut 8 squares
   5½ x 5½ in (14 x 14 cm)
From the sashing fabric, cut 10 strips each
   2 in (5 cm) wide across the width of the
   fabric. Cross-cut into 49 pieces 2 x 8½ in
   (5 x 21.5 cm)

Seam allowance

Quarter-inch (6 mm) seam allowances are
   used throughout

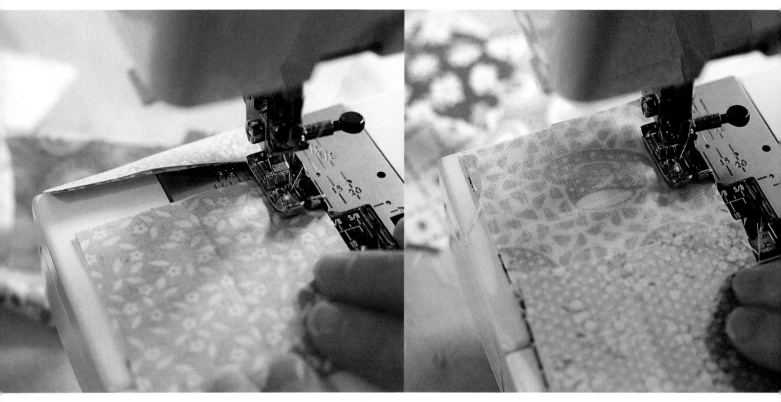

block B, step one Chain-piece pairs of 3 in (7.5 cm) squares together.

block B, step two Join pairs of squares to complete the central four-patch block

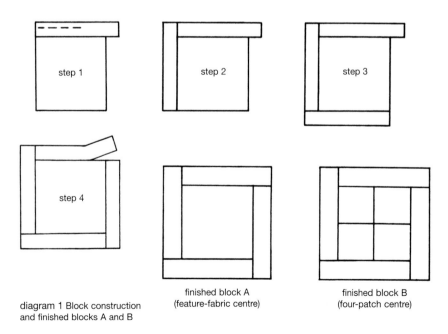

step 1

step 2

step 3

step 4

diagram 1 Block construction
and finished blocks A and B

finished block A
(feature-fabric centre)

finished block B
(four-patch centre)

CONSTRUCTION
Block A (make 8)

Finished size of the block is 8 in (21.5 cm).
Each block requires 1 square 5½ x 5½ in
(14 x 14 cm) and 4 rectangular strips each
2 x 7 in (5 x 17.5 cm).

1 Sew a rectangular strip to the feature-
print square, sewing only part of the first
seam as shown in Diagram 1. Press seam
toward coloured strip.

2 Add the remaining rectangular strips as
shown in Diagram 1, sewing from edge to
edge and matching each end. Sew the rest
of the unfinished first seam.

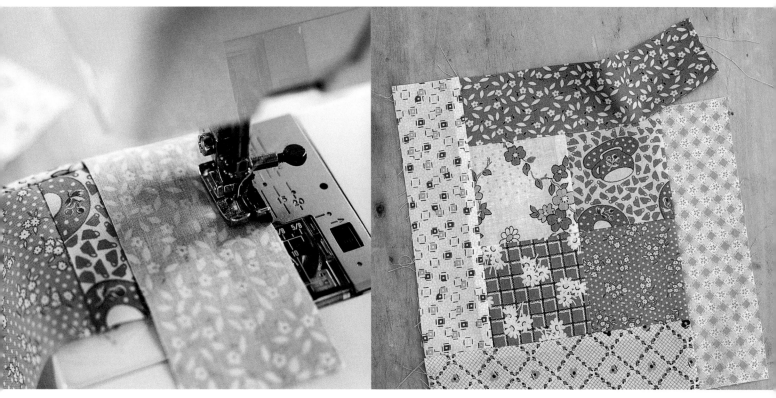

block B, step three Sew a rectangular strip to one edge of the four-patch block using a partial seam (end the seam 1 in/2.5 cm or so from the edge of the four-patch).

block B, step four Once all four rectangular strips have been added, the partial seam made for the first strip can be completed.

Block B (make 22)

Finished size of the block is 8 in (21.5 cm). Each block requires 4 squares each 3 x 3 in (7.5 x 7.5 cm) and 4 rectangular strips each 2 x 7 in (5 x 17.5 cm).

1 Sew the squares together in pairs.

2 Sew the pairs together to make a 5½ in (14 cm) square.

3 Sew the strips around the four-patch square in the same manner as for Block A.

4 Complete the partial first seam in the same manner as for Block A.

QUILT ASSEMBLY See Diagrams 2–5.

Sashing Rows Each row alternates 5 sashing strips and 4 setting squares, beginning and ending with a sashing strip (see Diagram 2). Sew 5 rows thus.

Block rows Each row alternates 5 blocks and 4 sashing strips, beginning and ending with a block. Arrange all the components as shown in Diagram 5, then sew the blocks and sashing strips together (see Diagrams 3 and 4). Sew 6 rows thus.

Alternate the block rows with the sashing rows, beginning and ending with a block row, to complete your quilt top (see Diagram 5).

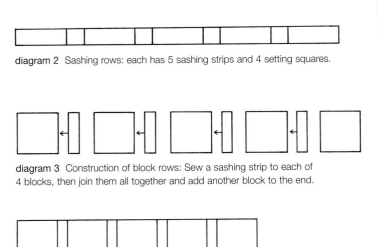

diagram 2 Sashing rows: each has 5 sashing strips and 4 setting squares.

diagram 3 Construction of block rows: Sew a sashing strip to each of 4 blocks, then join them all together and add another block to the end.

diagram 4 The finished block row.

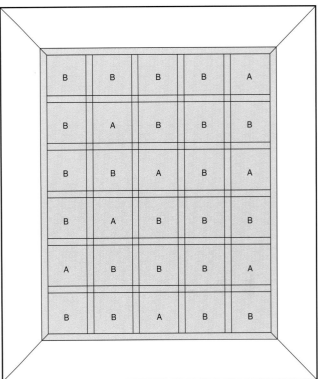

diagram 5 Quilt assembly: the blocks are separated from each other with sashing strips, and the block rows alternate with sashing rows.

Border 1 From the sashing fabric, cut 2 strips each 2 x 56 in (5 x 142.5 cm). Cut 2 strips 2 x 49½ in (5 x 126 cm). Sew the 2 longer strips to the sides of the quilt. Press. Sew the 2 shorter strips to the top and bottom of the quilt. Press.

Border 2 Cut 2 strips each 5½ x 59 in (14 x 150 cm). Cut 2 strips each 5½ x 59½ in (14 x 151.5 cm). Sew the first 2 strips to the sides of the quilt. Press. Sew the remaining 2 strips to the top and the bottom of the quilt. Press.

FINISHING

Cut the backing fabric in half widthwise. Sew the two pieces together along the selvedges. Place the backing right side down on a flat surface. Place the batting and the quilt on top of the backing, right side up. Pin and baste the layers together. Quilt as desired: our example is machine ditch-stitched along all seams, with a button sewn to the centre of each four-patch block.

BINDING

Across the width of the binding fabric, cut 7 strips each 2½ in (6.5 cm) wide. Seam the strips into a continuous length and proceed as instructed on page 175.

Pleated silk quilt

This highly textural, monochrome quilt will add

a touch of luxury to any room. If you can draw

and sew a straight line, you can make this; all

it requires is a little patience to sew the many

seams. As this quilt takes quite a lot of silk, it is

rather an investment, but if you wish to cut

costs, you could back it with a quilter's cotton

in a matching shade rather than with the silk.

Materials
All fabrics are 45 in (112 cm) wide.
10.5 yd (9.5 m) silk dupion for the quilt top,
    backing and binding
OR
6.6 yd (6 m) silk dupion for the quilt top
    and binding
    AND
4 yd (3.6 m) quilter's cotton in a matching
    shade for the backing and binding
Matching sewing thread
Batting at least 90 x 78 in (230 x 195 cm)

Tools
Long quilter's ruler
Tailor's chalk
Sewing machine with walking foot

Size
Approx. 83 x 69 in (210 x 175 cm)

Cutting instructions
Square up the fabric.
From the silk, cut 7 strips each 2½ in (6.5 cm)
    wide across the length of the fabric for
    the binding
For the quilt top, cut two pieces of silk each
    3 yd (2.7 m) long
For the backing, cut the remaining silk, or the
    quilter's cotton if using, into halves.

Seam allowance
Three-eighths inch (1 cm) seam allowances are
    used throughout

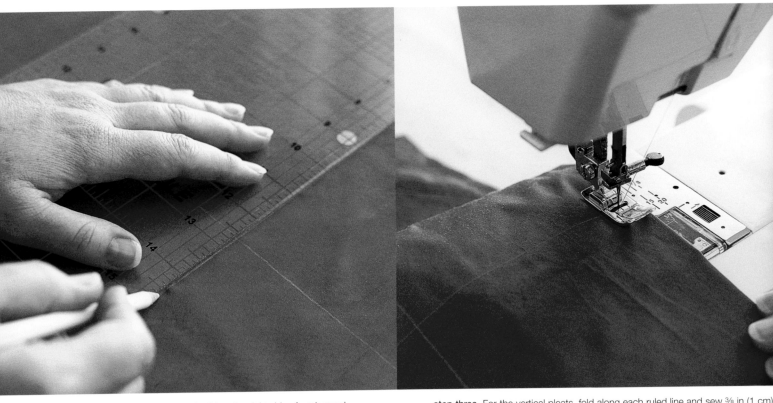

step two Rule and mark a 4¾ in (12 cm) grid on the right side of each panel of the quilt top.

step three For the vertical pleats, fold along each ruled line and sew ⅜ in (1 cm) from the fold line.

QUILT TOP

Refer to Diagram 1.

1 Square up the top edge of the fabric. Cut off and discard ⅜ in (1 cm) along the selvedges. Machine zig-zag along the sides and top edge of fabric to prevent fraying.

2 Using tailor's chalk and a long plastic quilter's ruler, mark out and rule a 4¾ in (12 cm) square grid on the right side of both panels. Once you have ruled all the lines horizontally and vertically, cut off excess fabric at bottom of fabric, leaving ⅜ in (1 cm) seam allowance. Machine zig-zag along the bottom edge, as before, to prevent fraying.

3 Sew the vertical pleats on each panel of fabric before joining the two panels together, as this will be less unwieldy. Crease along each vertical fold line. To make the pleats, machine-sew using a medium stitch length ⅜ in (1 cm) in from the fold line.

4 Once all the pleats are sewn on each panel, join the two panels: with RS together, match raw edges and fold lines, then sew a ⅜ in (1 cm) seam. (The finished seam will be concealed in a fold line.)

5 Sew all the horizontal pleats in the same manner as for Step 3.

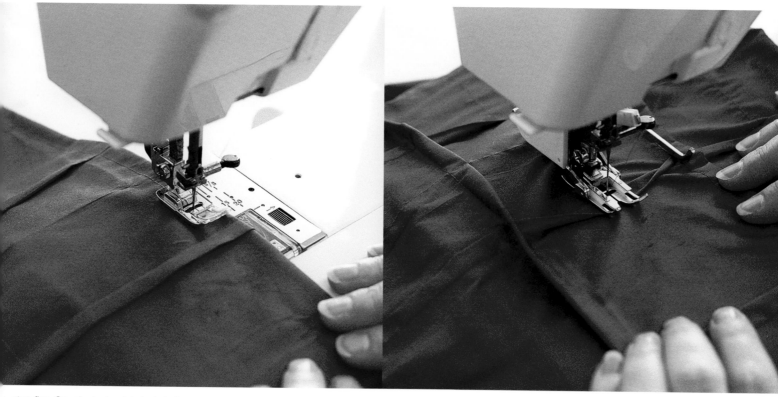

step five Sew the horizontal pleats in the same manner.

quilting Catch down the pleats in the quilting lines, sewing vertical lines in alternate directions and horizontal lines in the same direction. Use a walking foot, as shown.

FINISHING

For the backing, piece the two lengths of fabric together lengthwise. Place the backing right side down on a flat surface. Place the batting and quilt top on the backing, right side up. Pin and baste.

The pleats are caught down in the quilting lines, which are made halfway down each square of the grid. Many sewing machines have an adjustable arm that acts as a guide, allowing you to sew accurate lines by aligning the arm with a previously sewn straight line. Otherwise, rule the quilting lines, or do them freehand if you have an accurate eye.

Making sure all pleats are caught down in the correct direction, quilt the vertical lines, sewing them in alternate directions. Then quilt all the horizontal lines, sewing them in the same direction.

BINDING

Seam the reserved binding strips into a continuous length, making the joins at 45 degree angles, and proceed as described on page 175.

CARING FOR YOUR QUILT

Note that due to the nature and mixture of fabrics used, this quilt should not be washed; dry clean it instead.

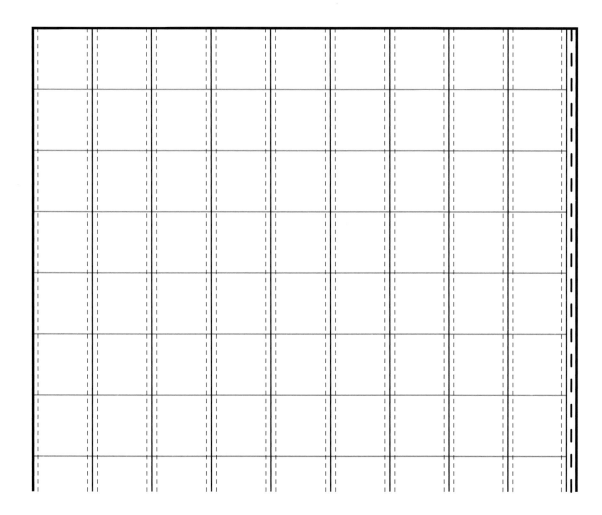

KEY

——————	Fold line
– – – – – – –	Sewing line for pleats
▬ ▬ ▬	Joining line for second length of fabric

diagram 1 The quilt top consists of two panels (this diagram shows only the upper part of one of the panels). Each is marked into a 4¾ in (12 cm) grid and the vertical pleats are sewn first. The two panels are then joined and the horizontal pleats are sewn next. After the quilt 'sandwich' is made, the quilt is machine-quilted to catch down the pleats.

Scrappy ninepatch quilt

Traditional quilt patterns often take their name from their method of construction, as is the case with this design, a ninepatch. Each block consists of three rows of three squares in two alternating colours. Despite the number of squares involved, this is a simple project suitable for a beginner. Quick quilting methods such as rotary cutting and chain-piecing make it easy to work both quickly and accurately.

Materials

All fabrics are 100% cotton, 45 in (112 cm) wide
For the cream squares, setting triangles and binding:
   4.4 yd (4 m) cream fabric
For the ninepatch squares: a total of 1.9 yd (1.7 m)
   assorted print fabrics (7 fat quarters or 14 fat eighths;
   or use fabric scraps)
For the backing: 4.1 yd (3.7 m) quilter's cotton
Matching sewing thread
Batting at least 80 x 75 in (200 x 185 cm)

Tools

Rotary cutter, ruler and mat
Sewing machine

Size

Approx. 75 x 69 in (190 x 175 cm)

Cutting directions

For the ninepatch blocks:
   From the width of each print fabric, cut 5 strips
     2 in (5 cm) wide
   From the width of the cream fabric, cut the
     same total number of strips 2 in (5 cm) wide
From the cream fabric:
   For the cream background squares, cut
     7 strips 5 in (12.5 cm) wide across width of fabric.
     Cross-cut into 63 squares 5 x 5 in (12.5 x 12.5 cm)
   For the setting triangles, cut 3 strips each 7½ in
     (19 cm) wide across the width of the fabric.
     Cross-cut into 15 squares 7½ x 7½ in (19 x 19 cm).
     Recut 11 squares on both diagonals to yield 44
     triangles (of which you will use only 42); see Diagram
     2 on page 197
   For the corner triangles, cut 2 squares each 4½ x
     4½ in (11.5 x 11.5 cm) and recut on one diagonal to
     yield 4 squares; see Diagram 3 on page 197

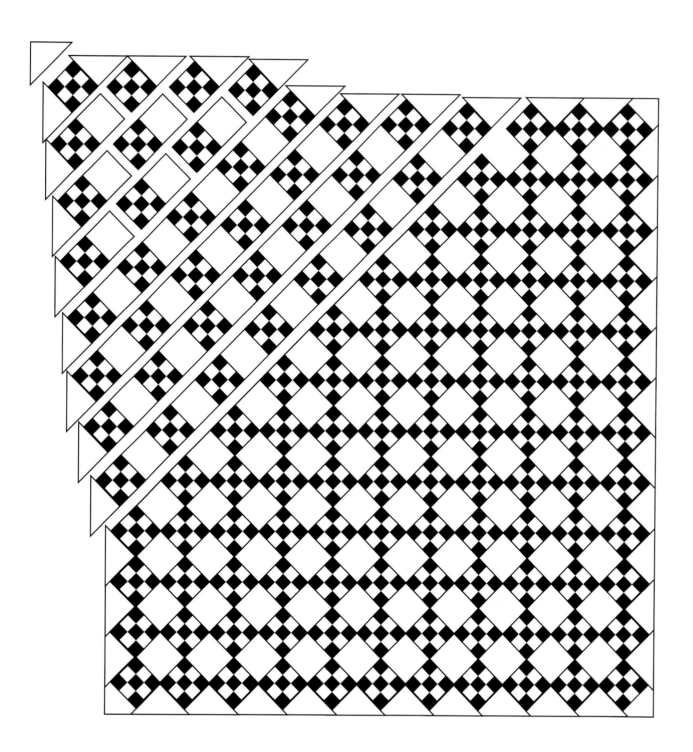

diagram 4 Quilt assembly: join the ninepatch blocks and cream squares into rows as shown, beginning and ending each row with a ninepatch block. Add the setting triangles to the end of each row and the corner triangles to the corners, then sew all the rows together to complete the quilt top.

Toile and ticking quilt

One of the simplest designs in this book, this

quilt is within reach of anyone with even

rudimentary sewing skills. Here, the plainness

of ticking makes an effective contrast to the

rococo qualities of the toile print. A black-and-

white colour scheme keeps the look restrained.

Materials
100 in (2.5 m) ticking, about 56 in (140 cm)
wide
100 in (2.5 m) toile, at least 45 in (112 cm)
wide
5.5 yd (5 m) black grosgrain ribbon, 5 cm
(2 in) wide
For the backing: 5.5 yd (5 m) backing fabric,
60 in (150 cm) wide; OR use a king-sized
cotton bed sheet
Black sewing thread
White sewing thread
For the binding: 24 in (60 cm) black quilter's
cotton, 45 in (112 cm) wide
King-sized thin batting
White quilting thread

Tools
Rotary cutter, ruler and mat
Sewing machine

Size
98 x 98 in (2.45 x 2.45 m)

Preparation
If your toile fabric is wider than 45 in (112 cm),
trim it to size, centring motifs if necessary
so that the panel is symmetrical

Seam allowance
Three-eighths inch (1 cm) seam allowances
are used throughout

CONSTRUCTION

Quilt top Cut the ticking fabric in half lengthwise to give two pieces each 28 in (70 cm) wide. With right sides together and matching raw edges, join a piece of ticking to each edge of the toile panel. Using a ⅜ in (1 cm) seam, machine-sew in place using white thread in both the needle and bobbin. Cut the grosgrain ribbon in half widthwise. Centre a piece of ribbon along each seam between the ticking and toile panels, making sure it is straight, then machine-sew in place close to each edge of the ribbon, using black thread in the needle and white thread in the bobbin. See Diagram 1.

FINISHING

Join the backing fabric, if necessary. Press the seams open. Place the backing fabric face down on a flat surface. Place the batting and the quilt top on top of the backing, right side up. Pin and baste. Quilt by hand or machine as desired, firstly marking the quilting design lightly with tailor's chalk or pencil. Our example is hand-quilted lengthwise with large stitches down the centre of each motif in the toile fabric and also down every 7th or 8th white stripe in the ticking fabric, and is also machine-quilted (with black thread in the needle and white thread in the bobbin) along every 7th or 8th black stripe in the ticking, next to the hand-quilted white stripes. Alternatively, you could hand-quilt around the motifs in the toile.

BINDING

Across the width of the fabric, cut 9 strips each 2½ in (6 cm) wide. Join strips into a continuous length and bind quilt as described on page 175.

diagram 1 Quilt construction: the toile panel is flanked by strips of ticking. Wide grosgrain ribbon separates the panels. The quilt is finished with a mixture of hand- and machine-quilting.

Pink silk button-tied quilt

This is an example of a tied quilt. Tying is an alternative to quilting as a means of finishing a quilt. It can be done with thread (either quilting or embroidery thread) or with buttons, as here.

The use of pretty flower-shaped buttons on pink silk results in an unapologetically girly quilt, but using a darker or cotton fabric and plainer buttons would give a totally different effect.

Materials
All fabrics are 44 in (112 cm) wide
5½ yd (5 m) pink silk or silk-look polyester fabric for quilt top
4¾ yd (4.4 m) white silk or silk-look polyester fabric for quilt back
Pink sewing and quilting threads
White sewing thread
121 buttons (it is advisable to buy a few extra in case of future loss or breakage)
Thick polyester batting at least 94 x 94 in (240 x 240 cm)

Tools
Rotary cutter, ruler and mat
Sewing machine
Quilting hoop (optional)

Size
Approx. 87 x 87 in (220 x 220 cm)

Cutting instructions
Ensure that the ends of both pieces of fabric are square.
From each piece of fabric, remove the selvedges. From the width of the pink fabric, cut 9 strips each 2.5 in (6 cm) wide for the binding. Set aside.
Cut both pieces of fabric in half widthways. Leave one pink and one white piece whole to make centre panels for front and back respectively. Cut the other 2 pieces in half lengthways to make side panels for front and back respectively

Care instructions
Silk or polyester quilts, or those with expensive buttons, must be dry-cleaned. Cotton quilts with inexpensive plastic buttons can be hand-washed carefully

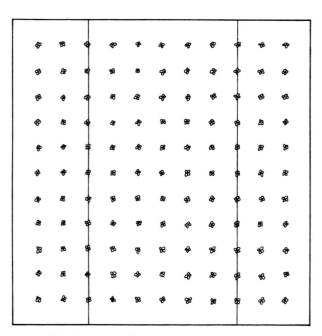

diagram 1: **Quilt assembly** Showing the seams along the centre panel and the placement of the buttons.

variation Quilt made with white cotton fabric and assorted buttons tied at random points, then bound with white grosgrain ribbon.

Variation

This design also works well in a crisp cotton fabric or a warm wool or flannel. If you prefer a random look to a regimented grid pattern, sew on the buttons at irregular intervals, or use a selection of many different buttons as shown in the example above.

CONSTRUCTION

1 For the front, sew a side panel of pink fabric to each side of the centre front panel. Press seams open using a cool iron.

2 For the back, sew a side panel of white fabric to each side of the centre back panel. Press seams open using a cool iron.

3 Using a removable marker or tailor's chalk, mark the grid for the buttons on the quilt top, as shown in Diagram 1. To calculate the distance between the buttons, measure the distance between the panel seams and divide by 6. First, place evenly spaced marks down each front panel seam,

then mark between and on either side of the panel seams.

4 Place the backing right side down on a flat surface. Place the batting and quilt top on top, right side up. Pin with safety pins.

5 Sew on buttons (this is most easily done with the fabric in a quilting frame) using quilting thread. Conceal the ends of the threads by running them into the wadding for 1 in (2.5 cm) or so, then bringing the needle up through the surface and cutting the thread off close to the surface.

6 Bind with reserved strips of pink fabric as described on page 175.

Giant hexagon quilt

The hexagon is a fascinating and versatile shape that most quilters equate with the popular 'grandmother's flower garden' pattern of the 1930s, in which many small hexagons are sewn by hand into rosettes. This quilt reinterprets that traditional design by using large hexagons, machine-sewing and bold Japanese fabrics.

An alternative colourway using soft, romantic florals is pictured on pages 160 and 211, showing how the same design in different fabrics can result in a vastly different effect.

Materials
All fabrics are 100% cotton, 45 in (112 cm) wide
For the large hexagons: 19 mixed bright floral fabrics, at least 13 x 13 in (33 x 33 cm)
For border 1: 1.1 yd (1 m) black quilter's cotton
For border 2: 2 yd (1.8 m) bold floral fabric
For the backing: 3.3 yd (3 m) plain fabric
For the binding: 20 in (50 cm) floral fabric
Matching thread
Batting at least 76 x 64 in (195 x 160 cm)
Thin cardboard or template plastic, for templates for large hexagons, half hexagons, and quarter hexagons
Thin cardboard, for templates for small hexagons

Tools
Rotary cutter, ruler and mat
Sewing machine

Size
Approx. 68 x 55½ in (173 x 141 cm)

Cutting directions
From the mixed bright floral fabrics, cut:
13 large hexagons from Template A
4 half hexagons from Template B
4 half hexagons from Template C
2 quarter hexagons from Template D, then reverse the template and cut 2 more

Seam allowance
Quarter-inch (6 mm) seam allowances are used throughout

preparing fabrics After cutting out the full, half and quarter hexagons, use a quilter's quarter and a pencil to mark precise ¼ in (6 mm) seam lines.

sewing Sew whole, quarter and half hexagons into rows, then machine-sew the rows together using a set-in seam.

CONSTRUCTION

Refer to Diagram 5 (see page 215).

1 After cutting out the pieces, lay them out on a flat surface and move them about until you have achieved an arrangement that you are pleased with.

2 Sew the pieces into rows, making sure that you sew *only* from seam allowance to seam allowance, not from edge to edge. This allows for a set-in seam to be more easily made in Step 3 (see Diagram 1). Press seams open.

3 Sew the rows together with a zig-zag set-in seam, beginning and ending each seam ¼ in (6 mm) in from the edge and pivoting the needle at the end of each seam in the previous row (see Diagram 2). Press seams open.

Border 1 Cut 2 strips 5½ x 48½ in (14 x 123 cm). Cut 2 strips 5½ x 42 in (14 x 107 cm). Sew the longer strips to the sides of the quilt. Press. Sew the shorter strips to the top and the bottom of the quilt. Press.

Border 2 Cut 2 strips 7½ x 58½ in (19 x 149 cm). Cut 2 strips 7½ x 56 in (19 x 142 cm). Sew the longer strips to the sides of the quilt. Press. Sew the shorter strips to the top and the bottom of the quilt. Press.

appliquéd diamonds The diamonds appliquéd to the outer border are composed of hexagons hand-sewn using the paper piecing method.

quilting This example in an alternative colourway shows the two hexagons quilted inside each large hexagon.

Appliquéd diamonds for Border 1

These are constructed using the paper piecing method (see page 168 and Diagrams 3 and 4, page 213) and are optional.

1 From thin cardboard, cut out small hexagons using Template E.

2 Using Template E and fabrics left over from large hexagons, pin a cardboard hexagon to wrong side of fabric. Cut out fabric, adding ¼ in (6 mm) seam allowance. Cut 7 small hexagons from each of 7 fabrics.

3 Fold the edge of the fabric over and tack all round, sewing through both cardboard and fabric. With right sides together and using a whip stitch, join 7 hexagons to make a rosette (see Diagram 3). Add an extra hexagon at each end to form a diamond (see Diagram 4). Press.

Make 7 units in this way.

Three diamonds are appliquéd to one side of the inner border and 4 to the other. Spray with starch and press well. Snip the tacking thread to release the cardboard and appliqué the diamonds into place, spacing them evenly and referring to the photograph on page 212 for placement.

TEMPLATE E
SMALL HEXAGON
FOR BORDER
APPLIQUÉ DESIGN

Template E Small hexagons for border appliqué design. Add ¼ in (6 mm) seam allowance when cutting fabric.

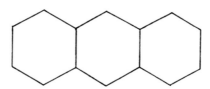

diagram 1 Sew the large hexagons into rows, beginning and ending seam ¼ in (6 mm) from edge.

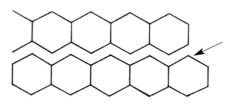

diagram 2 Sew the rows of hexagons together, using a zigzag set-in seam.

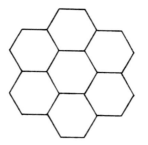

diagram 3 Hand-piece seven small hexagons into a rosette shape.

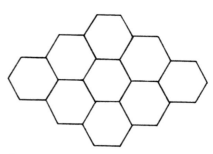

diagram 4 Add another hexagon to each end of the rosette to form a diamond shape.

FINISHING

Cut the backing fabric in half widthwise then join the two pieces together lengthwise to give a large enough backing. Place the backing right side down on a smooth surface. Place the batting and the quilt on top of the backing, right side up. Pin and baste the layers together. Quilt as desired: our example has been machine ditch-stitched along all the seams and around the appliquéd diamonds.

See the photograph on page 211 for an alternative hand-quilting suggestion.

BINDING

From width of the binding fabric, cut 6 strips each 2½ in (6.5 cm) wide. Seam the strips into a continuous length, then continue as explained on page 175.

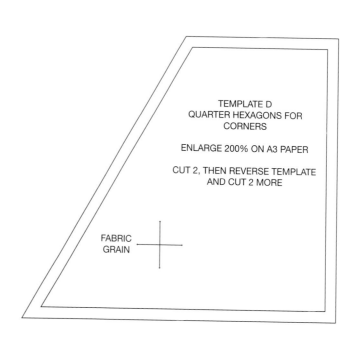

TEMPLATE D
QUARTER HEXAGONS FOR
CORNERS

ENLARGE 200% ON A3 PAPER

CUT 2, THEN REVERSE TEMPLATE
AND CUT 2 MORE

FABRIC
GRAIN

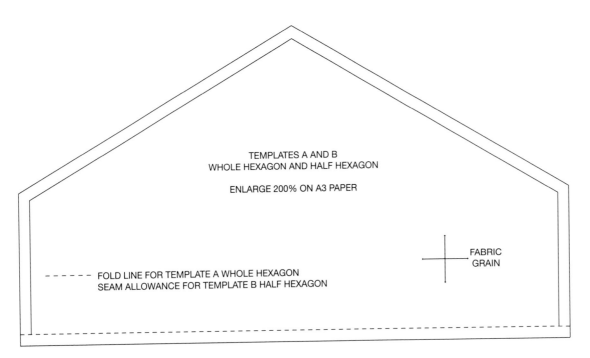

TEMPLATES A AND B
WHOLE HEXAGON AND HALF HEXAGON

ENLARGE 200% ON A3 PAPER

FABRIC
GRAIN

- - - - - FOLD LINE FOR TEMPLATE A WHOLE HEXAGON
SEAM ALLOWANCE FOR TEMPLATE B HALF HEXAGON

templates A and B: whole hexagons and half hexagons For the whole
hexagons (Template A), make 2 photocopies at 200% on A3 paper and join
accurately along the scored line to make the full template. For the half
hexagons (Template B), photocopy at 200% on A3 paper.

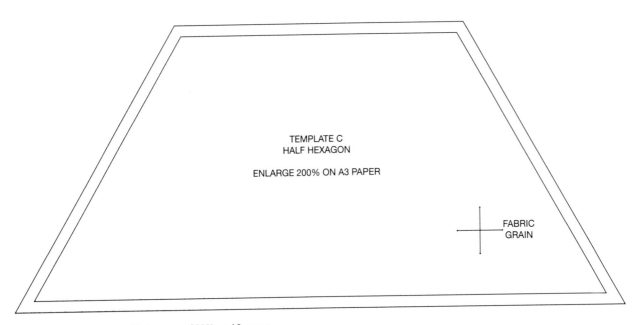

TEMPLATE C
HALF HEXAGON

ENLARGE 200% ON A3 PAPER

FABRIC
GRAIN

template C: half hexagons Photocopy at 200% on A3 paper.

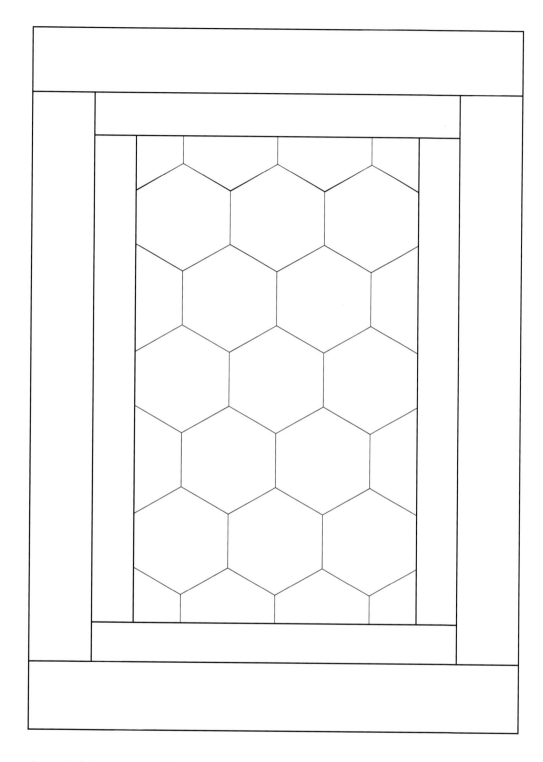

Labelling and dating quilts

Many quilters like to sign and date their quilts on the back as a record for future owners of when and by whom the quilts were made. Signing can be done with an indelible fabric marker directly onto the quilt if the backing is a pale fabric, or on a patch of pale fabric that is then sewn onto the back of a dark quilt. An alternative is to embroider the details onto a patch of fabric and sew the patch to the back of the quilt.

A signature can be as basic as the maker and year, or if the quilt is to be a gift, you might also like to include details of the recipient and the occasion for which the quilt was made.

diagram 5 Quilt construction: full hexagons, two different half hexagons (A and B) and quarter hexagons make up the centre of the quilt, and are surrounded by two borders.

Octagon illusion quilt

Octagons are attractive shapes, but they are not easy to piece as they require set-in seams. This ingenious yet simple quilt solves the problem by using only squares. The background consists of machine-pieced large squares, with smaller squares pressed over a cardboard template then appliquéd over the intersections of the larger ones, giving the illusion of an octagon. This quilt is the perfect showcase for a subtle blending of pale, floral fabrics.

Materials
All fabrics are 100% cotton, 45 in (112 cm) wide
For the large and small squares: a total of
    3⅓ yd (3 m) assorted floral fabrics
For border 1: 16 in (40 cm)
For border 2: 48 in (120 cm)
For the backing: 3¾ yd (3.4 m)
For the binding: 20 in (50 cm)
Matching sewing and quilting threads
Batting at least 79 x 68 in (200 x 175 cm)

Tools
Rotary cutter, ruler and mat
Sewing machine
Thin cardboard
Fabric starch

Size
Approx. 71 x 60 in (180 x 155 cm)

Preparation
From the thin cardboard, cut pressing
    templates C, D and E. (Cut a few of each;
    when one template becomes worn or its
    edges distorted through too much use,
    replace it with a new template)

Cutting directions
From the assorted floral fabrics:
    Cut 80 squares 6 x 6 in (15 x 15 cm)
    Cut 63 squares 3 x 3 in (7.5 x 7.5 cm)
    Cut 32 side triangles from template A
    Cut 4 corner triangles from template B

Seam allowance
Quarter-inch (6 mm) seam allowances are
    used throughout

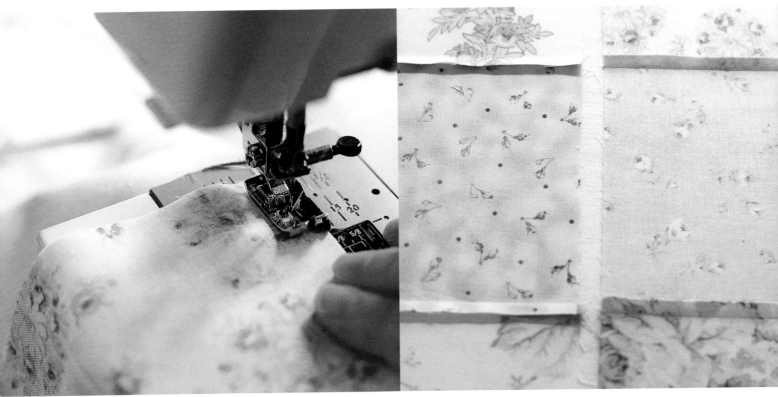

large squares Chain-piece pairs of large squares together.

large squares continued Piece pairs of squares into 8 rows of 10, pressing the seams of each row in alternate directions as shown.

CONSTRUCTION

Refer to Diagram 3, page 222.

Large squares Arrange the 6 in (15 cm) squares in 8 rows of 10, as shown in Diagram 3, and sew into rows. Press the seams of each row in alternate directions (see Diagram 1) so that when the rows are sewn together the seams are opposing (see Diagram 2). Sew the rows together.

Small squares Spray the 3 in (7.5 cm) squares lightly with fabric starch. Place the cardboard pressing template C onto the wrong side of the fabric square. Using a dry iron, carefully ease the seam allowance over the edges of the cardboard and press well.

Remove the cardboard and position the square on point over the joins of the large squares. Appliqué in place.

Side triangles Spray the fabric triangles lightly with fabric starch. Place the cardboard pressing template D onto the wrong side of the fabric triangle, aligning the long side of the template with the base of the fabric triangle. Using a dry iron, carefully ease the seam allowance over the short sides of the template to give sharp edges and points. Remove the cardboard and position the triangles along the sides of the background squares so that their raw edges align with those of the sewn squares.

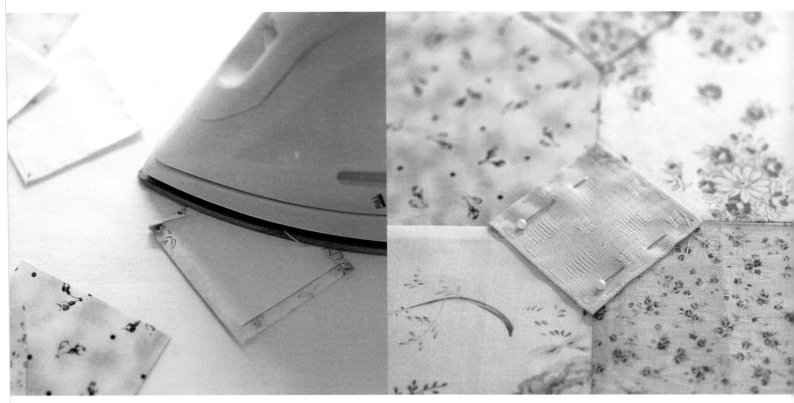

small squares Using a dry iron, carefully ease the seam allowance of the small squares over the edges of the cardboard pressing template.

small squares continued Align the pressed small squares with the intersections of the larger squares and appliqué into place.

Appliqué in place, leaving the raw edges to be sewn into the seams of Border 1.

Corner triangles Spray the fabric triangles lightly with fabric starch. Place the cardboard pressing template E onto the wrong side of the fabric triangle, aligning the 2 short sides of the template with the fabric. Using a dry iron, carefully ease the seam allowance over the long side of the cardboard only. Remove the cardboard and position the triangles so that their raw edges align with those of the corners of the quilt. Appliqué in place, leaving the raw edges to be sewn into the seams of Border 1.

Border 1 Cut 2 strips 2½ x 48½ in (6 x 123 cm). Cut 2 strips 2½ x 59½ in (6 x 152 cm). Allowing enough fabric to form the mitred corners, sew the 2 longer strips to the sides of the quilt. Press. Sew the shorter strips to the top and bottom. Press.

Border 2 Cut 2 strips 6½ x 61 in (16.5 x 155 cm). Cut 2 strips 6½ x 72 in (16.5 x 183 cm). Allowing enough fabric to form mitred corners, sew the 2 longer strips to the sides of the quilt. Press. Sew the shorter strips to the top and bottom. Press. Mitre corners as explained on page 172, beginning and ending seams a precise ¼ in (6 mm) from the outside edges. Press.

Mitred corners

When mitring corners, the additional lengths at each corner must be equal to the width of the borders. The seams must begin and end ¼ in (6 mm) from the outside edges — no more, no less.

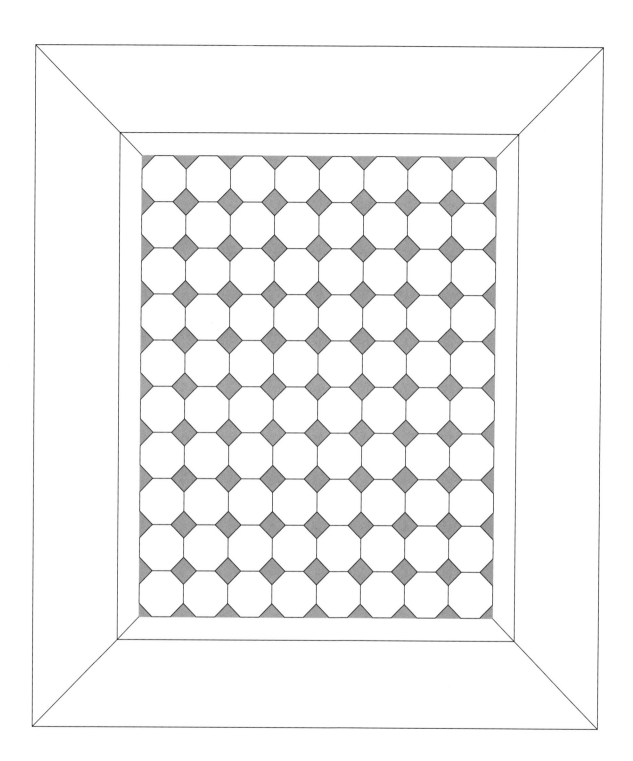

diagram 3 Quilt construction: the pieced large squares are intersected by small appliquéd squares, then surrounded by one narrow and one wide border, both with mitred corners.

Square-in-a-square quilt

Beautiful Japanese fabrics are the focus of this easy-to-piece quilt, with the dark indigos forming a sharp contrast to the cream centres, and both framed with russet sashing strips and borders.

Materials

All fabrics are 100% cotton, 45 in (112 cm) wide
For the blocks:
   A total of 1.9 yd (1.7 m) assorted Japanese print fabrics
   A total of 16 in (40 cm) assorted cream fabrics
For the sashing, border and binding: 2.1 yd (1.9 m)
   russet fabric
For the backing: 3 yd (2.7 m)
Matching sewing thread
Batting at least 68 x 54 in (175 x 140 cm)

Tools

Rotary cutter, ruler and mat
Sewing machine

Size

Approx. 64½ x 49½ in (163 x 125 cm)

Cutting directions

From the indigo fabrics, cut:
   For the blocks:
      96 strips each 3½ x 2 in (9 x 5 cm)
      96 strips each 6½ x 2 in (16.5 x 5 cm)
      (Note: if you want each square to have the same fabric
      on all sides, cut even numbers of each strip for
      each fabric)
   For the setting squares:
      35 squares 2 x 2 in (5 x 5 cm)
From the cream fabrics, cut 48 squares 3½ x
3½ in (9 x 9 cm)
From the length of the russet fabric, cut:
   For the border:
      2 strips 3½ x 59 in (9 x 150 cm)
      2 strips 3½ x 56 in (9 x 142 cm)
   For the binding: 4 strips 2½ in (6.5 cm) wide
   For the sashing: from the remaining russet
      fabric, cut 82 strips 6½ x 2 in (16.5 x 5 cm)

Seam allowance

Quarter-inch (6 mm) seam allowances are used throughout

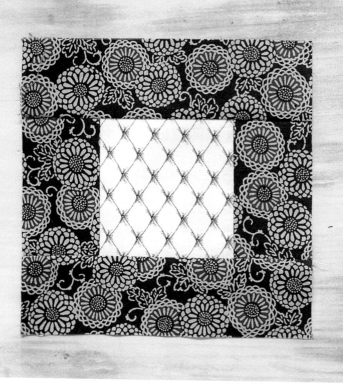

step one Sew a short indigo strip to opposite sides of a cream square.

step two Sew a longer indigo strip to the top and bottom of the unit formed in Step 1.

CONSTRUCTION OF BLOCK

1 Sew a 3½ x 2 in (9 x 5 cm) indigo strip to opposite sides of a cream square. Press seams towards indigo strips.

2 Sew a 6½ x 2 in (16.5 x 5 cm) strip to the top and bottom of the unit formed in Step 1. Press seams towards indigo strips.

Make 48 blocks. Avoid duplicating the same print combinations too many times.

SASHING

Block rows Each block row consists of 6 blocks alternating with 5 sashing strips (see Diagram 1). Each row begins and ends with a block. On a flat surface, arrange the blocks until you have an arrangement that you are pleased with. For a neat effect, make sure that the blocks are positioned so that the long strips on each side all face the same way. Make 8 block rows.

Sashing rows Each sashing row consists of 6 sashing strips and 5 setting squares. Each row begins and ends with a sashing strip. Join the sashing strips and setting squares to make 7 rows.

Stitch the rows together, alternating block rows and sashing rows, beginning and ending with a block row. See Diagram 1.

sashing rows Chain-piece indigo setting squares to russet sashing strips.

sashing rows continued Join 6 sashing strips to 5 setting squares to complete the sashing row.

BORDER

Sew the 2 longer strips to the side of the quilt. Press. Sew the 2 shorter strips to the top and bottom of the quilt. Press.

FINISHING

Cut the backing fabric in half widthwise. Join the two pieces lengthwise (along the selvedges). Press seam open.
Place the backing right side down on a flat surface. Place the batting and the quilt on top of the backing, right side up. Pin and baste the layers together. Quilt as desired: our example is machine ditch-stitched around the cream squares and along the sashing rows and border seam.

BINDING

Seam the reserved binding strips into a continuous length and proceed as described on page 175.

diagram 1 Lay out the blocks so that the longer side strips all face in the same direction. Join the blocks to sashing strips to form the block rows, and the sashing strips to the setting squares to form the sashing rows.

Stitch and slash quilt

The multiple layers of fabric used in this technique result in a wonderful texture that mimics chenille. There is no need for batting in this quilt, as the layers give adequate weight. Machine-washing frays the cut edges of the fabric and adds to the chenille effect. The more you wash it, the softer the quilt will become.

Materials

All fabrics are 100% cotton, 44 in (112 cm) wide
For the centre of the quilt: 32 in (80 cm) of
   each of 5 different fabrics:
   For the front border: 28 in (70 cm)
For the back border: 28 in (70 cm)
Non-fusible interfacing such as Pellon:
   28 in (70 cm)
For the binding: 20 in (50 cm)

Tools

Rotary cutter, ruler and mat
Sewing machine

Size

Approx. 41 x 53½ in (100 x 140 cm)

Seam allowance

Quarter-inch (6 mm) seam allowances are
   used throughout

step two Mark parallel diagonal lines ½ in (12 mm) apart on the right side of the fabric that will form the top of the quilt.

step six Sewing all lines in the same direction, machine-sew through all five layers along each of the marked lines.

Hints

The stitch and slash method uses five layers of fabric. Narrow diagonal lines are sewn across the layers, then the top three layers are cut to form the chenille effect. The fourth layer is thus exposed and forms the background to the main fabric. The fifth fabric makes up the back of the quilt.

In our example, the fabric for Border 1 is the same as for the top of the quilt, and the fabric for the back border is the same as for the back of the quilt.

CONSTRUCTION OF CENTRE

1 Trim each of the 5 fabrics for the front of the quilt to 31½ x 44 in (80 x 112 cm).

2 Place the fabric for the front of the quilt on a flat surface, right side up. Press well. Using a quilters' ruler and an erasable marker or pencil, draw parallel diagonal lines ½ in (12 mm) apart. Draw the first line from corner to corner. To draw the remaining lines, align the ½ in marking on the edge of the ruler with the previous line.

3 Place the fifth fabric (the backing fabric) on a flat surface, right side down. Press well.

4 Layer the other 4 fabrics, right side up, on top of the fifth fabric, placing the marked piece for the front of the quilt on top. Align all raw edges. Press well.

5 Pin the five layers together to minimize fabric movement.

6 Wind the bobbin of your sewing machine with thread matching the bottom layer of fabric and thread your machine needle with thread matching the top layer of fabric. Stitch along each of the marked lines in the same direction using a stitch length of 3. (Note that sewing all the lines in the same direction will cause the fabric layers to

step seven Carefully cut through the top three layers only, leaving the bottom two layers intact.

Borders Sew the border fabrics and Pellon the the edges of the quilt.

move slightly out of alignment; do not worry about this, as the rectangle will be trimmed later to square it up.)

7 When all the stitching is completed, carefully cut through the top three layers of fabric (see the photograph), leaving the bottom two layers intact. This creates the chenille effect.

8 When all the cutting is completed, lay out the rectangle on a cutting mat and, using a rotary cutter, trim it to square up the edges, so that it measures approximately 29½ x 42 in (75 x 106.5 cm).

BORDERS

Measure both the length and width through the centre of the quilt.

Side borders These are cut 6½ in (16.5 cm) wide by the length of the quilt. Cut 2 from the front border fabric. Cut 2 from the back border fabric. Cut 2 of Pellon. Pin the back border pieces to the side edges of the back of the quilt, right sides together. Pin the front border pieces to the side edges of the front of the quilt, right sides together. Pin the Pellon on top of the front border. The order of components on each side edge of the quilt should be: back border, quilt, front border, Pellon.

trimming borders Once the border pieces have been added, trim the ends if needed.

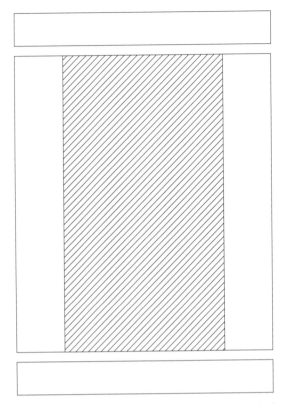

diagram 1 Side borders are sewn first to the central slashed panel, then the top and bottom borders are added.

Binding

From the width of the binding fabric, cut 5 strips each 2½ in (6 cm) wide. Seam the strips into a continuous length, making the joins at 45-degree angles, and proceed as described on page 175.

Stitch through all the layers on both edges. Fold the back border strips to the back of the quilt, the front border and Pellon strips to the front of the quilt, and press. Trim ends of borders if necessary. Pin the outer edge to hold the layers together.

Top and bottom borders These are cut 6½ in (16.5 cm) wide by the width of the quilt including the two side borders.
Cut 2 from the fabric for the front border.
Cut 2 from the fabric for the back border.
Cut 2 of Pellon.
Pin the back border pieces to the top and bottom edges of the back of the quilt, right sides together. Pin the front border pieces

to the top and bottom edges of the front of the quilt, right sides together. Pin the Pellon on top of the front border pieces. The order of components on the top and bottom edges should be as follows: back border, quilt, front border, Pellon.
Stitch through all the layers on both edges. Fold the back border strips to the back of the quilt, the front border and Pellon strips to the front of the quilt, and press. Trim the ends of the border if necessary. Pin the outer edge to hold the layers together.

FINISHING
Quilt a design in the border if desired.
Bind as decribed at left.

Ninepatch cot quilt

This bright and cheery cot quilt is quick and easy to make. The blocks are a variation on the traditional ninepatch design, with squares of printed fabric surrounding a plain centre.

Materials
All fabrics are 100% cotton, 44 in (112 cm) wide

For the coloured squares: a total of 32 in (80 cm) mixed scrap fabrics; or use 11 different fabric squares each 10½ x 10½ in (27 x 27 cm), or 11 strips each 44 x 2½ in (112 x 6 cm)

For the centre squares of the ninepatch, the sashing strips and the border: 1⅓ yd (1.2 m) white cotton

For the binding: 12 in (30 cm)

For the backing: 1.4 yd (1.2 m)

Tools
Rotary cutter, ruler and mat

Sewing machine

Size
Approx. 44 x 36 in (112 x 90 cm)

Cutting directions
From the mixed scrap fabrics, cut 172 squares each 2½ x 2½ in (6 x 6 cm) for the coloured ninepatch squares. The squares may be rotary-cut or cut out individually using templates, as preferred

From the white cotton fabric:

For the central ninepatch squares, cut 20 squares 2½ x 2½ in (6 x 6 cm)

For the sashing strips, cut 7 strips each 2½ in (6 cm) wide across the width of the fabric, then cross-cut into 31 rectangles each 2½ x 6½ in (6 x 16.5 cm)

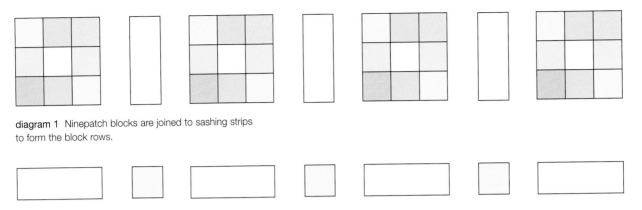

diagram 1 Ninepatch blocks are joined to sashing strips
to form the block rows.

diagram 2 Sashing strips are joined to 2½ in (6 cm)
setting squares to form the sashing rows.

diagram 3 The ninepatch block rows are alternated with
sashing rows, then a border the same colour as the block
centres and sashing strips is added.

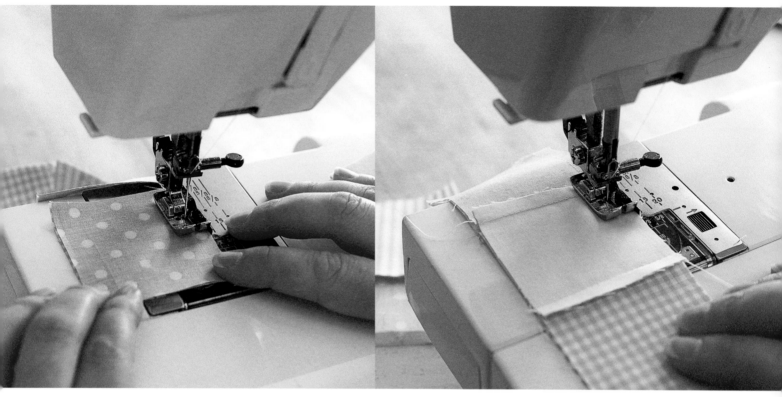

ninepatch blocks For the coloured strips, chain-piece pairs of coloured squares together, then add a single square to one end of each pair.

ninepatch blocks continued Sew a coloured strip to etiher side of a coloured-and-white strip to complete the ninepatch block.

CONSTRUCTION

Ninepatch blocks Each block consists of 8 coloured squares arranged around a white square (see Diagram 1). Piece the squares into strips first, then join the strips into blocks. Make sure there is a good range of prints in each block. Make 20 blocks.

ASSEMBLY

Block rows Sew 4 ninepatch blocks alternately with 3 sashing strips (see Diagram 1). Make a total of 5 block rows.

Sashing rows Sew 4 sashing strips alternately with 3 coloured setting squares. Make a total of 4 sashing rows.

Sew the block rows alternately with the sashing rows, beginning and ending with a block row, to complete the quilt centre.

BORDER

Find the length of the quilt by measuring vertically through the centre. From the white fabric, cut 2 strips each 3½ in (9 cm) by the length of the quilt (approx 38 in/ 96.5 cm). Sew in place and press.
Find the width of the quilt by measuring horizontally through the centre and including the two sewn side borders. Cut 2 strips each 3½ in (9 cm) by the width of the quilt (approx 36½ in/91 cm). Sew in place and press.

blocks The finished ninepatch block.

block rows and sashing rows Join blocks to sashing strips to form the block ro[w]
and coloured setting squares to sashing strips to form the sashing rows.

FINISHING

Place the backing right side down on a flat surface and smooth it out. Place the batting and the quilt on top of the backing, right side up. Pin and baste the layers together. Quilt as desired. The pictured example was machine ditch-stitched in all the horizontal and vertical seams.

BINDING

From the width of the binding fabric, cut 4 strips each 2½ in (6 cm) wide. Seam the strips into a continuous length, making the joins at 45-degree angles, and proceed as decribed on page 175.

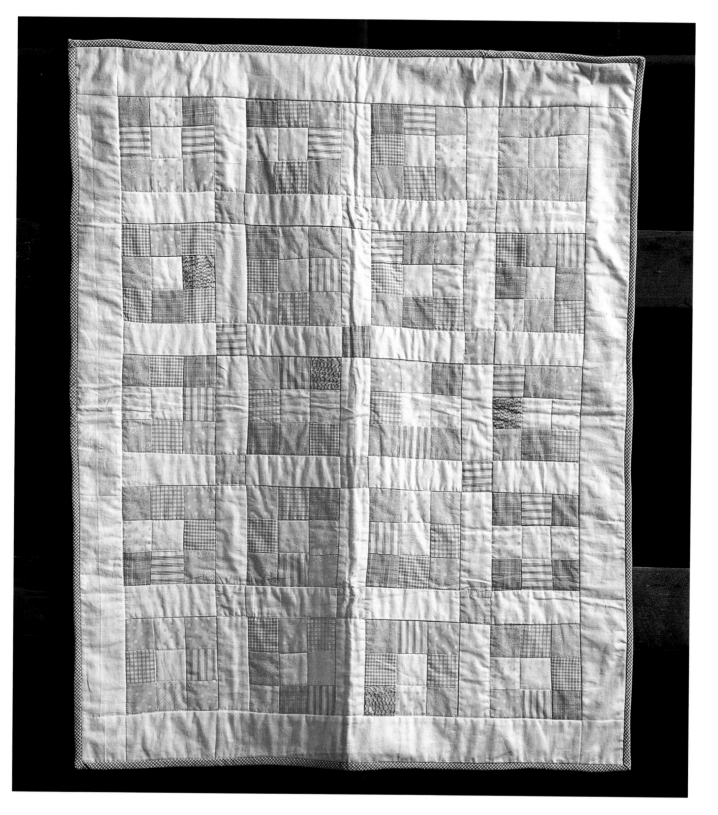

Folded Japanese quilt

This unusual folded quilt is surprisingly easy to make, as each block is simply a circle of fabric folded over a padded square, then quilted. This is a 'quilt-as-you-go' technique, meaning that batting and quilting are incorporated into each separate block, rather than being added once the quilt top is completed. For those who like the look of hand-quilting, but don't really enjoy the process, this technique breaks the task up into smaller, more manageable portions.

Materials

Mixed selection of Japanese indigo print fabrics to total 5.1 yd (4.6 m); for example, approx. 18 fat quarters, or 9 in (25 cm) of each of 15 different fabrics

Mixed selection of cream print fabrics to total 2 yd (1.7 m); for example, 81 squares each 5¾ x 5¾ in (14.5 x 14.5 cm), or 12 in (30 cm) of each of 6 different fabrics, or 6 in (15 cm) of each of 12 different fabrics

For the border (optional): 64 in (1.6 m) print fabric

For the binding: 16 in (40 cm) print fabric

Indigo sewing thread

Cream quilting thread

Thin cardboard for templates

Spray starch

Batting at least 70 x 70 in (175 x 175 cm) for quilt with border, or 60 x 60 in (155 x 155 cm) for quilt without border

Tools

Rotary cutter, ruler and mat

Sewing machine

Size

Approx. 60 x 60 in (155 x 155 cm) with border, 52 x 52 in (132 x 132 cm) without border

Cutting directions for fabric

Notes: Before cutting the fabrics, prepare the templates (see page 244). Cut fabric on the straight of the grain wherever possible

For the circles: Place the 8½ in (21.5 cm) circle template onto the wrong side of the indigo fabric and cut out a circle by hand, leaving a good ¼ in (6 mm) turning allowance all the way round

For the cream centres and batting: Rotary-cut 81 squares 5¾ x 5¾ in (14.5 x 14.5 cm) from both the cream fabric and the batting

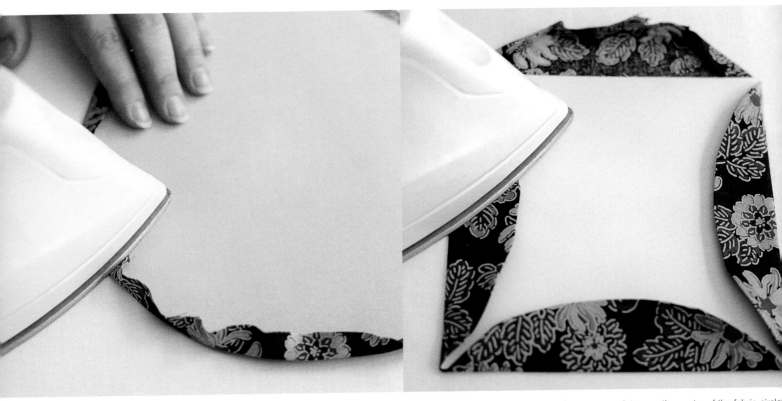

step one Lay the circle template on the wrong side of the fabric circle and press in the seam allowance over the template, using a dry iron.

step two Lay the 6 in (15 cm) square template over the centre of the fabric circle and press the edges of the fabric over the template.

Cutting directions for templates

From the thin cardboard, cut:
Circle 8½ in (21.5 cm) diameter
Square 6 x 6 in (15 x 15 cm)

Note: cut several of each, so that you have replacements for templates that become too worn or distorted.

CONSTRUCTION OF BLOCK

1 Spray the fabric circles with starch. Place the circle template in the centre of the wrong side of the fabric circle. Press in the seam allowance over the template using a dry iron (see photograph).

2 Lay the 6 in (15 cm) square template on the wrong side of the circle of fabric. Ensure that it is centred, and that the straight grain of the circle fabric aligns with the edge of the template. Fold the edges of the fabric circle over the template and dry press with a dry iron (see Diagram 1).

3 Open the flaps of the circle and replace the template with a square of wadding and a square of cream centre fabric.

4 Pin through the 4 layers using short appliqué pins. These permit you to stitch without catching the thread on each pin.

5 Using a small running stitch, quilt through all the layers approximately ⅛ in (3 mm) in from the edge (see photograph and Diagram 2). At each corner, make 3–4 small ladder stitches to bring the corner seams together. Make a total of 81 blocks.

step five Quilt through all the layers with an even running stitch.

assembly Join the finished blocks into rows by hand using a small ladder stitch.

ASSEMBLY

When you have completed quilting all the individual blocks, lay them out 9 across by 9 down, moving the blocks around to achieve a pleasing design. In our example, the blocks have been laid out alternating backs and fronts to give a reversible quilt. See Diagram 5 for an alternative layout. Join the blocks in each horizontal row, using a small ladder stitch. Then join the vertical rows in the same manner.

Border (optional) From the border fabric, cut 4 strips each 4½ x 54½ in (11 x 138.5 cm). Cut 4 strips each 4½ x 62½ in (11 x 160 cm).

From the batting, cut 2 strips 4½ x 54½ in (11 x 138.5 cm). Cut 2 strips each 4½ x 62½ in (11 x 160 cm).

With right sides together, pin a long strip of border fabric to one side of the front and back of the quilt. Place a strip of wadding on top and stitch ¼ in (6 mm) in from the raw edges. Trim evenly and press. Repeat for the other side, and then use the shorter strips for the top and bottom of the quilt.

BINDING

From the width of the binding fabric, cut 6 strips each 2½ in (6 cm) wide. Seam the strips into a continuous length, then proceed as described on page 175.

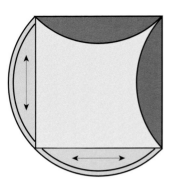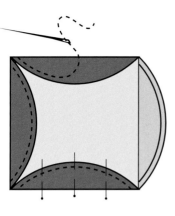

diagram 1 Align the straight grain of the fabric circle with the sides of the square template.

diagram 2 Quilt through all layers using a small running stitch.

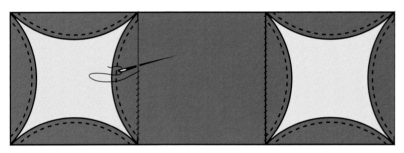

diagram 3 Join the finished squares into rows using a small ladder stitch.

feltmaking

Pleating and folding felt

Felt has a 'memory' for the shape in which it dries, so you can introduce pleats, folds and wrinkles if you want. Clothes pegs can be used to hold the folds while the felt dries, but keep in mind that the peg will leave an imprint. Alternatively, hold the pleats or folds in place with tacking stitches, unpicking them once the felt is dry.

What fibres can be felted?

Only wool makes true felt, as the structure of the felt depends upon the scaly structure of the wool fibres. Only sheep produce wool. Other fibre-producing animals include (but are not limited to) goats, alpacas, camels, rabbits, cats and dogs — all of which produce hair, not wool. Their product varies in usefulness; for example, the long, soft winter coat shed by horses and ponies in the springtime will not felt at all (even when blended with wool). Rabbit fur is the foundation of many felt hats, but is bonded using a highly toxic glue for durability. Industrial felt is usually made of synthetic waste products, bonded using a flat-bed needle-felting technique.

Various breeds of sheep produce wool suitable for felting, with different breeds giving different effects. Wool is classified as fine, medium or strong according to its thickness (usually expressed in microns; see opposite). The Australian Merino is the optimum breed for clothing felt, as it produces the finest wool (a British breed of sheep with strong wool could have a micron count up to twice that of a Merino). Merino wool is available throughout the U.K., Europe, Asia and North America.

In northern Europe, Friesian and Gotland sheep are popular for felting. In middle Europe, the Austrian Bergschaf is much used. In New Zealand, the locally bred Perendale is good for durable, sturdy felt. Stronger wools from breeds such as Leicester Longwool, Romney and Border Leicester are suitable for floor rugs. Merino crosses of these breeds will often produce good-quality, easy-felting wool.

In Mongolia, sheep's wool is principally used for yurts and gers, but also for rugs. Mongolian wool is available in Europe from felting suppliers.

Fibres other than wool can be used to decorate wool felt by either blending them with the sliver (the scoured, combed and carded wool fibres ready for felting) or simply laying them on the surface prior to felting. Silk, flax, hemp, ingeo (corn silk), alpaca and soy silk are all available in sliver form. Angora (rabbit fur), cotton fluff and mohair (from Angora goats) can also be incorporated into felt. Woven textiles will bond with wool, provided there are air spaces in the weave. A good test is to try to breathe through the textile; if breath passes easily through the cloth, wool fibres are likely to do so as well. Lovely effects can be achieved by felting onto patterned cloth.

special effects Leicester Longwool gives texture to the Shaggy rug with fleece curls (page 265).

Terms used in felting

Carding Wool is processed between two drums covered in small metal spikes to remove vegetable matter, soil and knots. Carded batting (which can also be produced on a small scale using a hand-operated drum carder) is a useful base for felting.

Combing After carding, wool is combed so that all the fibres lie in the same direction.

Crimp This refers to the natural waviness of the wool. The degree of crimp varies with the breed and the thickness of the wool.

Fleece wool Technically (in industry terms), fleece wool is the highest quality of the wool shorn from the sheep (generally wool from the side of the body).

Fulling This refers to the process of shrinking, firming and finishing soft felt (see page 254) so that it becomes dense and durable. This is generally done by rolling, but can also be achieved through dropping, kneading and beating.

Hard (or 'finished') felt Felt that has been fulled so that it no longer decreases visibly in size when rolled (however, vigorous machine washing can still shrink finished felt). It will feel firm to the touch and will be impossible to pull apart.

Lustre The brilliant glossy appearance of wool from British longwool breeds.

Microns The micron is the international unit of wool measurement. Although a micron is a mere one-millionth of a metre, experienced wool classers can usually make quite accurate estimates (to within 1–2 microns, particularly with regard to Merino wool). Wool of low micron count is generally referred to as being 'fine', whereas that of a high micron count is called 'strong' and requires considerable effort to felt. Merino wool comes in a range of 17–28 microns (the latter would be considered rather coarse, the former much in demand by Italian suit makers). Leicester Longwool

Equipment

Felting requires little specialized equipment. Most projects can be made using the following: soap; bubble wrap, for making templates and rolling up the item to be felted; a plastic non-slip mat or plastic fly-wire, useful as an intermediary or protective layer when rubbing soft, wet felt (fly-wire is particularly useful when bonding additional soft felts to the main body of felt using a scrunched piece of plastic or the wooden felting tool, shown above, to work the surface); a sushi mat and large bamboo blind, for rolling small and large items respectively; a watering can and hand-mister; and nylon cloth, for rolling up delicate felts at the beginning of the fulling stage after removing the felt from the mat or bubble wrap.

You may find it useful to buy wool carders (shown at the right of the photograph); these consist of two flat brushes studded with pins, between which fleece is stroked to straighten and separate the fibres. At the left of the photo is an improvized smoothing implement made from a cement-working tool with ribbed vinyl sheeting stapled over it; this is used to encourage fluffy parts to bond together or to add small pieces of pre-felt if repairing thin areas or adding decoration.

fulling This refers to the shrinking and hardening of felt, achieved through rolling or massage.

pre-felts These semi-felted pieces can be joined to each other, or to a background fabric.

Hint

You can make quite large felted pieces in a small workspace, by using a sushi mat to make small pre-felts then joining them together; this is the method used for the Patchwork blanket (page 273).

Washing and caring for felt

Contrary to popular belief, wool can actually be washed in hot water. The trick is not to vary the temperature of the water by more than 5°C (9°F) between successive baths or to agitate the wool. Once extremes of temperature and agitation or friction are introduced, felting is inevitable.

Because feltmaking is a continuous and irreversible process, any vigorous washing will shrink the felt. Big felt pieces are best laid on a mesh support or rolled in a bath, and gently hosed or sprayed. Small felt pieces should be very gently handwashed, making sure the temperature of the water is kept within a 5°C (9°F) range. Felt can be ironed while slightly damp, using a hot iron if desired. The important thing is always to dry the felt in the required shape, as it has a 'memory'. If folding felt for storage, acid-free tissue paper helps to prevent creasing, and good-quality moth repellent is essential.

To keep insects away, regular airing is important. Camphor-wood chips and boxes are both very good, and cedar balls also work quite well. Lavender, however, actually attracts moths due to its fragrance.

has a range of about 32–40 (in adult sheep), with rams generally having quite strong wool. Lincoln sheep are the strongest (British) longwool breed, with micron counts in the high 40s and low 50s. Their wool, which resembles curly human hair, is in demand for dolls' wigs, and was used to make human wigs in the past.

Pre-felt When the wool fibres have bonded sufficiently that the felt (when dry) holds together when lifted, but is still fluffy, the piece is called a pre-felt.

Raw fleece This describes unwashed (or unscoured) and untreated wool as shorn from the sheep. Raw wool contains vegetable matter picked up while the animal is grazing, natural secretions such as lanolin, and various other substances.

Roving See sliver.

Scouring Scouring is the process of washing the wool to remove the lanolin and dirt. After scouring, the wool is dried before being carded.

Sliver This refers to wool that has been scoured (washed), carded and combed, and formed into a thick, soft, straight (that is, untwisted) rope. This is how the wool is prepared for spinning into yarn. Felters find sliver most useful for making felt of an even thickness. In Britain, sliver is known as roving.

Soft felt At soft-felt stage, the work may be lifted and turned even though it is wet, and will not pull apart with the weight of the water. However, it still feels quite soft and can be easily stretched.

Staple The length of the wool fibre. Merino has a staple of 10–12.5 cm (4–5 inches); this is the growth for one year. Leicester Longwool can be up to 27 cm (11 inches).

Superwash wool This denotes wool with fibres that have been treated with silicon to ensure they don't felt while being washed; it is therefore totally unsuited to felting.

raw fleece Sheep produce fleece in various shades of cream, grey, brown and black.

sliver Sliver is cleaned, combed and carded wool that is ready to be spun or felted.

Making felt

To begin understanding felt, simply take a handful of wool fleece, wet it with hot, soapy water, and roll it around vigorously between the palms of your hands. In a very short space of time, the fluffy fleece will transform into a tight, firm woollen ball and you will have made felt.

Flat felt

The next step is to make flat felt. A simple and cheap piece of equipment for this is a sushi mat, which can be used on the kitchen sink. You can use raw fleece for the felting, or purchase wool sliver, which is more pleasant to use and has been scoured, carded and combed so that the wool is clean and the fibres are aligned.

1 Unroll the sushi mat. Gently pull tufts of wool from the end of the sliver and lay them on the mat so that they are all facing the same way, with each row slightly overlapping the previous one.

2 Lay out another layer, with the fibres at right angles to the first layer. Sprinkle the wool with warm, slightly soapy water (too much soap will create bubbles, which will decrease contact between the fibres).

3 Lifting the edge of the mat slightly, gently roll up the mat with the wool inside.

Using wetting agents

While it isn't essential to use a wetting agent when making felt, it does speed up the process. One or two drops of eco-friendly detergent to a 10-litre (2-gallon) bucket is enough to begin with. Then, as you work more with the piece, you'll find soap very useful, both to stick down any loose ends and hold them in place as you work, and as a lubricant so the felt doesn't catch on your fingers. While many people believe that the alkalinity of the soap promotes the felting, it has probably more to do with its lubricating and wetting qualities. If the fibres are well wetted, the little scales on the wool swell and lift up. As the felt is rolled, the individual fibres slide ever closer together. This is why felt appears to 'shrink' in the direction of the rolling action. When the finished felt has been rinsed and dried, the scales on the wool will have flattened again, and will have 'locked down' over any fibres that happen to be crossing them. This is what makes felt so strong, and why feltmaking is an irreversible and continuous process.

step one Pull wool from the end of the bundle of sliver and lay it on a bamboo mat.

step two Lay down the second layer of sliver, with the fibres running at right angles to the first.

step two continued Sprinkle the wool with warm, slightly soapy water.

Alternative method

Another felting technique, used for several of the smaller projects in this book, is to grasp and squeeze the felted item a number of times, first horizontally then vertically, rather than rolling it. Doing this in hot water then in cold hastens the felting process.

dampened sliver Once damp, the sliver will regain its natural wave as the fibres 'relax'.

Put a large rubber band over each end of the finished roll to keep it together. Then roll the bundle back and forth over the ridged draining surface of the kitchen sink. After 30 rolls, remove the rubber bands and unroll carefully. Use the mat to stretch the felt if any small wrinkles have formed. Re-roll the mat from the other end, re-apply the rubber bands and roll again 30 times. Undo the bundle again; the wool should now be sufficiently bonded that it can be picked up as one piece. The felt, though unfinished, is at a stage at which it may be handled. This is known as a 'pre-felt'. It is still quite soft, and may be bonded to other pre-felts.

4 Firm the edges of the felt by folding them inwards slightly and patting them with lightly soaped fingers. Alternatively, leave the edges flat and firm them by gentle 'massage', running soapy fingers over the surface in a light circular motion (initially using the sort of pressure one would use to apply cream to the face).

5 To finish the felt, keep rolling it from different directions until it is quite firm, adding more soapy water if required. This is called 'fulling' the felt. You will notice that the felt 'shrinks' in the direction of rolling. This is because the scales on the wool fibres allow them to travel in only one direction, so they must creep closer together as friction is applied. It is important to have wool fibres laid out crossing each other for the strength of the felt, and also to roll the felt in both directions to ensure proper bonding of the fibres. The finished piece of felt will only measure two-thirds of the size originally laid out. This is because the fibres have all moved closer together during the felting process.

step three Roll up the wool in the mat, lifting it a little to allow air to escape.

step three continued Roll the bundle back and forth the required number of times.

step four Use lightly soaped fingers to firm the edge of the felt.

Tips for felting

Using a washing machine

A front-loading washing machine is a wonderful felting tool. The fast-wash cycle can be used to rapidly finish felt where control of size is not critical — the felt will be very tough. This method is especially useful for making felt balls and sturdy bathmats. Wool- or hand-wash cycles are ideal for controlled finish of felt, repeating as necessary. Remember that machine-fulled felt tends to be somewhat fluffier than mat-rolled felt. Top-loading machines may be used to extract water by spinning, but are not helpful for felting flat pieces as the central agitator tends to rip the felt. However, small objects such as balls, bags and slippers may be fulled in a top loader. Protect them in a net washing bag and include them with a load of clothes (for additional friction).

Rolling

You may find that to finish your felt, you need to do more rolling than that suggested in the instructions. This is because there are many factors that can affect felting, including the strength (thickness) and breed of the wool, the temperature of the room or water and the pressure you exert on the work as you are rolling it. Even the quality of the water can make a difference; wool felts more rapidly when the water is alkaline. On the other hand, a heavy salt content will affect the behaviour of the soap or wetting agent. Experience will enable you to gauge more easily just how much effort will be required.

Try using a thick dowel or length of plastic down-pipe in the centre of your roll, whether using a bamboo mat or blind, or bubble wrap. This can make for more even felting, as sometimes when a felt is tightly rolled, the middle of the roll can felt more firmly than the outer edge.

Hints for making thick and thin felts

When making thick felts, wet each layer as you build up the wool layers.

Very fine felts can be strengthened by adding a layer of butter muslin (cheesecloth) between fine layers of sliver. This technique is sometimes referred to as 'nuno' felt ('nuno' being the Japanese word for cloth). The cloth may (but does not have to) be hemmed first. If you wish, lay extra sliver at the edges and fold the cloth over so that it creates a felted hem.

Using bubble wrap

Bubble wrap has various applications for felting. It is often used for making templates, and can also be employed to pick up a soft, wet, fragile piece of felt so that it can be turned (above); reverse-roll it by laying the wrap over the top of the piece, then pick up and roll the felt and bubble wrap together.

Bubble wrap can be used to make large areas of pre-felt quite rapidly. When used to roll felt, it has the advantage over using a bamboo mat in that the felt is easier to peel away from the plastic and that any applied moisture is retained in the roll. Also, bubble wrap is easily dried and stored away if space is short. The disadvantage is that one needs to be very careful about pressing air bubbles out of the wetted wool before rolling up the wrap, as there is no way for them to escape (unlike in the bamboo mat, where air can escape through the space between the slats). While bubble wrap is good for making garments, scarves and small items, thick rugs are still best made in bamboo mats or blinds in the traditional manner.

Plant dyes

All plants give some sort of colour in the dye pot, some more exciting than others. Avoid using protected or slow-growing plants and anything you can't identify.

Commonly available plant materials such as onion skins give delightful colours. Many weeds (such as *Hypericum perforatum*, or St John's wort, a weed of wastelands such as railway sidings and roadsides, and *Oxalis pes-caprae*, or soursob) are useful dye plants.

Eucalypts and acacias give colour, too. Leaves from the former can give colours ranging from green through gold to red and brown; leaves, seedpods and bark from acacia yield lovely golds and browns as well.

The scent of a plant is often a clue to colour; highly aromatic leaves contain acids and oils which either are dyes or will assist in the dye process. Eucalypts are a good example. Also, if colour can be rubbed from the leaf, it may (but does not always) indicate dye potential.

naturally dyed sliver All these bundles of sliver have been dyed using plant extracts.

Colour and decoration

Colouring your work

Sliver is available ready dyed in a range of colours. If you want to dye your own, you will need natural or synthetic dyes, and a traditional dye pot if using the stovetop, or a plastic container in a microwave oven. Brightly coloured drink concentrates often make excellent wool dyes. It is vital to heat and cool the sliver slowly, and not to stir it while it is being heated (or it will begin to felt).

If using plant extracts, make the extract first, then gently lower the dry sliver into the dye bath and heat for 30–60 minutes, keeping the temperature just below a simmer so that the surface of the dye bath is steaming slightly but not moving. Allow the sliver to cool in the solution, then place in a stainless steel, plastic or enamel strainer over a bucket to drain, and gently press out excess moisture. Dry in the shade. So long as toxic adjunct mordants (see below) are not used there will be no need to rinse, as this will occur during felting. If using synthetic dyes, adhere to the manufacturer's instructions for dye preparation, remembering not to stir the sliver. *It is most important never to dye anything in a pot that you use for cooking food, as the dyestuffs, whether natural or synthetic, may be toxic.*

A note on mordants

A mordant is a substance used to fix or alter colours obtained from dyes. Toxic adjunct mordants are the traditional metallic salt mordants such as chrome (potassium bichromate), tin (stannous chloride), copper (copper sulphate) and iron (ferrous sulphate). All are poisons and should not be used; they are dangerous in powdered form and difficult to dispose of responsibly in the spent solution. However, using pots made of these metals as the dye vessel can influence the colour of the dyebath. In general (but not always), iron shifts many dyes to purples and blacks; copper enhances greens; brass enhances greens and yellows, depending on the dye-plant that you are using; aluminium tends to enrich colours. Stainless steel is non-reactive. Otherwise, stick to mordants that you might find in and around the kitchen. Plant dyes for wool work best in an acidic environment (pH 7 or less). Vinegar will help lower the pH and also acts as a wool conditioner. Alum (potassium aluminium sulphate) is a traditional mordant for wool; use it sparingly, because it is an alkali and can make the wool quite 'sticky' to handle.

Decorating the surface

You may like to experiment with decorative effects for the surface of your felt. Remember that the design is more likely to stay where you've placed it if you work in reverse, that is, by building up layers from the front. You can make spots, stripes, flowers or various other abstract, geometric or figurative designs.

Sushi felt

Another way of making a pattern is to use the sushi felt technique (as shown in the photographs below). This produces spots with a swirly, spiral effect.

Begin by laying out sliver as though making a sushi roll; first lay down a wide strip of sliver in one colour, then add successive layers in other colours along one edge, each narrower than the last. All layers should be roughly the same length (there is no need to be exact; they will be trimmed later). Misting lightly with a water spray can help to keep the layers together.

Roll up the bundle carefully from one long side. Using sharp scissors, cut the log into slices about 1 cm (⅜ in) thick and arrange them decoratively on the bamboo mat or bubble wrap.

Cover the sushi decorations with two layers of sliver at right angles to each other, then dampen and felt in the usual manner.

decorations Crisp-edged spots can be formed on a bamboo mat.

adding texture Add texture to the decorations by forming holes with the fingers.

sushi felt Lay out sliver as though making a sushi roll, in successively narrower strips.

sushi felt, step two Roll up the sliver from one long side, then cut into slices.

sushi felt, step three Lay the sushi pieces onto the bamboo mat, then cover with sliver.

Taking care of your body

Make sure your felting table is at the correct height in relation to your body, so that no damage occurs to your back. A good height is 5–10 cm (2–4 in) below your navel when you are laying out wool. If you can sit on a stool that allows you to keep your back straight while you are rolling the felt, so much the better.

Have frequent breaks during long layouts and rolling sessions, stretching your arms, legs and back, rolling your shoulders and making sure that no areas of tension build up. Remember that wool can hold a great deal of water; for that reason, avoid trying to pick up large, wet rugs.

Spots

For spotted felt, roll a small amount of sliver between the palms of your hands to make loose, fluffy balls. Lay these on the felting mat and build up the layers as required. For rainbow spots, make sushi felt (see page 259).

Stripes

Cut sliver into lengths, and then split it. These stripes will be wavy after the felting process, once the wetted wool relaxes and regains its natural curl. For more precise stripes, make a pre-felt and cut it into strips. For a tartan effect, combine stripes as above with lengths of wool yarn to build up the desired pattern.

Blending colours

Take handfuls of sliver in the colours you wish to mix. Hold them one over the other and gently pull apart. Repeat until the colours are blended satisfactorily.

Adding texture

Wool's wonderful bonding qualities can be used to make richly textured decorative surfaces. Try felting natural fibres such as silk, flax and hemp (all available in sliver form) in fine layers on the surface. Soy silk, cotton waste and silk off-cuts left over from overlocking can also be used to add interest to your work.

stripes Make stripes by alternating pieces of sliver in two or more colours.

wavy lines Wetted wool relaxes and its natural wave returns, forming wavy lines in the sliver.

grid pattern For straight edges, cut pre-felts into the desired shape, then lay them flat or interlaced.

Tails, tassels and handles

Sliver can be made into ropes, for example as a tail or the handle on a bag. Take a section of sliver. If you intend sewing both ends to the item, felt the whole piece between your palms or on a mat. Or felt only the middle section or one end; the unfelted end(s) can then be felted onto the body of the item for a seamless join.

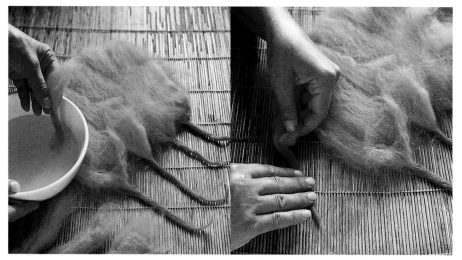

to make a tail, step one Wet sections of sliver with warm, soapy water.

tail, step two Felt one end. The other end is then felted to the item (such as the cat toys on page 285).

Making a flower

Quite delicate flowers can be made as part of a pattern on the surface of your felt, as shown in the three photographs below.

Take a short section of coloured sliver, then roll it up spiral-fashion with your fingers to make a flat circle. Lay this down on the bubble wrap or bamboo mat to form the centre of the flower.

To make petals with rounded ends, take a short section of sliver, lightly dampen each end, fold the sliver in half and twist the two ends together. Alternatively, to make petals with pointed ends, twist both ends of the folded piece of sliver, then fold up the wispy tail at the bottom to give a neat finish. Place the petals on top of the flower centre, then lay down sliver to form the background of the piece. Then begin felting as normal. To stop the flower pattern from moving about as you felt it, you can lay a piece of plastic fly-wire atop the design. Then begin felting through the fly-wire by rubbing with a scrunched-up plastic shopping bag.

petals, step one For rounded petals, fold the sliver in half and twist both ends together.

petals, step two Felt the folded end of the piece of sliver to create pointy petals.

flower Put a coloured centre down on the bubble wrap, then arrange the petals on top.

Shaggy rug with fleece curls

This rug has a surface layer felted from

raw (unprocessed) fleece. Try to find wool

from Leicester Longwool (used in the pictured

example), Lincoln, Friesian, Wensleydale or

other lustre-wool breeds that have a long staple

(see page 254). Adult wool will have the longest,

strongest locks; lambs' fleeces will make a

soft rug, ideal for a bedroom and bare feet.

The raw fleece may look and feel a little dirty;

however, it will soften and become clean during

the felting process.

Materials
Raw fleece curls, such as Leicester Longwool
Wool sliver: strong Merino (over 22 microns)
   or a medium crossbreed of 25–28 microns

Tools
Large bamboo blind
Plastic fly-wire
Plastic shopping bag
Soap
Cotton rag, for tying the felting roll
Vinegar, for rinsing

Size
Approximately 70 x 180 cm (27½ x 71 in)

step one Spread the curls of raw fleece (here, Leicester Longwool) on the bamboo blind, removing any seeds or foreign matter.

step two Cover the fleece curls with several layers of reasonably strong sliver, with each layer at right angles to the former.

1 Spread the unwashed fleece evenly across a large bamboo blind. If you spot any grass-seeds or other foreign bodies, remove them. If space is a problem, the rug can be laid out and rolled up in sections. It doesn't matter if the fibres are going in all different directions on this layer, as there will be substantial layers of felt forming the backing.

2 Over this layer, lay a reasonably strong Merino or medium crossbreed sliver to help bond the fleece curls. The rug will need at least four layers of wool at right angles to each other, in addition to the surface layer.

3 Because the rug will be quite thick, it is helpful to sprinkle the layers with water as you build them up. However, because wool 'relaxes' and remembers its original structure when wet, it is important not to leave a carpet half-finished and damp overnight. In the morning, the damp fibres will have regained their original curl, which may affect the design.

4 When the rug is fully laid out and wetted, lay a sheet of plastic fly-wire across the top. Using a scrunched-up plastic bag, and working in sections, rub gently across the surface in a circular motion to remove air bubbles and spread the moisture evenly

Flipping the rug Flip the heavy, wet felt safely and easily by reverse-rolling it (see Hints, right).

Checking progress Unroll the flipped rug to inspect it. Pick out any seeds that have come to the surface, and continue to roll until a satisfactory firmness is obtained.

throughout. It may help to rub a bar of soap lightly across the fly-wire, and then sprinkle with more water. When the air bubbles have been released and the fibres are wet, tightly roll the bamboo blind, lifting it slightly as you roll, so that water or air bubbles underneath can escape. Tie the roll firmly in three or four places, using strips of cotton rag (the knots are less likely to work loose than if you use string).

5 The rug must now be rolled back and forth about 200 times, before unrolling and reversing the direction. It may be rolled with the arms on a bench, or placed on the floor and rolled with the feet, from a

standing or sitting position. If working outside on a paved area, it is wise to wrap the bamboo roll in an old sheet, tying it off securely before rolling, in order to protect the bamboo blind from damage.

6 When the rug has been rolled 200 times from each direction (a total of 400 rolls), it should be turned over and the process repeated. After a further 2 x 200 rolls, the rug should be of a sturdy texture, and can be thoroughly rinsed and dried flat. Add half a cup of white vinegar to the final rinsing water. Vinegar is an acid and counters the alkalinity of the soap, acting as a conditioner.

Hints

To flip a heavy, wet article such as this rug, reverse-roll it. Take the front edge of the bamboo blind and roll it under, towards you, carefully rolling the felt with it. When the whole roll is unrolled again, the blind will have flipped.

Stone door prop

step one Roll up the stone in the square of pre-felt, easing and adjusting the pre-felt to ensure the stone is well covered.

step three Wet the stone in hot, soapy water then rub it with your hands or roll it about on a piece of bubble wrap until well felted.

This simple and satisfying project produces a useful door prop with a rustic, dinosaur-egg appeal.

Materials
Wool sliver to make pre-felt
A smooth river or beach stone
about the size of a brick
(or use a house brick)
Wool yarn

Tools
Large darning needle
Bucket
Soap
Towel
Bubble wrap

1 Make a piece of pre-felt, about 60 cm (24 in) square, using four layers of wool. If you wish to incorporate patterning, do it on the part of the square that will be on the outside of the bundle. Lay the pre-felt pattern side down. Put the stone on the pre-felt and roll it up, easing and adjusting the pre-felt so the stone is well covered.

2 Using wool yarn and a large darning needle, secure the pre-felt with some stitches. These can become a decorative feature; they don't need to be too neat.

3 Dip the woolly stone into a bucket of hot soapy water, and begin to rub it gently with your hands. Keep working your way around the stone, becoming more vigorous as the felt begins to firm. You may find that rolling the stone around on a pad made of a folded towel, covered by a piece of bubble wrap (bubble side up), is helpful.

4 Continue rubbing and rolling the stone on the bubble wrap until the felt is firm. Rinse, then allow to dry. The felt-covered stone prop will be much quieter than a bare one.

Champagne cooler

This Champagne cooler is made in two parts.

The inner sleeve is fitted to the bottle and

provides a base; the outer sleeve, which can be

made as thick as you wish, is both decorative

and insulating. For picnic portability, add a carry-

strap. The template can be sized to suit any type

of bottle. Such a cooler is excellent for a water-

bottle, with or without a carry-strap; the felt will

keep a pre-frozen drink cool for hours.

Materials
Wool sliver
Buttons, beads and thread, for embellishment
  (optional)

Tools
Used Champagne or other bottle
Bubble wrap, for template
Bamboo mat or bubble wrap, for rolling
Chalk
Soap
Towel

inner sleeve, step one Once the layers of wool are laid out on the marked area of the bamboo mat or bubble wrap, moisten the central section only.

inner sleeve, step two Lay the template on the central section of the wool, pressing down gently to remove any air bubbles.

Making the template

Measure the circumference of your chosen bottle, add 50 per cent (to allow for shrinkage of one-third) and divide the total by 2 to give you the width of your template. Decide how tall you wish your cooler to be, and add 50 per cent to give the height. Cut a template from bubble wrap, about 15 cm (6 in) longer than the required height and exactly the width you have calculated. Mark the required height with a waterproof marker.

INNER SLEEVE

1 Make a template (see left). Then lay the template on the bamboo mat or bubble wrap that you will use for rolling the felt. Using chalk, draw a line around the template, about 8 cm (3¼ in) away from the edge, marking the height required. Put the template aside, then lay out three or four layers of sliver at right angles to each other, filling out to the edges of the chalked line. Carefully sprinkle the middle of the wool pile with warm, soapy water, using the template as a guide. It is important not to wet the sides, or they will become difficult to handle.

2 Lay the bubble wrap template on the wool, pressing down gently (but without popping the cells). Pat the template using the fingertips to gently push out any air bubbles from the wool.

3 Very carefully fold the edges of the wool up and inwards, over the edges of the template and towards the middle. Sprinkle them gently with water as you go, so that they don't spring back. Fill in the middle of the template with as many layers of wool as were used underneath, making sure all the layers overlap. Sprinkle the whole with warm water.

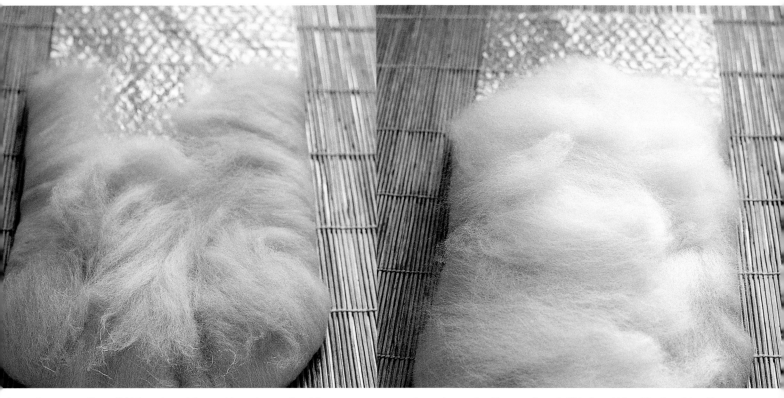

inner sleeve, step three Fold the edges of the wool inwards, over the sides of the template and towards the middle.

inner sleeve, step three continued Fill in the middle of the template with as many layers of wool as were used on the first side.

4 Taking a bar of soap, gently soap your wet hands. Begin to carefully pat the soap on to the wool. You will notice the felting process beginning. Re-soaping your hands frequently, make sure the surface of the parcel is soaped and wetted out. Carefully turn the pile over and repeat.

5 When you are sure that both sides are wetted out and there are no air bubbles in the wool, roll the parcel up gently in the bamboo mat. Roll it about 20 times, not pressing down too hard. Unroll and repeat from the other direction. Keep repeating this process, changing the direction of the little woolly parcel within the mat.

6 Keep note of the edges of the parcel, and keep smoothing around the edges of the template with your hands. When the felt feels strong enough, remove the template and turn the sleeve inside out. Continue to full the felt by gentle kneading, rolling and dropping; you can also shock the felt (see right) if you wish. Insert the bottle and rub the felt gently, forming it to the shape of the bottle, remembering to leave the neck of the cooler open so that the bottle can be removed. Massage the bottom of the felt pocket so that it forms to the punt (the indentation at the base of the bottle). Rinse and set aside, leaving the pocket on the bottle for now.

'Shocking' the felt

You can hasten the process of felting by dipping the felt alternately in very hot and very cold water. This is called 'shocking' the felt and will make it quite tough.

Patchwork blanket

This blanket can be made in a very small house or apartment, as it is constructed from small pre-felts made with a sushi mat. These are then sewn together and the blanket is felted in the bath or shower.

Materials

Wool sliver in various colours, for making pre-felts

Wool yarn

Tools

Bamboo sushi mat, for making pre-felts

Darning needle

Large bamboo mat (optional)

Vinegar, for rinsing

1 Using a variety of colours, make a range of fairly firm, small pre-felts using a bamboo sushi mat at the kitchen table or sink. You may like to introduce simple patterns or designs. Use two layers of wool sliver, laid at right angles to each other, in addition to the design layer. All of the pre-felts should be of similar texture, as it is more difficult to bond felts of dissimilar strength. You will need about 30 pre-felts for a baby rug, or as many as 600 for a large bed blanket.

2 Sew the pre-felts together using a large darning needle and wool yarn in a matching or contrasting shade. Overlap the patches slightly, and allow the blanket to grow in an organic fashion. You can use large or small stitches, in running, cross or seed and/or chain stitch. In the end, all of the stitches will be felted into the blanket, becoming part of the surface. If there are odd-shaped gaps, fill them with small pre-felt shapes and a few interesting stitches.

3 When all of the patches are stitched together, take the blanket to the bath or shower. Wet it thoroughly with warm, soapy water, and roll and drop-full it until the felt is the firmness you want. If you have the space, roll the blanket in a large bamboo mat; this process allows more control over felting and makes the felt crisper.

4 If you have a front-loading washing machine, and the blanket is not too big, you can complete the felting by washing the blanket on a wool or handwash cycle, after you have begun the process in the bath. Be aware, though, that the washing machine is a most efficient felting tool, and that things can rapidly get out of hand. Felt fulled in a machine tends to be fluffier than felt fulled by rolling in a mat or bubble wrap.

5 When it is fully felted, rinse thoroughly, finishing with a water and vinegar rinse. Spin excess water out, and dry in shade.

Variations

Make the squares using butter muslin (a very open-weave muslin) or cheesecloth and wool for a very lightweight blanket.

Make all of the squares in white wool, and overdye the pre-felts using shibori techniques before stitching.

Add decorations such as beads and buttons, or even small pockets for secret notes.

For a truly warm and cuddly baby blanket, line the felted blanket with soft silk cloth, simply tacking it to the back by hand.

Reverse inlay rug

The design on this boldly patterned rug is laid

out working from the front surface back. While

this means you won't see the pattern properly

until the first time you turn the felt over, its

advantage is that the pattern will be well bonded

with the rest of the rug. Layers of sliver are built

up on top of the design to give a sturdy and

hard-wearing rug.

If planning a complicated design, you could

rough it out on a large sheet of paper first and

use this as a guide when laying out. If you have

more experience or confidence, lay the pieces

straight onto the bamboo mat, rearranging them

to your satisfaction before laying sliver on top.

The same technique, with more layers of wool,

can be used to create a bathmat (see page 277).

Materials
Pieces of sliver, loose fleece or shapes cut
    from pre-felt, for the inlay pattern
Wool sliver

Tools
Bubble wrap
Large bamboo blind
Chalk
Plastic fly-wire
Plastic shopping bag
Soap
Strips of cotton rag, for tying

step two Begin to build up the pattern on the bamboo blind, working from the front to the back of the rug.

step three Infill the design with sliver, building up four layers and ensuring there is an even thickness across the whole rug.

Calculating dimensions

Layout area	Approximate finished size
90 x 90 cm (35½ x 35½ in)	60 x 60 cm (24 x 24 in)
120 x 180 cm (47 x 71 in)	80 x 120 cm (31½ x 47 in)
150 x 150 cm (59 x 59 in)	100 x 100 cm (39½ x 39½ in)

1 Chalk your design onto the bamboo mat. Remember that the finished felt will only be two-thirds the area of the laid-out fleece. The layout should equal the desired finished size plus 50 per cent. The chart at left may be helpful.

2 Lay out the pattern, working from the 'top' (the front surface) back. You can cut lengths of sliver, use loose fleece or cut shapes from pre-felt to develop the design for your rug. It doesn't matter that the fibres are going in all different directions on this layer, as there will be substantial layers of felt forming the backing.

3 The rug will need at least four layers of wool, in addition to the design layer. Put each layer of sliver at right angles to the previous, and make sure that the thickness is even across the whole rug. You may find that a 90 x 150 cm (35½ x 59 in) rug will require 1 kg (2 lb 4 oz) of wool. It is helpful to sprinkle the layers with water as you build them up. However, it is important not to leave a rug half-finished and damp overnight, as wool has a 'memory'; in the morning, the damp fibres will have regained their original curl (which was straightened during combing and carding), and this may affect the design.

step five After the rug has been rolled 200 times in each direction, unroll it to reveal the design. Then re-roll the parcel and roll it back and forth a further 2 x 200 times.

variation A sturdy bathmat (tailored to the size and shape of your bathroom floor, if you like) can be created using the same technique, with or without a pattern.

4 When the rug is fully laid out and wetted, lay a sheet of plastic fly-wire across the top. Using a scrunched-up plastic shopping bag, rub gently across the surface in a circular motion to remove air bubbles and spread the moisture evenly throughout. It may help to rub a bar of soap lightly across the fly-wire, and then sprinkle water over the top again. When the air bubbles have been released and the fibres are wet, tightly roll the mat, lifting it slightly as you roll, so that water or air beneath does not affect the design. Tie the roll firmly in three or four places, using strips of cotton rag (the knots will be less likely to work loose than if you use string).

5 The rug must now be rolled back and forth about 200 times, before unrolling and reversing the direction. It may be rolled on a bench, or placed on the floor and rolled with the feet, from a standing or sitting position. If you wish to work outside on a paved area, it is wise to wrap the bamboo roll in an old sheet, tying it securely, before rolling, to protect the mat from damage. When the rug has been rolled from both directions (a total of 400 rolls), turn it over to show the design, then repeat the rolling process. After a further 2 x 200 rolls, its texture should be sturdy. Rinse thoroughly, adding half a cup of white vinegar to the final rinsing water, then allow to dry flat.

Bathmat variation

For a bathmat, lay out wool about 90 x 60 cm (35½ x 24 in) for a rectangular or oval mat, or 90 x 90 cm (35½ x 35½ in) for a round mat. The mat will need at least six layers of wool, in addition to the design layer. Extra texture may be added by laying whole lengths of sliver into the felt at intervals. Construct and roll the mat as described at left. The bathmat will keep felting throughout its life, becoming firmer and more compact as people walk on it with wet feet.

Baby blanket

This project is suitable for a beginner, and will

make a beautiful yet hard-wearing gift for a baby.

Use the finest Merino sliver for a soft, cosy rug.

Materials
White raw lambs' curls
Small amounts of yellow and pale pink wool sliver
White wool sliver

Tools
Bubble wrap or large bamboo mat
Soap
Towel

Size
Approximately 85 x 64 cm (33½ x 25¼ in)

step one Arrange the curly fleece in a spokelike pattern. Put a small circle of yellow sliver in the centre, then top it with a larger circle of pink sliver.

1 Cut a piece of bubble wrap about 77 x 105 cm (30 x 41 in), or mark an area this size on a bamboo mat. Arrange the lambs' curls in a spokelike fashion in the centre. Put a small circular patch of yellow sliver in the centre of the spoke pattern, then add a larger circle of pink sliver. Put two layers of white sliver on top, at right angles to each other, extending the sliver to the edges of the template.

2 Soft-felt the blanket, then hard-felt it for about 20 minutes. Stroke hard on the centre to flatten the pattern, then turn over and repeat.

3 Roll up the blanket and bubble wrap or mat together horizontally, then grasp and squeeze about 50 times. Immerse alternately in hot and cold water, grasping and squeezing as before, then unroll, re-roll vertically and repeat.

4 Put the felt on a work surface, pattern side up, and hard-felt it for about 10 minutes. Then roll it up vertically (minus the mat or bubble wrap) and grasp and squeeze from end to end about 50 times. Check the edges occasionally, firming them with the fingers to ensure they are crisp.

5 Do the pinch test (see page 299). When it passes the pinch test, roll it in a towel to remove excess water (do not wring it), then stretch the felt out in both directions to the finished size of approximately 85 x 64 cm (33½ x 25¼ in). Allow to dry flat in shade.

Variations

Other designs can be laid out in the centre of the template, such as flowers (see page 261), a bunny or, for a less traditional look, a geometric pattern.

Donut pet bed and toy accessories

This cosy, donut-shaped bed will make a snug nest for your cat or dog. The instructions given will make a bed for an average-sized cat or a small dog, but the bed can be tailored to most sizes of pet (see page 283). Alternatively, the bed can be constructed from two flat pieces of felt if desired, and made in any shape you like.

To make your pet's happiness complete, also included are instructions for two simple toys; one formed around a ping-pong ball, the other in the shape of a mouse. They will prove so popular that you may find yourself making frequent replacements!

Materials
Wool sliver
Wool yarn
Stuffing: various materials are suitable, including washed fleece, old clothes, commercially available polyester fibrefill, or odd socks from the washing basket; even newspaper will do at a pinch

Tools
Bubble wrap, for template
Large bamboo blind
Chalk
Soap
Plastic fly-wire
Plastic shopping bag
Large darning needle

Simple pod bag

This organic-looking round bag, constructed around a simple donut-shaped bubble-wrap template, is easy to make. The handle can be left plain, as in the photograph at right, or wrapped, as in the examples on the following pages.

Adjust the size of the template to produce a bigger or smaller bag, making the template about 50 per cent larger all round than you want the finished bag to be.

This technique can also be used to make a beret (see page 289). For a small beret, cut a bubble-wrap template 30 cm (12 in) in diameter; for medium, it will need to be 35 cm (14 in); and for large, 40 cm (16 in).

Materials
Wool sliver
Pre-felt, for reinforcement
Wool yarn or other thread, if making wrapped handle
Petersham ribbon, if making the beret variation (optional)

Tools
Bubble wrap, for template
Darning needle, if making wrapped handle
Soap
Bubble wrap or bamboo mat

Size
Approximately 28 cm (11 in) in diameter

step two Once you have laid out the layers of sliver, put the template on top, then the donut-shaped piece of pre-felt.

ready to felt Once the overlapping felt is folded in, the handle attached and the thing wetted, roll the bag in bubble wrap or a bamboo mat and begin felting.

Hints

To help reinforce the edge of the bag, cut a donut shape from a piece of pre-felt, about 35 cm (14 in) wide and with a 12 cm (4½ in) central hole.

To add decoration to a bag, put the pattern down first, on top of the bamboo mat or bubble wrap. Then layer sliver on top of the pattern, then the template, and proceed as instructed. To decorate the beret, however (which is constructed inside out), lay the design on the layer that precedes the template.

1 Cut a circular template from bubble wrap, about 40 cm (16 in) in diameter. Cut a reinforcing piece of pre-felt (see left).

2 Lay out four or five layers of sliver, about 7 cm (2¾ in) larger than the template all round. Wet the pile (no closer than 7 cm/ 2¾ in to the edge). Put the template on top, then the circle of pre-felt.

3 Fold in the edges, and build more sliver onto them, laying extra around the inside of the circle. The hole in the middle should be between one-half and one-third of the diameter of the pile; because felt shrinks as it is fulled, the holes actually get bigger.

4 For the handle, take two pieces of sliver; their length should be about two-thirds the diameter of the bag. Put them together (parallel), fold in half, and holding them by the ends, dip the middle part in warm soapy water. Pat this middle bit together a little. Spread the soft (dry) ends slightly, then lay the handle across the bag. Lay some extra sliver across the soft ends to strengthen the join. If you wish to wrap the handle with thread (see opposite), this needs to be done before the handle is wetted.

5 Dampen the whole, and begin felting by patting with the hands. When the parcel is nicely wetted and beginning to bond, roll it

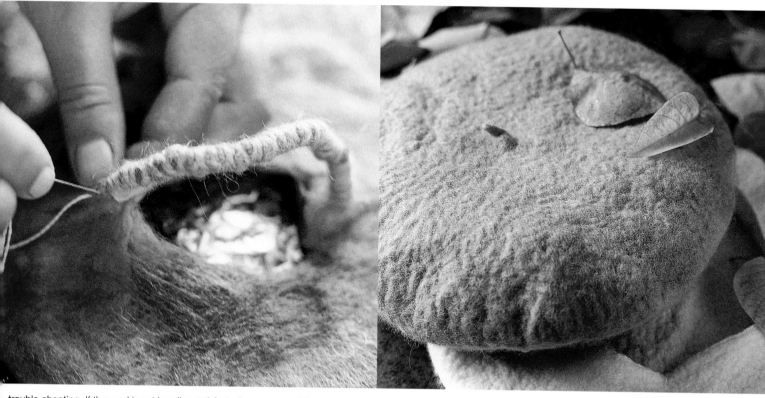

trouble-shooting If the wool is not bonding satisfactorily, you can pull it together with a few stitches.

beret variation A smaller version of the bag, minus the handle and the pre-felt reinforcement, makes a beret. Add a little tail to the top for decoration if you wish.

in a bamboo mat or bubble wrap, changing directions and turning over frequently until the template begins to wrinkle.

6 Remove the template, turn the bag right side out and continue fulling. If you wish to deepen the shape, you can mould the bag by gently pushing with your fist from the inside against a firm surface such as the draining ridges of the kitchen sink.

7 Continue rolling and moulding until the texture is nice and strong, then rinse and dry. When drying, first line the bag with a plastic shopping bag, then stuff with newspaper or more plastic shopping bags.

Variation: beret

Build up three layers of fine wool sliver, the first in a radiating pattern, the second circular and the third radiating. This will avoid ridged areas at the edge of the beret. Wet the wool. Lay a bubble-wrap template (sizes are given on page 286) on top, and fold in the edges. Lay on extra wool so that the hole is about one-third of the diameter of the template; it will become larger as you proceed. Felt as for the pod bag, turning inside out when the template is removed. Shape a little edge for the hole. Allow to dry; then, if desired, stitch some petersham ribbon around the inner edge.

Wrapped handle

To decorate and strengthen the handle, it can be wrapped using wool thread. Do this before the parcel is wetted and felted. Wrap the thread around the handle, or stitch it on using blanket stitch, then fasten off securely, leaving 7–8 cm (about 3 in) fluffy sliver at each end. Dampen the handle in the middle, where it is wrapped. Roll this part between the palms to firm it. Then lay the handle on the bag, roll the whole up in a bamboo mat or bubble wrap and felt in the usual manner.

Origami bag

This sturdy bag is constructed from four squares of pre-made, finished felt folded to give roomy pockets. You can vary the size of the bag by changing the size of the squares you start with. The tote bag pictured here is made from pieces 50 cm (20 in) square. The bag could also be made as a handbag or, if you're really keen, a weekender. Requirements for these other sizes are given on the following pages.

The handles can be varied. Making them from the same flat felt as the body of the bag creates strong handles that will sustain a fair load, necessary for the tote or weekender. For a smaller bag that will carry a lighter load, you could make a handle from a rope of felt.

Materials (for the tote bag)
Completely fulled felt, from which to cut the pieces

Thread for machine-sewing and/or stranded or pearl cotton for hand-sewing

Two felt balls or bobbles (see below), or purchased round buttons

Cardboard, for making the insert for the base of the bag (optional)

Tools
Sewing machine

Large sharp or crewel needle

Size
Approximately 35 x 35 x 15 cm (14 x 14 x 6 in), for the tote bag pictured at left; for other sizes, see pages 292 and 293

Making felt balls or bobbles
To make a small felt ball, cut wool sliver into 3 cm (1¼ in) lengths, tease it out with your fingers, dampen it with warm, soapy water and roll it between the palms of the hands until felted, about 10 minutes. Go softly at first, until you feel the felt begin to harden a little, then apply more pressure.

To make a bigger bead or a small ball, take a handful of washed fleece (or even a scrap of rag), scrunch it into a ball shape and wrap a length of spare yarn around it to keep the shape together. Then wind small strips of sliver around the outside, building them up until the core is well covered. Moisten the whole with warm, soapy water, and soap the outside a little as well so that it doesn't stick to your hands. Finish the felt by rolling it between your hands, on a piece of bubble wrap, or on the draining ridges of the kitchen sink. Rinse well and allow to dry, then use as desired.

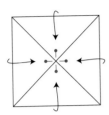

diagram 1 Taking one felt square, fold each corner into the centre and pin in place.

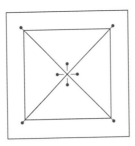

diagram 2 Centre the folded piece on one of the other squares and pin in place.

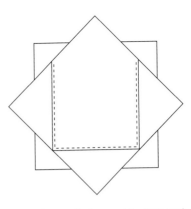

diagram 3 Open out the flaps and sew a little way inside the fold lines along the sides and bottom as shown.

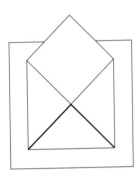

diagram 4 Open out the top flap, then sew together the seams indicated by the bold line.

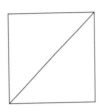

diagram 5 Cut the smaller felt square on the diagonal to make the pocket extension pieces.

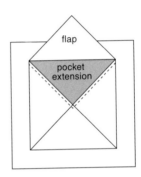

diagram 6 Sew the pocket extension piece behind the pocket formed by the lower three triangles.

To make a handbag

Pocket pieces: four squares 40 x 40 cm (16 x 16 in)

Pocket extension pieces: one square 18 x 18 cm (7 x 7 in), cut in half diagonally

Handles: twine together two pieces of sliver about 1.3 m (51 in) long, wet them with warm, soapy water and roll between your hands until firm. This creates a strap about 90 cm (35½ in) long

Button tabs: two pieces 6 x 3 cm (2½ x 1¼ in)

Side straps (optional): two pieces 12 x 2 cm (4½ x ¾ in)

PREPARATION

When cutting pieces from felt, it will be easier to make the felt slightly larger than the required size then trim it to the right shape and size; or make one large sheet of felt and divide it into squares.

You can vary the look of the bag by making either one colour felt, or felt with different colours on either side.

For the pocket pieces, cut four squares of felt 50 x 50 cm (20 x 20 in). It is most important that they all be perfectly square and the same size.

For the pocket extension pieces, cut one square 20 x 20 cm (8 x 8 in). Cut it in half diagonally (see Diagram 5) to give two identical triangles.

For the handles, cut two pieces 50 x 10 cm (20 x 4 in).

For the button tab, cut one piece 12 x 3 cm (4½ x 1¼ in).

For the optional side straps, if using, cut two pieces 12 x 2 cm (4½ x ¾ in).

step two Place one folded and one unfolded square together and stitch along the lines as shown in Diagram 3, using one or two rows of stitching as you prefer.

steps three and four Stitch the lower edges together to form a pocket. Using a flat seam, attach the pocket extension piece to make the pocket deeper.

MAKING THE POCKETS

1 Take one square and fold the corners towards the centre, so that they meet in the middle (see Diagram 1). Pin them down.

2 Pin this (now smaller) square to one of the remaining squares (see Diagram 2), placing the pins at the corners. After they are positioned, open out the flaps (see Diagram 3). Use the dotted line on this diagram as the stitching guide (you can stitch by machine or hand, as you prefer). Stitch slightly in from the fold lines, and don't go too close to the corner, as it becomes too difficult to stitch neatly. Also, the pockets will have a more interesting shape, and will be able to hold wider

objects, if not too closely stitched to the main body of the bag.

3 Fold in the bottom and two side flaps again. Referring to Diagram 4, stitch together the edges marked by a bold line, leaving the top flap free.

4 To finish the pocket, place the pocket extension piece (see Diagram 5) behind the pocket formed by the three lower triangles (see Diagram 6). Using a flat seam, hand-sew the extension piece in place.

Repeat Steps 1–4 with the remaining two squares to make another pocket piece.

To make a weekender

Pocket pieces: four squares 70 x 70 cm (27½ x 27½ in)
Pocket extension pieces: one square 33 x 33 cm (13 x 13 in), cut in half diagonally
Handles: two pieces 30 x 10 cm (12 x 4 in)
Button tabs: two pieces 6 x 3 cm (2½ x 1¼ in)
Side straps (optional): two pieces 15 x 3 cm (6 x 1¼ in)

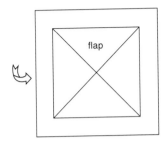

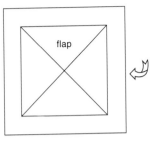

diagram 7 Sew the bottom and sides of the two pocket pieces together, right sides facing.

fold line

fold line

diagram 8 For the handles, fold each piece of felt in half lengthways, wrong sides together. Sew along the dotted lines, beginning and ending about 9 cm (3½ in) from each short end.

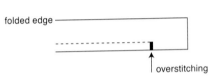

folded edge

overstitching

diagram 9 To reinforce, overstitch the ends of the handle seams at the points shown.

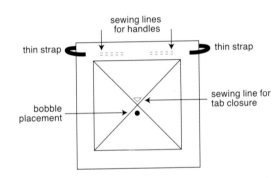

sewing lines for handles

thin strap

thin strap

bobble placement

sewing line for tab closure

diagram 10 Showing sewing and placement lines for attaching all the components.

Lining

You may wish to line the bag with a woven fabric. Simply stitch a square of your chosen fabric to each felt square before beginning to assemble the bag.

SEWING THE BAG

Place the two pieces with the right (pocket) sides facing each other, making sure that the pocket openings are at the top (see Diagram 7). Stitch them together at both sides and along the bottom. Then taking the bottom corners, stitch diagonally across them about 3 cm (1¼ in) from the corner point, at right angles to the bottom seam. Turn the bag right side out. You will see that it now has a flattish base. You can make this firmer by covering a piece of stiff cardboard in cloth or felt, and placing it in the bottom of the bag. The length of this piece of cardboard should be 8 cm (3¼ in) shorter than the height of the bag.

FINISHING

To make the handles, fold each piece of felt in half lengthways, wrong sides together. Beginning and ending about 9 cm (3½ in) from each short end, sew along the dotted lines indicated in Diagram 8. To reinforce, overstitch several times at the points indicated by the dots (see Diagram 9).

Pin the ends of the handles to the bag, about 5 cm (2 in) down from the top and about 14 cm (5½ in) in from the side seams (see Diagram 10). Before stitching, make sure you are happy with the placement and that the handles are level. Sew by hand, using two lines of stitching.

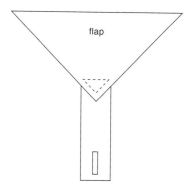

diagram 11 Sew the button tab to the point of the pocket flap, then cut a slit in the end just large enough for the button.

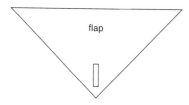

diagram 12 Alternative closure: rather than attaching a button tab, simply cut a slit in the point of the pocket flap.

For the flap closures, make two small felt balls or bobbles (see page 291), and sew them just below the point where the triangles of the outer pockets meet. Sew a button tab to the point of each pocket flap (see Diagram 11). Cut a slit in the other end for the bobble or button. Alternatively, rather than making a button tab, carefully cut a small vertical hole in the point of the overhanging flap, just big enough for the bobble or button to slip through.

You may wish to make small gathers across the top of the side seams and attach small, thin straps, to give the bag a more rounded shape (see Diagram 13).

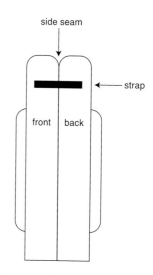

variation For a handbag, an alternative handle can be made from a rope of felt that is then stitched securely at each side seam.

Variations

When sewing on the outer pockets, simultaneously add inner pockets (this means you will need six squares to begin with). Or, for less bulk inside the bag, cut four squares of felt the same size as the folded squares to make patch pockets.

After placing the pockets and before stitching together the two panels, add a zipper to the top of the big internal pocket by stitching it in, with right sides facing up, while the pieces are flat. Then fold the bag inside out to stitch the side seams.

diagram 13 If desired, gather in the sides of the bag a little and secure with a small strap to give the bag a more rounded shape.

Glasses case

A soft felt case will ensure that your glasses

don't get scratched or damaged. This easy

project lends itself to personalized decoration,

as shown in the pictured examples; lay down

spots, or teardrop-shaped pieces of sliver to

suggest raindrops, or add lines of hand-stitching,

a crochet trim or a pattern of beads.

Materials
Wool sliver
Beads, buttons and yarns for stitched and
    crocheted embellishments (optional)

Tools
Bubble wrap
Soap
Scissors

Size
Approximately 20 x 9.5 cm (8 x 3¾ in)

step two Decorate the felt by laying down a pattern before covering it with sliver. To create small dots, form thin lengths of sliver into spirals.

step two continued Begin to lay the pattern down on the bubble wrap.

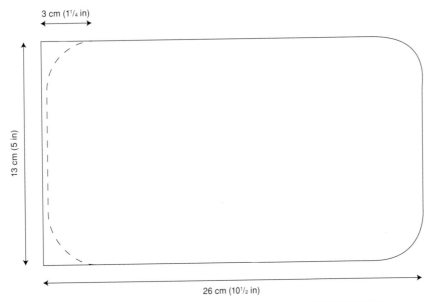

3 cm (1¼ in)

13 cm (5 in)

26 cm (10½ in)

template Round off the lower corners of the template. Once the pouch is felted and dry, cut the top of the pouch to form a curve, as indicated by the dotted line.

1 Cut bubble wrap to make a template.

2 Pull a little wool from the sliver and make a pattern, as desired. Lay it on the bubble wrap and gently sprinkle each layer of pattern with warm, soapy water; this ensures the pattern won't slip and makes it easier to attach it to the background.

3 Put two layers of sliver in the background colour over the top, each layer at right angles to the other, allowing 4 cm (1½ in) overlap around the edges. Sprinkle warm, soapy water only on the parts of the wool that cover the template (do not wet the overlap, and take care to avoid making the

step two continued Laying larger circles of sliver over small ones will create a two-toned dot on the surface of the felt.

finishing Crochet around the top edge of the case, or add beads or embroidery to embellish. As here, you can add a beaded loop to keep the pouch closed.

wool spread out due to water pressure). Gently press with soapy hands to make sure that all fibres are wet. Stroke the wool very gently with your palm to make the surface of the wool flat, then continue until soft felt forms.

4 Turn the whole thing over and fold the overlapping edges of the wool inwards.

5 Put two layers of sliver on top, allowing 4 cm (1½ in) overlap around the edges. Sprinkle with warm, soapy water. Gently press with soapy hands to make sure that all the fibres are wet.

6 Gently massage until soft felt forms, tucking in any wool that is sticking out. Hard felt for about 15 minutes each side until the surface is smooth. Immerse the felt in hot water and grasp and squeeze about 50 times in each direction, then immerse in cold water and grasp and squeeze about 50 times more in each direction.

7 Do the pinch test (see at right); if you can grasp single fibres from the felt, it needs more massage. When it passes the pinch test, cut the top of the case into a curve (as shown on the template). Allow to dry in shade, then add a button and button loop, and embellish if desired.

The pinch test

The pinch test is a useful way of determining whether your felt is adequately fulled. Pinch the felt between your fingertips; if you can grasp single fibres from the felt, it needs more fulling. Keep massaging until it passes the pinch test; this will ensure a firm and durable felt.

Wallet

This cute, sturdy little wallet acts as a mini handbag, with two pockets (one for banknotes, one for coins), a carry strap and even a photo pocket. To make a flower decoration, as on the example pictured here, see page 261.

Materials

Grey wool sliver
Small amounts of yellow and white sliver
  (or colours as desired), for the flower design
9 cm (3½ in) zipper, or size to suit your wallet
Embroidery threads (optional)
Bead(s) or button for closure

Tools

Bubble wrap
Soap
Sharp or crewel needle

step six Cut down the marked side to form two pockets, then turn right side out to expose the flower design.

photo pocket Attach the photo pocket to the inside of the wallet using blanket stitch. Leave the top edge open to allow for insertion of the photo.

1 Cut bubble wrap to make the template.

2 To make the flower pattern (see page 261), first put a yellow dot in the centre of one end of the template, then arrange petals around it. Sprinkle with warm soapy water.

3 Put two layers of grey sliver on top, at right angles to each other, allowing 4 cm (1½ in) overlap around the edges. Put a small amount of contrasting sliver on top of the pile to act as a marker, so that you know which is the design side when you later cut the wallet to form the two pockets. Gently stroke and massage until soft felt forms.

4 Turn the whole parcel over and fold the overlapping edges of wool inwards. Be careful that the wool is not piled on top of itself, especially at the corners. Put two layers of grey sliver on top, at right angles to each other. Massage until soft felt forms, tucking in any wool that is sticking out.

5 Hard-felt for about 15 minutes on each side until the surface is smooth. Immerse the felt in hot water and grasp and squeeze about 50 times in each direction, then immerse in cold water and grasp and squeeze about 50 times more in each direction. Do the pinch test (see page 299); massage more if needed.

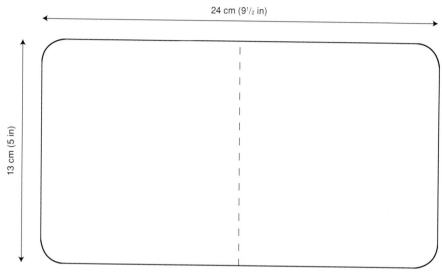

24 cm (9½ in)

13 cm (5 in)

template Cut a piece of bubble wrap to these dimensions for the template.

6 Cut widthways down the centre of the side that you marked with the contrasting sliver, as indicated on the template, using a pair of sharp scissors. Allow to dry in shade.

7 When completely dry, turn the wallet right side out, exposing the flower design, and insert a zipper into the cut that you made in Step 6.

HANDLE

1 Pull off pieces of sliver to give a length of about 60 cm (24 in). Form the sliver into a circle, making sure the ends overlap by about 8 cm (3¼ in). Dip the overlapping part into warm, soapy water.

2 Roll the sliver between your palms so that the wool hardens and the circle ends up about 20 cm (8 in) in diameter. Allow to dry, then securely hand-stitch it to the underside of the wallet, along the fold line.

PHOTO POCKET

Make a piece of matching felt at least 11 x 11 cm (4½ x 4½ in). When dry, cut it to 10 x 9 cm (4 x 3½ in), or the same size as your wallet. In the centre, cut a window 7 x 7 cm (2¾ x 2¾ in), or a size to suit the intended photograph. Blanket-stitch the pocket to the inside of the wallet, matching the raw edges and leaving the top edge open. Finish as instructed at right.

Finishing

Sew a button loop to one end of the wallet (adding beads if desired, as on the pictured example) and a button or bead closure to the other end.

Bag with mobile-phone pouch

The body and pouch of this bag are felted together, which is an advanced skill. A separate rope of felt is used for the handle. However, if your felting skills are less developed but you still want to make a similar bag, you could make the bag minus the pouch, and cut a patch pocket out of a piece of matching pre-prepared, completely fulled felt. Then, when the bag is fully felted and completely dry, stitch the patch pocket to the outside of the bag.

The white variation pictured has no pouch. It uses raw fleece curls to form a fringe, and the body and handle are felted together.

Materials
Wool sliver
Curly fleece (if making the white variation
    pictured at right)
Strong sewing or embroidery thread
Beads (optional)

Tools
Bubble wrap
Soap
Towel

handle For the handle, roll the wetted middle section of a long piece of sliver between your hands until well felted.

pouch Felt the lower section only, leaving the top part on both sides unfelted so that it can later be melded with the body of the bag.

HANDLES

Take two pieces of sliver, each 100 cm (39½ in) long. Wet the central section of one piece with hot soapy water and roll the wetted part in your palm for 20 minutes, leaving about 10 cm (4 in) unfelted at each end. Repeat the process with the other piece to make the second handle.

POUCH

1 Cut a piece of bubble wrap 15 x 9 cm (6 x 3½ in) for the template, rounding off the bottom corners. Put two layers of sliver on the template, at right angles to each other, allowing 3 cm (1¼ in) overlap at the edges. Sprinkle with warm soapy water.

Turn the whole thing over and fold the overlapping wool inwards.

2 Put two layers of sliver on the template, at right angles to each other (no overlap is needed). Felt the lower part of the pouch, leaving about 5 cm (2 in) at the top unfelted; this will be used to attach the pouch to the bag. Do not remove the template.

BAG

1 Cut a piece of bubble wrap 38 x 33 cm (15 x 13 in) for the template. Cut a horizontal slit in the template, about 9 cm (3½ in) long, and beginning 9 cm (3½ in) down from the top edge.

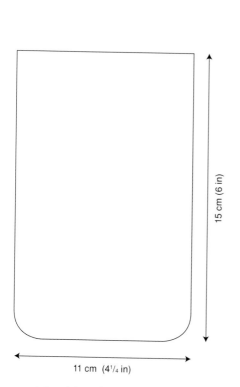

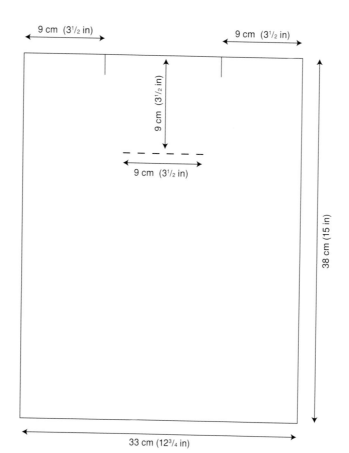

9 cm (3½ in)

9 cm (3½ in)

9 cm (3½ in)

9 cm (3½ in)

38 cm (15 in)

15 cm (6 in)

11 cm (4¼ in)

33 cm (12¾ in)

pouch template and mask Cut a piece of bubble wrap to these dimensions.

bag template Cut a piece of bubble wrap to these dimensions. The dotted line indicates where to make the slit to insert the pouch.

2 Insert the pouch into the slit cut in the bag template, leaving the bubble-wrap template in the pouch to act as a mask. Leave the unfelted top part of the pouch protruding through to the upper side of the template. Fold the wool at the back of the pouch upwards; fold the wool at the front of the pouch downwards (see photograph on page 308). This helps encourage the wool at the top of the pouch to meld with the rest of the sliver that you lay down for the body of the bag.

3 Put one layer of sliver on the template, allowing 7 cm (2¾ in) overlap at the edges. The unfelted top of the pouch should be

above this layer. Then put another layer of sliver at right angles to the previous, allowing 7 cm (2¾ in) overlap at the edges. The unfelted top of the pouch should now be trapped between these two layers.

4 Sprinkle with warm, soapy water, press the wool with your hand, fold the overlap inwards and massage until soft felt forms. Pay special attention to the entrance of the pouch, massaging more here to make a smooth connection with the body of the bag. Be careful that the position of the pouch doesn't move when you are stroking the piece, and that the pouch sticks to the body of the bag.

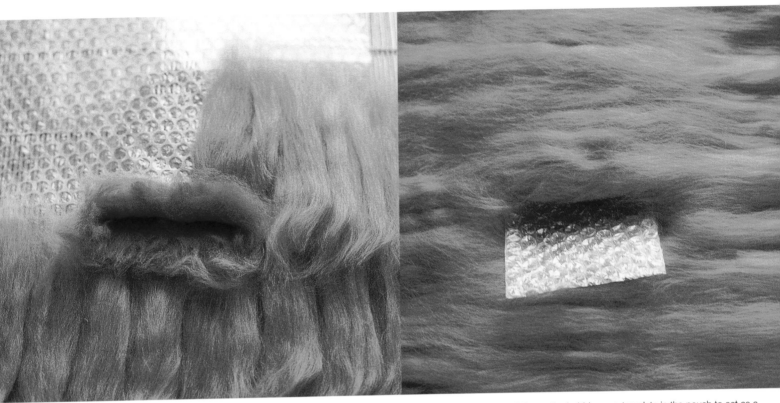

step two Insert the pouch into the slit in the bubble-wrap template, then lay out sliver to cover the template, allowing overlap at the sides.

step two continued Leave the bubble-wrap template in the pouch to act as a mask, so the insides do not felt together and the mouth of the pouch remains open.

5 Turn the whole parcel over and fold the overlapping edges of wool inwards. Be careful that the wool is not piled on top of itself, especially at the corners. Put two layers of sliver on top, at right angles to each other. Massage until soft felt forms, tucking in any wool that is sticking out.

6 Immerse the felt in hot water and grasp and squeeze about 50 times in each direction, then immerse in cold water and grasp and squeeze about 50 times more in each direction.

7 Roll the felt in a towel to remove excess water (do not wring). Stretch the bag in both directions until it is flat and evenly shaped. Allow to dry in shade.

8 Attach the handles to the bag, placing them about 9 cm (3½ in) in from the sides of the bag and the same distance down from the top, making sure they are even. Stitch securely, adding beads if you like.

White curly fleece bag

1 Cut a bubble-wrap template 33 x 30 cm (13 x 12 in). There is no need to make a slit in the template for the pouch.

step four To attach the top of the pouch to the body of the bag, put your fingers inside the pouch and the other hand on top of the bag and massage well.

step five Once the first side of the bag is felted, turn the whole thing over and fold in the overlapping edges of wool, before adding two more layers of sliver.

2 Make the handles as described for the bag with pouch.

3 Lay the curly wool on the template, placing the cut ends about 10 cm (4 cm) from the bottom, allowing the curly ends to hang free over the edge of the template.

4 Put one layer of sliver on the template, allowing 7 cm (2¾ in) overlap at the edges. Put one handle piece at the top edge, positioning each end about 9 cm (3½ in) in from the sides. Put one layer of wool sliver on top, at right angles to the previous layer. Sprinkle with warm, soapy water, press with your hand and fold the overlap inwards.

5 Felt the bag and handle together, being careful that the position of the handle does not move when you are stroking the piece.

6 Turn the whole thing over and repeat Step 3, then repeat Steps 4 and 5.

7 When the felt passes the pinch test (see page 299), allow the bag to dry in shade, then finish as instructed at right.

Finishing

When the bag is completely dry, sew a row of white beads 10 cm (4 in) from the bottom, along the line where the top of the curly fleece ends. Using backstitch and strong thread, stitch firmly, as this line will form the base of the bag.

Soft cloche hat

This hat is shaped like a bell, hence its name; cloche is French for bell. Fitted hats such as cloches normally need to be formed on a hat block; as this is not something that most people have, this hat is made from a bubble-wrap template tailored to the head of the wearer. The beauty of the bubble-wrap template is that you can cut virtually any shape you like, with spikes and blobs, extended crowns and brims, and then felt it.

Materials
Merino sliver

Tools
Bubble wrap, for template
Scissors
Bamboo mat or bubble wrap, for rolling
Soap
Towel

step three Press down gently on the bubble-wrap template to ensure that there are no air bubbles underneath it.

step four Once the hat is soft-felted, roll it up on itself and roll it back and forth about 20 rolls at a time, checking on the edges and seams as you go.

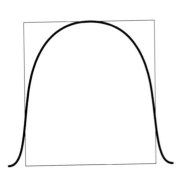

The template is formed from a rectangle calculated on your own head size, which then is rounded off at the top corners and widened at the bottom into a bell shape.

1 To make a hat blocked (formed) on your own or another's head (in the absence of a hat block), you will need to make a template. Measure around the head, add 50 per cent of the measurement and then divide the total by 2, to give you the width of the template. Then measure from the centre crown to the middle of the ear, add 50 per cent of the measurement, and divide the total by 2, to give you the height of the template. Draw a rectangle using the height and width you have calculated. Trim the top corners to curves and very slightly widen the bottom edge so that you have a sort of bell shape (see Diagram 1). Cut out a template to this shape from bubble wrap.

2 Trace around the outside of the template onto the mat or the bubble wrap in which you will roll the felt, adding about 7 cm (2¾ in) around the edge, except at the brim edge. Remove the template, then, using the traced line as a guide, lay out sliver in four thin layers. Reinforce the brim slightly by laying a little extra sliver along the edge.

3 Sprinkle the middle of the layers with warm, soapy water. Lay the template on top, pressing down gently to remove air bubbles. Fold the edges of the wool in over the template, and fill in the middle of the template so that the thickness of wool is even over the whole. Remember to create a

the finished 'hood' The felt is now ready for blocking or shaping.

variation The crown of the hat can be depressed to give a different shape.
A ribbon or a felt rope, as shown, can be tied around the base for decoration.

slight overlap with the folded-in edges, and to repeat the reinforcement of the brim.

4 Wet the whole parcel, and begin the felting process by patting it gently with the fingers. Pay attention to the edges of the template, watching for holes and making sure that no ridges form. If they do, smooth them out with the fingers. Then roll the hat, about 20 rolls at a time, checking the edges and seams in between each set of rolls.

5 When the felt is strong enough to turn over, firm the brim edge of the hat. Soap the fingers and very gently rub the edges of the felt, using a circular motion and about

the same pressure one would use for washing one's face. You will notice the felt visibly shrinking and firming.

6 Once the hat begins to exert pressure on the template, remove the template. You can now start to full quite vigorously, rolling the hat between the hands, dropping, dipping in hot and cold water, and rolling it on the mat. Try the hat on from time to time, to make sure it doesn't become too small. When it reaches the required size, rinse in warm water, press out in a towel (do not wring) and put it on, smoothing it and shaping the edge. Line with a plastic shopping bag, stuff with crumpled newspaper and leave to dry.

Hint

When laying out the sliver to form the hat, remember that several thin layers are better than fewer thick ones, making a stronger and more even felt. The finer the sliver you use, the softer the hat, which is why high-quality Merino is specified. If you wish to use stronger wool, the hat may need to be lined with silk or cotton fabric, to prevent an itch problem.

Cobweb scarf

Cobweb scarves are very fine and delicate but beautifully warm, as they trap warm air around the body. The pictured example has wisps of soy silk laid down first for embellishment.

This project will require its own room for a few hours; as the shawl is so fine, it is best laid out in a room where there will be no sudden drafts of air to waft away the sliver. Also, it needs to rest for a couple of hours, so construct it somewhere where pets or other people cannot disturb it.

Sliver can be prepared for cobweb felting well in advance. Spread it in sections, using butter paper or waxed lunchwrap to support it, rolling it up as you go for later use.

Materials
Fiine Merino sliver
Soy silk or other fibres for embellishment
 (optional; see page 317)

Tools
Bubble wrap, about 2.5 m x 40 cm
 (98½ x 16 in)
Hand-mister
Towel
Soap

Size
Approximately 40 x 150 cm (16 x 59 in)

Note
The finished scarf will be wider than the sliver that is originally laid out. This is because there is no lateral bonding of the fibres, as they are all laid out longitudinally, so the scarf can actually spread sideways during the felting process. It will only decrease in size lengthways

Calculating quantities

It is difficult to give precise quantities of sliver required for felting projects, as the same volume of wool from different breeds will have different weights; for example, a bag made of Leicester or Lincoln could weigh at least half as much again as one of a similar size and thickness of felt made from Merino. The following rough guidelines may be helpful, however.

A lightweight shawl measuring approximately 90 x 180 cm (35½ x 71 in) might require 300–500 g (10½ oz–17½ oz), depending on its thickness and pattern. If making 'nuno' felt (using a woven backing), you can get away with as little as 100 g (3½ oz), when using fine Merino sliver. A heavy rug might need as much as 700 g–1 kg (1 lb 9 oz–2 lb 4 oz). It is safest to buy more rather than less; any leftovers can be used to create pre-felts or to make decorations for other projects.

step two Carefully spread out the sliver laterally into a fine, even layer about 30 cm (12 in) wide.

1 Lay the bubble wrap on a long table or on the floor, bubble side down. Take a length of wool sliver about 2.5 m (98½ in) long and lay it along the length of the bubble wrap.

2 Very carefully begin to pull the sliver laterally, spreading the fibres without pulling them apart lengthways. Work slowly and carefully so that the fibres will be spread evenly across the bubble wrap. You should be able to spread them about 30 cm (12 in) wide. They will look quite delicate and thin.

3 Using a hand-mister, gently mist the spread wool sliver along its whole length, using *cold*, slightly soapy water. Once it is

completely misted, leave it undisturbed for at least two hours, or preferably overnight.

4 After two hours, you will see that the wool fibres will have relaxed under moisture, that they will be quite wavy, and that a lacy pattern will have begun to appear. Gently sprinkle all of the wool with warm, slightly soapy water. Carefully roll up the bubble wrap, and very lightly begin to squeeze the bundle. Gently roll it back and forth. Re-roll in the other direction, and repeat the process. Cobweb felt must be made slowly and gently as it has a delicate and fragile textile.

step four Make sure the wool is thoroughly wetted before rolling up the bundle.

Using templates

Many felted items require a template made from bubble wrap (or a similar recyclable flexible non-stick material). Flat objects such as scarves do not need a template. The felt for a three-dimensional object such as a bag is made around both sides of the template. For some items, the template is laid down first, then the sliver put on top; for others, the sliver is laid out first, then the template added. As you become adept at felting, you will be able to choose which method is most appropriate for the item you are making.

When using a template, chalk its outline on the bamboo mat or bubble wrap. Use this as a guide when laying down the sliver, allowing sufficient sliver (7–10 cm/2¾–4 in) to fold over the edge. Once the wool is laid out, wet the centre area, making sure the edges to be folded remain dry. Lay the template down, patting firmly from the middle outwards to ensure wetting and to remove air bubbles. Fold in the edges, fill in the remaining area to the same thickness as the rest, and proceed with felting.

When using a template you may choose to make the article 'inside out', as it is easier to make decorative designs stay exactly where you want them. Also, any solid ridges at the edges can be trimmed or hidden on the inside of the item.

5 The felt may also be helped along by slipping two large elastic bands around the rolled bubble wrap, and simply picking up and dropping the whole bundle a few times. In fact, if the bundle is well secured, it can be kicked gently around the floor as the felt gets stronger. After an hour or so of gentle massage, rolling and dropping (re-rolling the work from time to time to ensure even felting), remove the felt from the bubble wrap and gently rinse in lukewarm water. Place in a towel, roll up, and then place the rolled towel on the floor. Stand on the towel a few times to squeeze the moisture out of the felt (never wring the felt). Unroll and allow the felt to dry in the shade.

Variations

Once the sliver has been laid out, and before the misting, small scraps of silk and wool threads and yarns can be added to the scarf, either at random or laid as a pattern. You can even add soft feathers if you wish. (These embellishments can be laid at right angles to or parallel with the sliver, as you wish; each way will create a slightly different look.) Then felt as described above.

To encourage bigger holes in your cobweb felt, gently prise apart the fibres of the sliver, rounding the edges with your fingers.

Beaded scarf

This unusual scarf is made of two narrow pieces of felt embellished with curly fleece and joined by two rows of beads. The larger beads shown here are made of felt (see page 291), but you could use any type of bead.

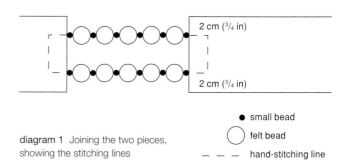

diagram 1 Joining the two pieces, showing the stitching lines

- ● small bead
- ○ felt bead
- − − − hand-stitching line

2 cm (³/₄ in)

2 cm (³/₄ in)

Materials
Curly wool
Wool sliver
Wool yarn
10 beads, about 2 cm (³/₄ in)
    in diameter
12 felt beads, about 8 mm
    (³/₈ in) in diameter (see
    page 291)

Tools
Bubble wrap, cut to 20 x
    100 cm (8 x 39½ in)
Soap
Scissors
Sharp or crewel needle

1 Arrange strands of curly wool horizontally along the bubble wrap. Top with two layers of wool sliver, at right angles to each other, to cover the area of the bubble wrap only (without any overlap). Sprinkle gently with warm, soapy water (avoid making the wool spread out due to water pressure).

2 Press with your palms until the wool is thoroughly wet and any air bubbles have been pressed out. Stroke very gently (as though giving a baby its first bath) to make the surface of the felt flat. To make the edges round, massage them with your fingertips. When you feel the wool begin to harden, you can exert more pressure. Keep massaging for about 5 minutes.

3 Turn the felt over and remove the bubble wrap. Sprinkle with warm, soapy water and keep massaging for about 5 minutes. If the curly wool isn't sticking to the felt, turn the scarf back over to the first side and keep massaging until it does (you won't need the bubble wrap for this step).

4 Immerse the felt in hot water and grasp and squeeze about 50 times in each direction, then immerse in cold water and grasp and squeeze about 50 times more in each direction.

5 Put the felt on a work surface and sprinkle with warm, soapy water. Massage for about 10 minutes on each side, or until it is well fulled.

6 Cut across one end of the felt to give a clean line, then cut the piece of felt in halves lengthways. Allow to dry in shade.

7 Thread a sharp or crewel needle with wool yarn. Starting at a point about 2 cm (³/₄ in) in from the sides and 1 cm (³/₈ in) in from the cut end, sew a line of running stitch (see Diagram 1), then string 6 large beads alternately with 5 smaller beads. Sew another line of running stitch at the cut end of the second piece of felt, then string the rest of the beads. Join to the first piece of felt and fasten off securely.

Baby shoes

For these soft, pretty first shoes, use lambs' curls and the finest Merino sliver to suit a baby's delicate skin. Or vary the design by using wool sliver alone, as shown in the variations pictured on page 323. Once the baby has grown out of them, the shoes will make a lovely keepsake.

For safety, if attaching beads or buttons to the shoes, stitch them on very securely with strong thread so that they will not easily become detached.

Materials
Raw lambs' curls
Fine Merino sliver
Beads, buttons or embroidery thread (optional)

Tools
Bubble wrap
Soap
Scissors
Tissue paper

Size
Approximately 12 cm (4½ in) long

Making a felted bunny
The bunny is made using a needle-felting process, in which the wool is stabbed with a special needle that has rough, notched edges. These force the fibre down, making it entangle with other fibres and form felt. Using a needle to felt small areas gives precise control, so is ideal for areas of small detail such as the bunny's features.

Roll a ball of sliver between your palms until it hardens, then place it on a sponge or a piece of foam rubber. Stab it with a felting needle for about 20 minutes, turning the ball to stab evenly all over, until it felts. To make the nose and cheek, stab in little circles on the felted ball so that indentations form. For the nose, roll a small amount of pink wool into a ball. Place in position on the larger felt ball and stab to fix it in place. For the eyes, do the same with orange wool. For each ear, fold a piece of brown sliver in half widthways then place it on a sponge or other surface that you can stab into. Stab one end until it becomes hard, leaving the other end unstabbed. Position the ear on the larger felt ball. Stab from the back, on the previously unstabbed end, to fix the ear to the head.

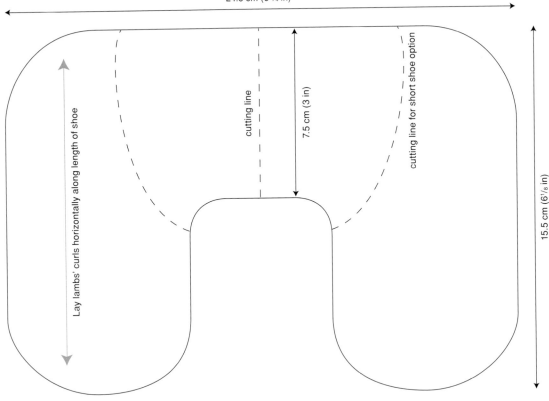

24.5 cm (9³/₄ in)

Lay lambs' curls horizontally along length of shoe

cutting line

7.5 cm (3 in)

cutting line for short shoe option

15.5 cm (6¹/₈ in)

template Cut the template from bubble wrap (this shape will make two shoes at once).

1 Cut out the template from bubble wrap. Note that you will be making both shoes at once; they will then be cut down the middle and separated.

2 Lay the lambs' curls horizontally on top of the template (no overlap is needed). Put two layers of wool sliver on top, allowing 4 cm (1½ in) overlap around the edges.

3 Sprinkle warm, soapy water only on the wool covering the template (do not wet the overlap). Gently massage until soft felt forms.

4 Turn the whole parcel over. Lay lambs' curls horizontally on top of the template (no overlap is needed), then fold the overlapping edges of the Merino sliver inwards. Make sure that the wool is not piled up onto itself at the edges and that there are no lumps.

5 Put two layers of Merino sliver on top, with each layer at right angles to the previous. Sprinkle warm, soapy water over the whole. Gently massage the wool until soft felt forms, tucking in any wool that is sticking out.

step two Lay the lambs' curls horizontally on top of the template.

embellishment The shoes can be decorated with stitching, beads, buttons, straps or animal faces (see 'Making a felted bunny', page 321), if desired.

6 Hard felt on both sides until the surface is smooth, about 10 minutes.

7 Cut down the centre of the felted piece, as indicated on the template, to separate the two shoes. Put your fingers inside each shoe and stroke the felt until smooth, paying particular attention to the corners.

8 Turn each shoe inside out and stroke the surface until it is hard and smooth, about 10 minutes.

9 Immerse in hot water and grasp and squeeze about 50 times in each direction,

then immerse in cold water and grasp and squeeze about 50 times in each direction.

10 Do the pinch test (see page 299); if you can grasp single fibres from the felt, it needs more massaging.

11 When it passes the pinch test, stuff each shoe with tissue paper and allow to dry in shade.

12 If desired, cut the top edge of each shoe to give a scalloped effect, as shown in the photograph on page 321. Embellish with beads, buttons or stitching (as shown in the photograph above) if you wish.

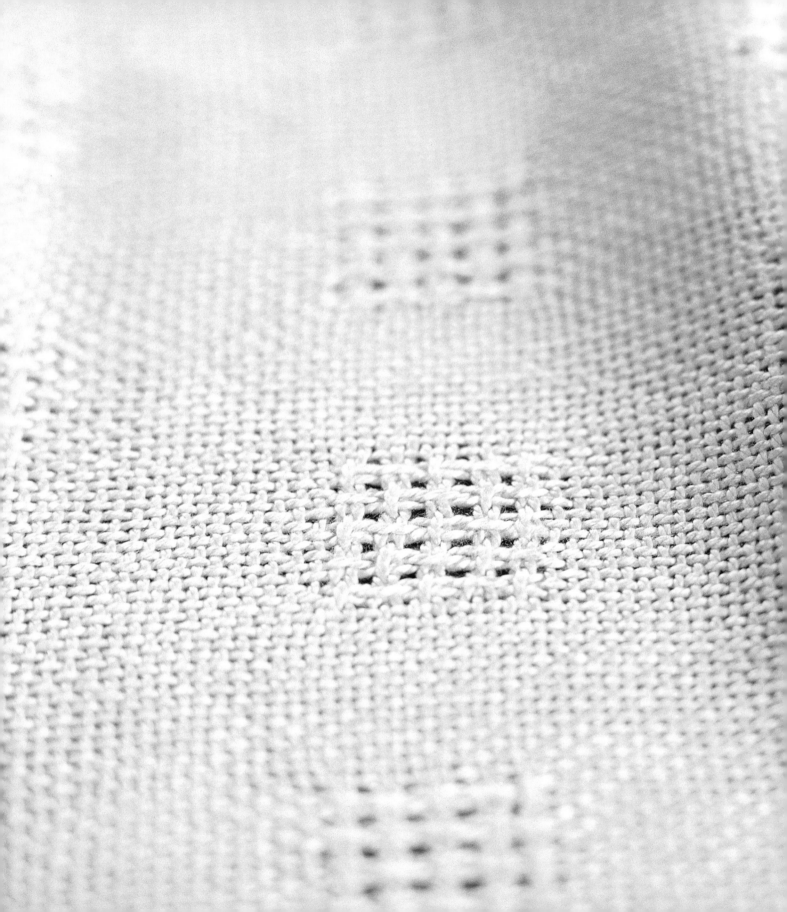

weaving

Weaving basics

Any piece of woven cloth consists of vertical or lengthwise threads, which are known as the warp, interlaced at right angles with horizontal or crosswise threads, called the weft. The first stage of weaving is to measure and wind the warp threads (see pages 330–331). The warp threads are then attached to the loom (see pages 332–333) and put under tension. The weft yarn (which may or may not be the same as the warp yarn) is wound onto a shuttle that is then passed back and forth across the warp to form the cloth.

Every loom has a 'shedding' device; this separates some of the warp threads from the others so that the shuttle carrying the weft thread can be passed through that space, which is known as a shed. Changing between one shed and the other on successive passes serves to interlace the warp and the weft to form the woven fabric. After each pass of the shuttle, the weft thread is packed firmly into place by means of a moving device known as a beater.

A single thread of warp is known as an end. Every weave has a certain number of ends per inch (epi) or ends per centimetre (e/cm); this is the number of ends per inch or per centimetre across the warp. This is also known as the sett; for example, a sett of 20 epi means that there are 20 warp ends per inch. A single thread of weft is known as a pick. Picks per inch (ppi) or picks per centimetre (p/cm) refers to the number of weft threads, or picks, per inch or per centimetre.

The loom has a series of shafts; these horizontal frames serve as the loom's shedding devices. A loom must have at least two shafts to create a shed through which the shuttle can pass. To the shaft are attached heddles — lengths of string or thin metal with a small hole, or 'eye', at the centre, through which a warp end is threaded. In a floor loom, the shafts are attached to treadles, which are operated with the feet. Depending on the sequence in which the treadles are operated, different warp threads are picked up on successive passes of the shuttle; it is these different sequences that produce the pattern of the weave.

Once the entire length of cloth has been woven, it may be hem stitched (see page 344), then it is cut from the loom. Handwoven cloth should be washed and pressed; it can then be used as is (as a scarf, shawl or table runner, for example), or cut up and then sewn into homewares or garments.

There are many different types of loom, and more than one way to prepare a loom. For best results, familiarize yourself thoroughly with your particular loom and its use. The beginner weaver would be well advised to attend a course in weaving; seeing the craft demonstrated will make the process much clearer.

table loom A table loom (the one pictured has eight shafts) is ideal for weavers who lack the space for a floor loom, or who wish to weave only smaller pieces. With a table loom, the shafts are lifted with levers.

floor loom To weave larger pieces or more complex patterns, a floor loom is required. This example has eight shafts; in floor looms, the shafts are lifted and lowered by depressing the treadles.

Looms

Looms vary greatly in size and complexity. Most beginner weavers learn on a table loom and progress to a floor loom. All but three of the projects in this book were created on floor looms, of which there are a number of different types.

Counterbalance Usually limited to four shafts, this loom works with two shafts up and two shafts down. The tie-up is fairly simple but it is difficult to weave unbalanced weaves (see page 334) on this loom.

Countermarch This loom is the most preferred by professional weavers because it will give a perfect shed with any number of shafts. Each shaft works as an independent unit, with the rising and falling controlled by the treadles. The countermarch loom can have from four to 16 shafts.

Jack The simplest of the floor looms, this has four or eight shafts. The shafts rise only (rather than both rising and falling) and so tying them to the treadles is comparatively simple.

Other types of loom

Table looms The most commonly used table looms have four or eight shafts, although table looms with more shafts and with only two shafts are also available.

Small hand looms These looms consist of square or rectangular wooden frames with small nails set in them; yarn is wound around the nails from one side of the loom to the other, in three alternating layers. The final layer, which serves to interlace the fabric, is created using yarn threaded into a long needle.

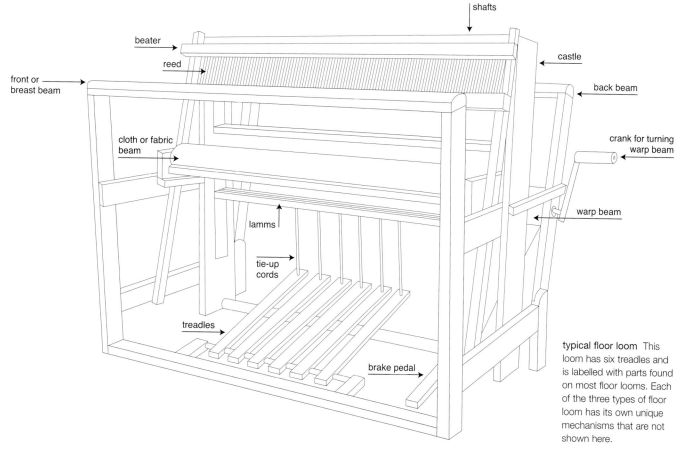

beater
reed
shafts
castle
back beam
front or breast beam
cloth or fabric beam
crank for turning warp beam
warp beam
lamms
tie-up cords
treadles
brake pedal

typical floor loom This loom has six treadles and is labelled with parts found on most floor looms. Each of the three types of floor loom has its own unique mechanisms that are not shown here.

Other equipment

As well as a loom, the following equipment is needed before weaving commences:

Bobbin winder A bobbin winder is designed to wind yarns onto bobbins for use in a boat shuttle. Bobbin winders come in different shapes and with different drive mechanisms, both manual and electric.

Cross sticks When measuring the warp, the cross is the figure-of-eight that is made at both ends of the warp to prevent tangles later on. The cross sticks are used to put in the cross on the warp once it has been removed from the warping board. Threading the warp through the heddles is done from the cross sticks once the warp has been attached to the loom.

Raddle Looms can be warped up from front to back, or back to front. If warping back to front, a raddle is needed. This length of wood has pegs or nails at even intervals, and is used when rolling onto the warp beam to separate and spread the warp to the correct width.

Reed The reed sits inside the beater (see also page 337), and consists of vertical teeth set at regular intervals within a frame. (The teeth used to be made of actual reed, hence their name; now they are either carbon or stainless steel.) Each space in the reed is known as a dent. The reed acts as a spacer for the warp yarn, which is threaded through it, usually one or more threads per dent. Reeds come in various sizes based on the number of dents per inch; most weavers will have

Shuttles

The various types of shuttles are designed for different tasks and uses. Three of the most commonly used are as follows:

Boat shuttle This is the quickest to 'throw' (or to pass through the shed), as the yarn is wound on a bobbin and feeds from it automatically as the shuttle passes through the shed. One disadvantage of boat shuttles is that they cannot hold as much heavy yarn as, for example, a ski shuttle.

Ski shuttle This is used for heavier yarns and rug weaving. The yarn is wound directly onto the shuttle, between two 'horns' on its upper surface, without the use of a bobbin.

Stick shuttle A simple shuttle with a notch in each end through which the yarn is wound; good for carrying small amounts of yarn. These are the cheapest shuttles to buy (and are also easy to make yourself) and come in many styles and lengths. They can be used in narrow or wide warps, and should be a little wider than the weaving. Stick shuttles are also less expensive than other shuttles, as they do not require a bobbin winder.

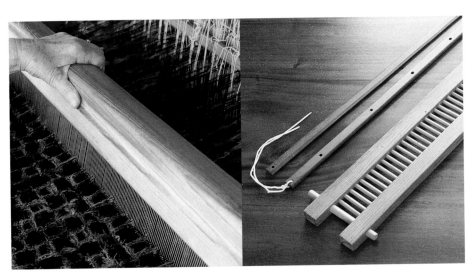

beating The beater, which contains the reed, is used to pack the weft threads into place.

left to right Cross sticks (also known as lease sticks) and a raddle.

several reeds to allow for different setts. Reeds also come in different widths; for example, a 24-inch (60 cm) reed is 24 inches wide and can weave a 24-inch wide warp. A warp is centred on the reed. The term 'sley' means to insert a warp thread through a dent in the reed.

Reed hook This small, flat tool (also known as a sley hook) assists in 'sleying the reed', or pulling the warp through the dents in the reed.

Temple Also known as a stretcher, this tool can be adjusted to various widths and is used to keep the width of a weaving constant.

Threading hook Also known as a warp hook or heddle hook, and used to thread a warp end through a heddle (although some weavers prefer to thread the heddles using their fingers).

Warping board Before the warp is attached to the loom, it must first be measured. This is the purpose of a warping board, a square or rectangular frame with a series of pegs around the outside. A warping mill (see page 330) performs a similar function to a warping board but is generally used for longer warps. Either tool permits a long warp to be measured in a very compact way. The required length of warp is calculated, and then the warp thread is passed back and forth between a series of pegs to give the correct length for one end of warp. This process is continued until enough thread has been wound for the required number of warp ends; the warp is then transferred to the loom (see page 332). See pages 330–331 for more detailed instructions on using a warping board.

small looms For very compact and portable weaving, small looms are ideal. The one pictured produces squares measuring 4 in (10 cm). Such looms can be found under various proprietary names, including Weave-It. Small looms of other dimensions, as well as rectangular and triangular versions, are also available.

left to right Boat shuttle, bobbin winder, stick shuttle, threading hook, stick shuttle, ski shuttle.

warping mill Here, the cross can be seen around the two pegs at the top and bottom.

Using a warping board

Warping boards have a number of pegs and holes so the pegs can be moved around depending on the length of the warp. The pegs are about 5 in (13 cm) apart. The distance between a peg on the left side of the warping board and one on the right side is usually a standard measure (for example, one yard or one metre, or half that), making it easy to work out how many pegs must be traversed to give the correct warp length. If constructing your own warping board, keep this in mind when designing it.

If threading the loom with a raddle, the cross is usually made around the first two and last two pegs on the warping board. If threading from front to back, it is easier to have a distance between the cross and the end of the warp — say 5 in (13 cm).

Warping

The simplest way to wind a warp is on a warping board. Most warping boards will take up to about 10 metres or 10 yards of warp. However, when winding a longer warp, a warping mill is used. The most important thing when winding a warp is the cross (also known as the lease); this is the intersection between one warp end and the next, and is made by taking the yarn in a figure-of-eight pattern around the last two pegs on the warping board, so that the yarn crosses over itself. The purpose of the cross is to keep the ends separate and secure, and to prevent tangles later. The warp is best wound with a cross each end for safety, so that if one cross comes undone you still have another.

Setting up the guide string

Before winding the warp, you will need to work out the path that your warp will take on the board. First, calculate the required length of one warp end. If using one of the projects in this book, the required warp length is given in the instructions; if making up your own project, see page 340 for how to calculate warp length. Cut a piece of waste yarn this length, plus enough extra to allow for tying both ends to the pegs. This will be your guide string; make it a contrasting colour from the warp yarn so that it is easily distinguished.

warping board Yarn is wound around the pegs to a pre-determined length to create the warp.

guide string Here, the guide string (in red) can be seen under the wound warp.

counting thread Showing a counting thread inserted in the warp.

Tie one end of the guide string to one of the pegs on the warping board. Next, find a path on the warping board that produces the correct warp length. Once you have found a correct path, tie the other end of the guide string in place. You are now ready to wind the warp, following the path of the guide string.

When winding the warp, put in a counting thread every 1 in (2.5 cm) or, say, every 10 or 20 warp ends. This helps to count the number of warp ends and makes it easy to spread the warp evenly in the raddle to the correct width. If the first pass is made from top to bottom of the warping board, the second pass is made from bottom to top. Continue in this manner until you have wound the correct number of warp ends. If you need to join in a new cop or cone of yarn, always make the join at either end of the warp, using a knot. Avoid any knots in the middle of the warp. Before removing the warp from the board, tie the cross securely (see right) to maintain the order in which the warp has been wound.

Tying the cross

Before removing the warp from the warping board, it is vital to tie the cross securely so that it does not come undone while the warp is being transferred to the loom or during tying on. Ties should be made on either side of the cross, as shown in the photograph below, and also around the cross itself.

Chaining the warp

When removing the warp from the warping board or mill, it is formed into a chain, which keeps it from becoming tangled, especially if it will not be used immediately. To chain the warp, make a loop in one end, then draw the body of the warp threads through the loop to form another loop (as though making crochet chains). Continue in this manner along the length of the warp. To stop the chain from unravelling, make a tie between the last loop and the unchained end of the warp.

cross ties Showing a tie on either side of the cross to help keep it secure.

chaining the warp Make a loop in the bundle of threads, then draw the threads through the loop.

the chained warp Continue in this manner along the length of the warp.

Threading up and tying on

The process of putting the warp on the loom is known as 'dressing' the loom. The warp is threaded from the cross, with each thread being taken in the same order in which the warp was wound. This stops the threads from becoming tangled with each other.

The loom can be dressed from back to front or front to back; each weaver will choose the method that best suits him or herself, and the particular loom. Whatever method is used, the warp should always be centred in the loom, so it is necessary to know the width of the warp in the reed. Always check before threading up that the reed is centred in the beater. It is a good idea to mark the centre of the reed, either by tying a thread in the centre of the reed, or by marking the centre of the beater with a marking pen. Also mark the centre of the beater frame — this mark will ensure that you hold the beater in the centre to beat.

threading Showing warp ends threaded through the heddles.

Dressing the loom from back to front

This method requires a raddle, which is essentially a coarse reed with round pegs, and is used to distribute the warp evenly across the warp beam. Some raddles have a removable cap, which is used to keep all the threads in place.

tying on Pass two groups of ends under the stick, which is tied to the apron.

tying on, continued Bring the groups up and around the stick, then tie them together.

tying on completed Proceed along the width of the beam until all ends are tied on.

You will also need cardboard or paper, or preferably warp sticks, inserted between the layers of warp. This is to prevent the warp yarn from biting down unevenly through the layers of threads and to prevent threads at the edge of the warp from slipping off. Cross sticks (see also pages 328 and 337) are inserted in the cross and are used to help thread the warp ends in the correct order through the heddles.

To begin dressing the loom, push the heddles on all the shafts well away to both sides, and work from the back of the loom. Remove the stick that is tied to the apron on the back beam and thread the loops at the end of the warp evenly onto the stick. Then reattach the stick to the apron.

Centre the raddle and attach it to the loom, then spread the warp evenly across the raddle using the counting thread (see page 331). Attach the cap of the raddle (if it has one) to keep the threads in place.

Once these steps are completed, wind the warp onto the back beam using cardboard or warp sticks between each layer of warp. If using a floor loom, it is easier if you have a helper to wind on while you hold the warp under tension. When about 30 in (76 cm) of the warp remains, insert the cross sticks in the cross and thread the warp through the heddles and the reed, then tie it onto the front beam, making sure the tension is even. The loom is now ready for weaving.

Dressing the loom from front to back

This method does not require a raddle. The cross sticks are inserted and the warp is first threaded through the reed, then the heddles, and tied onto the back beam. It is then wound onto the back beam under tension, inserting cardboard or warp sticks between each layer of warp. The warp is then tied onto the front beam and the loom is ready for weaving.

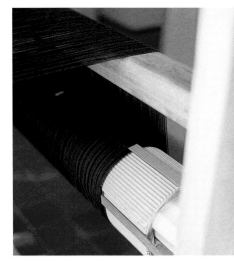

winding on to the back roller Showing sticks and cardboard between each layer of warp.

using a threading hook This tool assists in threading the warp ends though the heddle.

Balanced and unbalanced weaves

A weave can be balanced or unbalanced. Balanced weaves are those in which the number of weft threads per inch or centimetre is the same as the number of warp threads. In unbalanced weaves, the thread count per inch or centimetre differs for warp and weft.

Reeds and sleying

Looms are usually supplied with a 12-dent reed (that is, one that has 12 dents, or spaces, to the inch). In general use, one or two threads are passed through each dent of the reed, with perhaps double threads for a selvedge; however, a weaver should have reeds of different dentages for a variety of fabric weights. A second choice would probably be either ten or eight dents. A four-dent reed is suitable for rugs and can be used as a raddle.

To obtain the maximum value from any single reed, warps may be sleyed at one, two or three ends per dent, or alternating one end and two ends per dent. These methods of uneven denting will leave reeding marks in the woven fabric, particularly if the sley repeat does not divide into the weave repeat. For example, 2/2 twill has weave repeats on four ends and is best sleyed one, two or four per dent, not three per dent; mock leno has weave repeats on six ends and is best sleyed one or three per dent, not two or four.

Depending on the yarn and weave, reeding marks may disappear after the fabric is removed from the loom and washed, although they generally remain.

four-shaft double weave This is an example of a balanced weave.

dents A close-up of dents in the reed; the wooden frame that encloses the reed is the beater.

Weaving

Before weaving commences, the weaver must decide what type of shuttle to use. A stick shuttle works well for narrow weaving, but if weaving a wider piece a boat shuttle makes the weaving process much quicker and easier. If using a mohair or heavier yarn for the weft, a ski shuttle enables more yarn to be wound and is easy to throw across any width of weaving (see also page 328). If you are using two wefts, you will need two shuttles.

The weaving process may appear to be a mechanical sequence of actions — treadle depression, shed opening, weft insertion and beating — however, to weave a variety of cloth weights and qualities takes both skill and experience. A steady rhythm is essential for even weaving. The quality of a piece of handwoven cloth depends on the evenness of the tensions of the warp and weft threads. An even beat is very important and the weft should never be pulled tightly, but entered in the shed at a 45-degree angle. The weft is packed into place with the beater, the shed is changed and the process repeated. This simple operation can have many variations, each suitable for different types of weaving. The weaver may vary the moment at which he or she beats — sometimes it is better to change the shed, beat, throw the shuttle and beat again.

At the beginning and end of a piece, weave a header (several picks of plain weave) in a thicker yarn to draw the threads together. These threads prevent the cloth from unravelling when cut from the loom.

Joining in new weft threads

During the weaving, when the yarn on the bobbin or shuttle runs out, a new thread will need to be joined in. When starting a new bobbin of the same colour, you can overlap the new thead with the old weft for about 1 in (2.5 cm) in the same shed. If using a thick plied yarn, the old and new threads can be split so the overlapping area is not too thick. If using wool, often the new and old threads can be spliced together. If starting a new colour, finish the old colour by taking the yarn back on itself in the same shed at the selvedge for about 1 in (2.5 cm). The new colour is added in the same way.

header Two warp sticks are used as a header here instead of several picks of plain weave.

weft pick Pass the shuttle through the shed so that the weft enters at a 45-degree angle.

beating Beat the weft to pack it firmly into place.

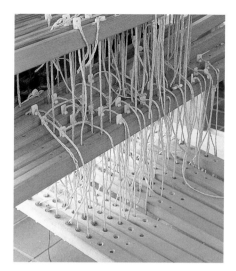
treadles and lamms on a floor loom

Design Diagram of cloth structure obtained by combining the threading draft and the lifting plan (see also pages 342–343).

Direct system A means of measuring the size of yarn (see also page 341).

Draft A graph that indicates the order in which the ends are drawn through the heddles on the shafts.

Drawing-in See Threading.

Dressing a loom All the processes of preparing a loom for weaving.

E/cm Ends per centimetre.

End A single warp thread. The term refers to the entire length of the thread, not just the actual end of it.

End and end Alternating single ends of warp in two colours.

Epi Ends per inch.

Fell The fell line of the cloth is the front or forward edge of the weaving, or the point where the last weft pick has been inserted.

Filling Another term for the weft.

Finishing Work done on cloth after it has been removed from the loom, for example washing, hem stitching or pressing.

Float An end or pick that goes over or under two or more warp ends or two or more picks; for example in a twill weave, the weft goes over and under two warp threads.

Floating selvedge A warp end at either side of the warp which is not threaded through a heddle eye, but is sleyed through the reed.

Grey cloth Cloth in its loom state prior to finishing.

Guide string A preliminary measuring thread used to determine the correct warp length and the pattern of winding on the warping board; see also page 330.

Harness Another name for a shaft; used more in America than elsewhere.

Header Picks woven at the beginning of the warp to test its threading and tension.

Heddles Strings or wires suspended between the shafts, with eyes through which the warp ends are threaded.

Indirect system A means of measuring the size of yarn (see also page 341).

Lamms Horizontal pieces positioned between the treadles and shafts.

Lease See Cross.

Lease sticks (rods) See Cross sticks.

Lifting plan (peg or pegging plan) A plan showing the order in which the shafts are to be operated.

Loom waste The unweavable portion of the warp threads that are required for tying on to the loom, and which are cut off at the end of the weaving process.

Over-dyeing The process of dyeing a second colour over a previous one.

P/cm Picks per centimetre.

Peg (or pegging) plan See Lifting plan.

Pick A single pass of weft. Also known as a shot or filling.

Pick and pick Alternating single picks of weft in two colours.

shafts, warp threads and heddles

Pick-up stick A smooth stick with a pointed end; used to pick up selected warp ends.

Plain weave (or tabby) A basic weave of one up and one down in both the warp and the weft.

Ppi Picks per inch.

Raddle A frame (often with a removable cap on top), having pegs set at equal intervals; used for spreading the warp to its correct width when beaming.

Reed A comb-like frame composed of thin metal slats, which is used for spacing the warp ends and beating in the weft. The reed is held in place by the beater.

Reed hook (or sley hook) A thin, flat, S-shaped hook used for sleying the reed.

Rolling on See Beaming.

Selvedge The point at which the weft binds the warp to form a firmly woven closed edge on each side of the cloth. It may consist of only one thread, or several.

Sett The number of warp threads (or ends) per inch or per centimetre as determined by the yarn thickness and the particular end use. Spelled 'set' when used as a verb and 'sett' when used as a noun.

Shaft (or harness) A unit composed of heddles and heddle bars or frames.

Shed The opening between the layers of warp threads; made by raising or lowering one or more, but not all, of the shafts. The loaded shuttle is passed through the shed when weaving in order to deposit the weft thread, or pick.

Shot One pick of weft (or filling).

Shuttle A tool on which the weft yarn is wound so it can be passed through the shed.

Sley hook See Threading hook.

Sleying The threading of the warp ends through the dents of the reed.

Tabby Another term for plain weave.

Temple (tenterhook) An implement used for preventing the selvedges pulling in too much. Placed on the woven cloth in front of the reed.

Tex The size of a yarn in the direct system (see also page 341).

Threading (drawing in) The threading of the warp ends through the eyes of the heddles according to the draft.

Threading hook Used for threading the warp ends through the eyes of the heddles.

Tie-up Instructions for a floor loom — how the shafts are to be tied so that a foot pedal operates them.

Treadling plan The order in which the treadles of a floor loom are to be operated. The treadling plan, tie-up and threading draft combine to produce the design or draw-down.

Warp The threads running the length of the loom, which are held under tension. These run lengthwise in the woven cloth.

Warping board A board or frame set with pegs which is used for winding the warp.

Web A piece of woven fabric.

Weft The thread carried by the shuttle which is passed through the shed to interlace with the warp ends. These run widthwise in the woven cloth.

shed in warp The space between the lifted and lowered warp threads is known as the shed. It is through this space that the shuttle is passed, or 'thrown'.

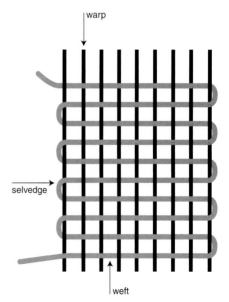

selvedge The selvedge is the closed edge of the fabric, and the point at which the weft threads wrap around the warp.

Yarn calculation

Calculation for the warp is the width of the weaving multiplied by the ends per inch or per centimetre multiplied by the length of the warp. (Work in metric or imperial; don't mix the two.) For example:

If working in inches: For a warp 24 inches wide, sett 10 epi, length 72 inches:
24 x 10 x 72 = 17,280.

Divide the result by 36 inches to give the number of yards needed:

17,280 ÷ 36 = 480 yards.

If working in centimetres: For a warp 60 cm wide, sett 5 e/cm, length 200 cm:
60 x 5 x 200 = 60,000.

Divide the result by 100 cm to give the number of metres needed for the warp:

60,000 ÷ 100 = 600 metres.

Calculation for the weft is the width of the weaving multiplied by the picks per inch or per cm multiplied by the length of the weaving. For example:

If working in inches: For a weft 20 inches wide, 10 picks per inch, length 36 inches:
20 x 10 x 36 = 7,200 inches.

Divide the result by 36 to give the number of yards required for the weft:

7,200 ÷ 36 = 200 yards.

If working in centimetres: For a weft 50 cm wide, 4 picks per cm, length 200 cm: 50 x 4 x 200 = 40,000.

Divide the result by 100 to give the number of metres required for the weft:

40,000 ÷ 100 = 400 metres.

Yarns

A warp yarn can be composed of any fibre so long as it can sustain both considerable tension during weaving and the friction caused by the movement of the shafts and the reed. The yarn needs to be chosen for its strength, elasticity and abrasion resistance.

Weft yarns are not subject to the same strain or abrasion and therefore almost any type of yarn can be used. The weft yarn does not have to be the same type of yarn as the warp; for instance, a soft wool yarn can be used with a cotton warp. Avoid highly twisted yarns, as they do not pack down well in the weaving and can distort the weave. They can be used for special effects by experienced weavers, but are best not used by beginners.

Try a weft of the same or an analogous colour or texture (white and cream used together for warp and weft are very effective), or mix textures — for example, shiny and dull, rough and smooth, dull and metallic.

Pulling in can occur if the weft is pulled too tightly, thus forcing the cloth out of shape. Also, the reed may wear the selvedge threads. Be careful of the non-elasticity of some fancy yarns, as often the pulling in is not apparent until too late.

warp yarns These should be chosen for their strength and abrasion resistance.

weft yarns Fancy and textured yarns, as well as plain, can be used for the weft.

Count system

The count system refers to the measurement of the thickness of yarns. There are two systems, direct and indirect.

Indirect

This Imperial system is very complicated, as yardages vary for different types of yarn. The unit length of 1s count (that is, one unit length to 1 lb weight) varies with different fibres and different spinning systems, for example:

Woollen spun Galashiels	cut	200 yards
Yorkshire	skein	256 yards
West of England	hank	320 yards
Worsted	hank	560 yards
Linen	lea	300 yards
Cotton	hank	840 yards
Spun silk	hank	840 yards

When a yarn in any of the above systems is plied — that is, when two yarns of identical count are twisted together — the yarn is twice as thick and the length of a pound weight is halved. For example, with 2/8s cotton, the length of this yarn would be 8 x 840 ÷ 2 = 3360 yards. Fortunately today most yarns have the yardage noted on the package, which makes calculation for your weaving much easier.

Direct

The direct, or Tex, system is based on a fixed-length system, that is, weight per unit length. The Tex count is a metric system, and represents the weight in grams per kilometre of yarn. For example, a yarn numbered 10 Tex measures 1 kilometre and weighs 10 grams. The Tex number increases with the size of the yarn. The term 'folded' is used in preference to 'plied' yarn when two or more yarns are twisted together, and the direction of the twist is included in the information. For example, 20 Tex/2S indicates that two threads of 10 Tex are folded in an 'S' direction. The resultant count will be 20 Tex because the weight is exactly doubled. It is hoped that this system will be adopted universally as it is much easier and applies to all yarns.

Sett

A quick way of working out the sett of a yarn is to wind the yarn around a ruler over 1 inch (2.5 cm) so that the threads just touch each other. When the warp and weft are of the same yarn, the sett will be half the number of threads that wind to 1 inch (2.5 cm) for plain weave. Add about a third more ends for twill. When calculating the amount of warp yarn needed, allowances must be made for tie-ups at the front and back of the loom, take-up of yarn when weaving, and shrinkage. On a floor loom, allow an extra yard or metre — on a table loom, half a yard or half a metre is usually all that is needed.

The weft usually takes about three quarters as much yarn as the warp, as you don't have to allow for warp take-up and tying on. It is always better to be generous when calculating how much yarn is needed. See opposite for more detail on yarn calculation.

testing sett Winding the yarn around a ruler will help you to calculate its sett.

Reading drafts in handweaving

A 'draw down' — sometimes known as a 'comprehensive draft' — gives a picture of the three components of pattern making on a loom: the threading draft, the lifting plan and the design resulting from a combination of these two.

In threading, the warp threads are drawn through the heddles in a pre-determined sequence; changes in this sequence alter the resultant pattern. The simplest threading is the straight (or twill) threading. On a four-shaft loom, the first warp thread is drawn through the first heddle on shaft 1; the second warp end through the first heddle on shaft 2; the third warp end through the first heddle on shaft 3; the fourth warp end through the first heddle on shaft 4; the fifth warp end on the second heddle on shaft 1; the sixth warp end on the second heddle of shaft 2, and so on. This is continued across the width of the loom — on an eight-shaft loom, the same sequence is followed through to the eighth shaft.

The symbols used to represent drafts vary between publications, but the principles remain the same. The simplest and least confusing method is to use numbers referring to the number of the shaft on which that end is threaded, written on squared paper so that each vertical space represents a warp thread; see Diagram 1.

If you read from left to right, then thread from left to right. If you read from right to left, thread from right to left. On a balanced weave, it makes no difference in which direction you thread; if there is a different pattern at one end, then it would just be reversed. A lifting plan relates directly to the draft, and shows the order in which the shafts are lifted after they have been threaded. This is written on squared paper with crosses (see Diagram 2) to indicate a lift of warp over weft. A lifting plan also uses each vertical row to represent a warp thread — a horizontal row refers to one pick.

Straight draft   Fancy draft

diagram 1 **Threading draft** Shown for both
a straight and a fancy weave

Drafts, lifting plans and designs

A lifting plan is read from the bottom up, as shown in Diagram 2. By looking at each vertical row in the lifting plan in turn, the action of each warp thread can be seen. For example:

Thread number 1: lifts, falls, lifts, falls
Thread number 2: falls, lifts, lifts, falls
Thread number 3: lifts, falls, falls, lifts
Thread number 4: falls, lifts, falls, lifts

A lifting plan can only be as wide, or over as many ends, as there are shafts threaded. For example, on a four-shaft loom, the lifting plan will be four ends wide. However, it can be as long, or over as many picks, as required.

A design is a combination of these two. With a straight draft, the design and lifting plan will be the same, but any variation in the threading will produce a different design. The design will be as long as the lifting plan and as wide as the draft; see Diagram 3.

When using a floor loom, the same rules apply, except now you have a draft, tie-up and treadling plan. The tie-up shows how the shafts are tied to the treadles. The draft is read from right to left and the treadling plan is read from top to bottom. It works the same as for a table loom, except with a floor loom the treadles lift the shafts; see Diagram 4.

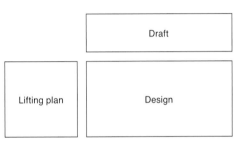

				Pick	Shafts
		X	X	4	3 and 4
X	X			3	1 and 2
	X		X	2	2 and 4
X		X		1	1 and 3

diagram 2 Lifting plan

	Draft
Lifting plan	Design

diagram 3 Design with draft and lifting plan for a table loom

Draft	Tie up
Design	Treadling plan

diagram 4 Design with draft, tie-up and treadling plan for a floor loom

Wool and mohair wrap

This cosy wrap in heather tones uses a combination of wool and mohair yarns for a luxurious effect.

The basketweave blocks among the plain weave result in an almost embossed effect.

Size 20 x 84 in (50 x 214 cm)

Equipment Eight-shaft loom, 24 in (60 cm) weaving width, ski shuttle

Techniques Basket weave and plain weave

Warp and weft yarns 4½ oz (125 g) space-dyed blue-black bouclé mohair, 4½ oz (125 g) 3-ply green wool, 1 oz (25 g) 2-ply dark grey mohair, 4½ oz (125 g) 6-ply fuzzy taupe mohair, 1 oz (25 g) 2-ply mauve mohair

Reed 10 dents per in (2.5 cm)

Sett 12 ends per in (2.5 cm). Sley 1 green wool and 1 dark grey mohair together

Selvedge 3 ends per dent twice on each side

Width in reed 24 in (60 cm)

Finished width 22 in (55 cm)

Weft sett 12 picks per in (2.5 cm)

Warp length 120 in (305 cm), which includes ties, loom waste and take-up

Number of ends 328

Designer Helen Frostell

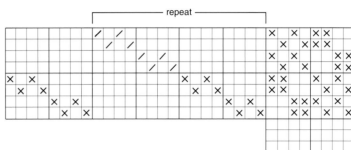

Warp and weft colour order

					End	
Green 3-ply wool	8		8	8	8	8 (x5) = 168
Blue/black mohair bouclé		8				(x5) = 40
Dark grey mohair			8			(x5) = 40
Fuzzy taupe 6-ply mohair				8		(x5) = 40
Mauve mohair					8	(x5) = 40
TOTAL						328

✕ green
╱ mohair
follow warp colour order

WEAVING

As mohair tends to stick, this can be overcome by opening the following shed while the beater is still at the fell line. Leave 8 in (20 cm) of warp at each end for fringing. Weave a header at both ends to hold weave firmly.

FINISHING

Remove from loom. Make a twisted fringe (see page 345) with about five threads in each hand. Twist to the right, then let the two cords twist back around each other in the opposite direction. Finish with an overhand knot. Hand-wash in warm, soapy water and agitate firmly. Rinse. Spin dry for 10 seconds. Roll firmly around a large tube for 24 hours, then dry flat. Trim fringes.

Three lace scarves from the same warp

Making more than one item from the same warp reduces the time needed for the lengthy process of warping. Each of these three delicately patterned scarves uses a different three-end huck lace design. A natural mulberry silk yarn is used here, but the weave patterns could easily be adapted for thicker yarns or, equally well, for larger garments.

Size of each scarf 7 x 73 in (18 x 185 cm)

Equipment Eight-shaft loom, throw shuttle

Technique Three-end huck lace

Warp and weft yarn For three scarves: 10½ oz (300 g) 20/2 mulberry silk. Add 3½ oz (100 g) for any additional scarves

Reed 10 dents per in (2.5 cm)

Sett 20 ends per in (2.5 cm). Sley 2 ends per dent

Width in reed 8 in (20 cm)

Weft sett 20 picks per in (2.5 cm)

Warp length 8¼ yds (7.5 m); add 2⅔ yds (2.4 m) for any additional scarves

Number of ends 163

Designer Mary Hawkins

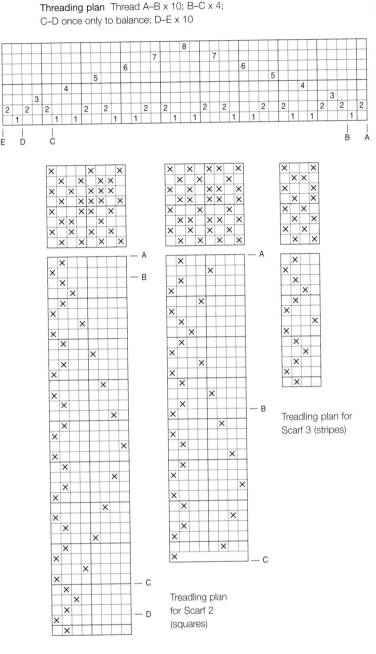

Treadling plan for
Scarf 1 (diamonds)

Treadling plan
for Scarf 2
(squares)

Treadling plan for
Scarf 3 (stripes)

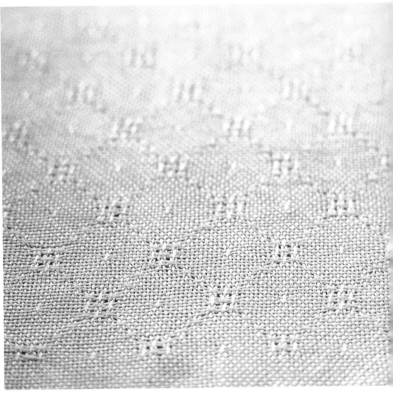

scarf 1 Diamonds and lace squares

THREADING

Thread from A–B 10 times (for plain weave border); from B–C four times (pattern repeats); from C–D once only (to balance pattern); and from D–E 10 times (for remaining border).

SCARF 1: DIAMONDS

Allow 7 in (18 cm) for the fringe (part of this can come out of the tie-on). Weave A–B (plain weave) for 2 in (5 cm), then follow treadling plan 1; weave B–C for 75 in (1.9 m), ending with C–D once only to balance the design. Weave 2 in (5 cm) plain weave. Allow 7 in (18 cm) fringe for Scarf 1, then 7 in (18 cm) fringe for Scarf 2.

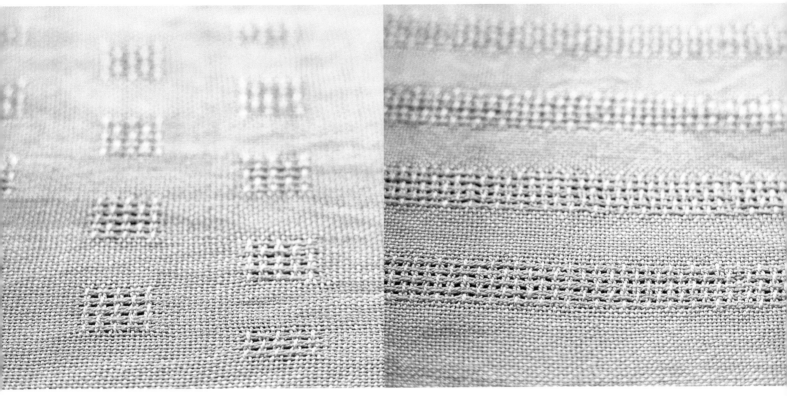

scarf 2 Lace squares

scarf 3 Lace stripes

SCARF 2: SQUARES

Weave 2 in (5 cm) of plain weave, as for
Scarf 1, then follow treadling plan 2 for
A–B, then 15 picks plain weave, then B–C
as per treadling plan, then 15 picks plain
weave. Continue thus for 75 in (1.9 m).
Weave 2 in (5 cm) plain weave. Allow 7 in
(18 cm) fringe for Scarf 2, then 7 in (18 cm)
fringe for Scarf 3.

SCARF 3: STRIPES

Weave 2 in (5 cm) of plain weave, as for
Scarf 1, then follow treadling plan 3 for 75 in
(1.9 m). Weave 2 in (5 cm) plain weave.
Allow 7 in (18 cm) fringe.

Remove the fabric from the loom. Cut the
three scarves apart.

FINISHING

Finish each scarf with a twisted fringe (see
page 345). Wash in wool-approved detergent
and rinse in fabric conditioner. Roll in a
towel to remove excess moisture (do not
wring). Dry flat in shade. When almost dry,
iron to complete the drying process.

Bouclé mohair wrap

This autumn-toned wrap is woven in bouclé mohair yarn and a fine 2/20 wool. Combining the bouclé with two picks of 2/20 wool in between each bouclé pick creates a lighter fabric.

Size 22 x 72 in (55 x 182 cm)

Equipment Four-shaft loom, with 24 in (60 cm) weaving width, ski shuttle, throw shuttle

Technique Plain weave and 1/3 twill

Warp yarn Bendigo Woollen Mills 2-ply pure wool, 336 yds (307 m) of each of three colours to match the mohair weft yarn

Weft yarn Touch Yarns (New Zealand) variegated bouclé mohair, 304 yds (278 m); and olive green 2/20s pure wool, 610 yds (558 m)

Reed 12 dents per in (2.5 cm)

Sett 12 ends per in (2.5 cm)

Selvedge Double thread through heddle at each end

Width in reed 24 in (60 cm)

Finished width of fabric 22 x 72 in (55 x 182 cm)

Weft sett 18 picks per in (2.5 cm): six picks bouclé yarn and 12 picks fine yarn

Warp length 3½ yds (3.2 m)

Number of ends 288

Designer Wendy Cartwright

WINDING THE WARP

Wind a warp in the 2-ply Bendigo wool from Bendigo using the three colours; these can be wound together with a finger between each thread to prevent tangling. The three ends can be taken through the cross together and threaded through the reed in the order preferred.

WEAVING

Use a ski shuttle for the mohair yarn and a throw shuttle for the fine yarn. Start the weaving with four plain-weave picks of the 2/20s wool, then weave one pick of bouclé and two picks of 2/20s yarn. Weave for approximately 76 in (193 cm), leaving 5 in (13 cm) of warp at each end for a fringe, and hem stitching each end while the fabric is still on the loom.

End the weaving with four plain-weave picks in the 2/20s wool; these extra four picks at each end make the hem stitching easier.

The finished size will be 22 x 72 in (55 x 182 cm); always measure on the loom without tension. Some length and width are always lost in the finishing process.

FINISHING

Cut the wrap from the loom and twist the ends of the fringe (see page 345) before washing. Wash in a wool-approved detergent, then put through the spin cycle on a washing machine and steam press. Line dry and steam press again.

X tie-up

⁄ treadling plan

F 2/20s wool

B bouclé

Ruana

This simple but elegant garment is woven in a shadow weave (see the explanation on page 357). It is constructed from two pieces of fabric that are seamed together at the back only; the fronts are left open so that they can be pinned together, or one side draped across the shoulder.

Size One size fits most; length from shoulder approximately 39 in (100 cm)

Equipment Four-shaft loom, 24 in (60 cm) weaving width, two throw shuttles

Technique Shadow weave

Warp and weft yarns Grignasco Tango: six 1¾ oz (50 g) balls of each of Colours 221 and 218. For the purposes of this project, the green yarn will be referred to as dark and the pink as light

Reed 10 dents per in (2.5 cm)

Sett 10 ends per in (2.5 cm)

Selvedge Double thread through heddle at each end

Width in reed 24 in (60 cm)

Finished width 22 in (55 cm)

Weft sett 10 ends per in (2.5 cm), alternating between the two yarns

Warp length 5½ yds (5.1 m)

Number of ends 240

Designer Wendy Cartwright

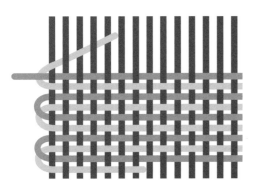

diagram 1 While weaving this shadow weave, you can keep your weft turns even by holding the unused weft taut as you turn the active weft around it.

detail The combination of pink and green yarns produces a heather-toned effect.

WINDING THE WARP

Wind a warp with 1 end dark (green) yarn and 1 end light (pink) yarn. When winding the warp, the two colours can be wound together with a finger between each to prevent tangling.

WEAVING

This piece is woven as drawn in. Determining the correct shuttle order for the wefts to interlock at each edge avoids floats up the edges. You can keep your weft turns even by holding the unused weft taut as you turn the active weft around it; see Diagram 1.

Weave two lengths of fabric, each 2 yards 10 in (209 m) long. Leave 5 in (13 cm) of warp at the beginning of the weaving and 10 in (25 cm) of warp between the two lengths, as well as 5 in (13 cm) at the end of the weaving for a fringe. Hem stitch at the beginning and end of each piece while the fabric is still on the loom.

The finished size of each piece should be 22 x 78 in (55 x 198 cm).

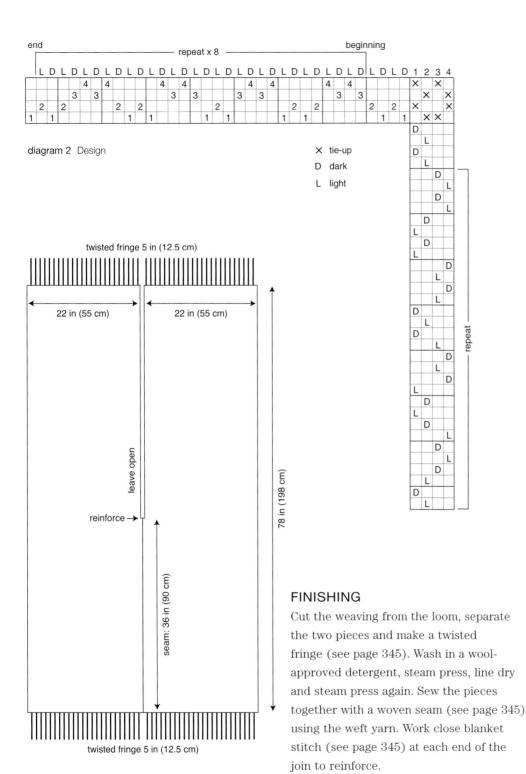

diagram 2 Design

end — repeat x 8 — beginning

L D L D L D L D L D L D L D L D L D L D L D L D L D L D L D L D L D   1 2 3 4

× tie-up
D dark
L light

twisted fringe 5 in (12.5 cm)

22 in (55 cm)   22 in (55 cm)

leave open

reinforce →

seam: 36 in (90 cm)

78 in (198 cm)

twisted fringe 5 in (12.5 cm)

diagram 3 Assembly

repeat

Shadow weaves

The shadow weave is a block weave, and is woven warp and weft in a 1 and 1 colouration — that is, one dark and one light end in the warp and the same in the weft. This is a two colour weave. With four shafts you can have four blocks, as follows:

A 1–2
B 3–4
C 2–1
D 4–3

The shaft in bold type carries the dark thread.

FINISHING

Cut the weaving from the loom, separate the two pieces and make a twisted fringe (see page 345). Wash in a wool-approved detergent, steam press, line dry and steam press again. Sew the pieces together with a woven seam (see page 345) using the weft yarn. Work close blanket stitch (see page 345) at each end of the join to reinforce.

Wrap with mohair tufts

This wrap is woven in a 2/2 twill with a mohair weft. It is loosely woven, producing a light, nicely draping fabric. The multicoloured tufted yarn used in the weft provides an interesting texture.

Size 76 x 23 in (193 x 65 cm), excluding fringes

Equipment Four-shaft table loom, 24 in (60 cm) weaving width, ski shuttle

Technique 2/2 twill

Warp yarns Bendigo Woollen Mills 2-ply pure wool, approximately 301 yds (275 m) in each of four colours; and one 1¾ oz (50 g) ball Heirloom Jazz

Weft yarn Four ⅔ oz (20 g) balls British Spinners 8-ply (DK) mohair

Reed 8 dents per in (2.5 cm)

Sett 2-ply wool, 16 ends per in (2.5 cm); Heirloom Jazz, 8 ends per in (2.5 cm)

Selvedge 3 ends per dent in the first four and last four dents, using the 2-ply wool

Width in reed 25 in (63 cm)

Finished width 25 in (63 cm)

Weft sett 8 picks per in (2.5 cm)

Warp length 3½ yds (3.2 m)

Number of ends 86 ends in each colour of 2-ply wool, plus 27 of Heirloom Jazz

Designer Wendy Cartwright

WARPING

Wind two warps 3½ yards (3.2 m) long — the first in the four colours of the 2-ply Bendigo wool, winding 86 ends of each colour, and the second with 27 ends of the Heirloom Jazz yarn. The four colours of the 2-ply yarn can be wound together with a finger between each to prevent tangling. When threading, every 13th thread, excluding the selvedges, is Jazz. Thread the selvedge (three ends per dent in the first four dents) then four ends of 2-ply wool, then one end Jazz; continue alternating 12 ends 2-ply and one end Jazz, ending with four ends 2-ply ends and another selvedge of three ends per dent in the last four dents. Thread the 2-ply yarns through the dents in random order.

WEAVING

Leave about 8 in (20 cm) at each end for the fringe. Weave for approximately 78 in (198 cm), hem stitching at the beginning and end of the piece.

FINISHING

Cut the wrap from the loom and make a twisted fringe (see page 345) before washing. Wash in a wool-approved detergent, spin in the spin cycle of your washing machine, steam press and line dry. When dry, steam press again.

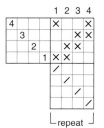

× tie-up
╱ treadling plan
repeat

Twill wrap

A very elegant garment using a sombre but rich combination of midnight blue and black.

The wool and chenille yarns give a beautifully luxurious texture.

Size 84 x 23 in (214 x 58 cm)

Equipment Eight-shaft loom, ski shuttle

Technique Twill

Warp yarn 1530 yds (1400 m) 2/20 wool (2-ply worsted, 5,600 yds/lb)

Weft yarns 8½ oz (240 g) rayon chenille plied with 700 yds (640 m) fine 3-ply wool (1,300 yds/lb)

Reed 16 dents per in (2.5 cm)

Sett 16 ends per in (2.5 cm)

Selvedge 2 ends twice in each heddle, twice on each side

Width in reed 24 in (60 cm)

Finished width 23 in (58 cm)

Weft sett 8 picks per in (2.5 cm)

Warp length 130 in (330 cm)

Number of ends 384

Designer Helen Frostell

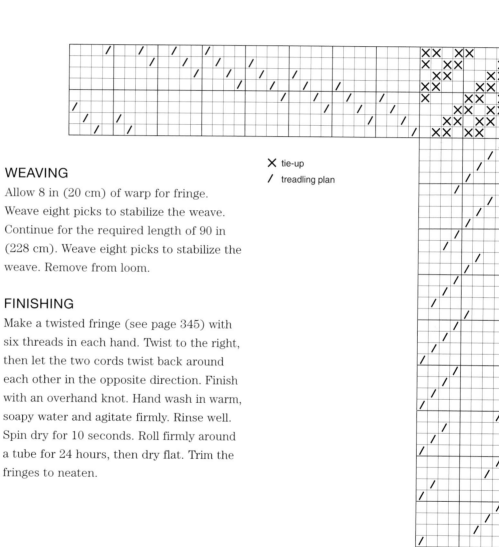

X tie-up

/ treadling plan

WEAVING

Allow 8 in (20 cm) of warp for fringe. Weave eight picks to stabilize the weave. Continue for the required length of 90 in (228 cm). Weave eight picks to stabilize the weave. Remove from loom.

FINISHING

Make a twisted fringe (see page 345) with six threads in each hand. Twist to the right, then let the two cords twist back around each other in the opposite direction. Finish with an overhand knot. Hand wash in warm, soapy water and agitate firmly. Rinse well. Spin dry for 10 seconds. Roll firmly around a tube for 24 hours, then dry flat. Trim the fringes to neaten.

Multi-yarn scarf

This scarf is a good way to use up small amounts of yarn left over from other projects. You can mix textures and different weights of yarn in the same warp. When using yarns of various textures and compositions, it is necessary to keep one constant yarn that is used throughout the piece, at the rate of at least 2–3 threads per in (2.5 cm). This way you avoid a differential take-up, which can occur when different types of yarn are used.

Finished size 7¼ x 58 in (18 x 147 cm)

Equipment Two- or four-shaft loom, ski shuttle

Technique Plain weave on four shafts

Warp yarns Wind a warp 2½ yds (2.3 m) long and 8 in (20 cm) wide. The number of ends depends on yarns used. The base yarn in this scarf is a 2-ply Bendigo Woollen Mills wool in various colours, plus a mixture of yarns (mohair, silk, bouclé, and other fancy yarns). The fine yarns are set at 2 ends per dent and fancy yarns at 1 end per dent in an 8-dent reed

Weft yarns 8-ply mohair at 8 picks per in (2.5 cm). For the weft, choose any yarn used in the warp, or another toning yarn. If using mohair, you need fewer picks per inch

Reed 8 dents per in (2.5 cm)

Selvedge 3 ends per dent for first 3 and last 3 dents, using the 2-ply wool

Width in reed 8 in (20 cm)

Finished width 7½ in (19 cm)

Warp length 2½ yds (2.3 m), or length desired

Number of ends Depends on the yarns used

Designer Wendy Cartwright

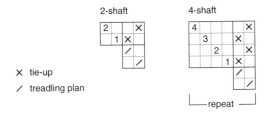

✕ tie-up
╱ treadling plan

Two designs are shown, for either a two-shaft or four-shaft loom.

WEAVING

Allow about 5 in (13 cm) at each end of the scarf for a fringe. Weave in plain weave for approximately 60 in (152 cm), or the length desired. Hem stitch each end of the scarf (see page 344) while it is on the loom.

FINISHING

Cut the hem-stitched scarf from the loom and make a twisted fringe (see page 345) before washing. Wash in a wool-approved detergent, then spin dry in the spin cycle of the washing machine. Steam press with a cloth, especially if using synthetic yarns, line dry, and steam press again.

Lace weave wrap

Here, an open weave gives a garment with a beautifully soft drape. A variegated mohair yarn

in muted, earthy colours is used on a black background.

Finished size of garment 95 x 21 in
(240 x 53 cm)

Equipment Four-shaft loom with 24 in (60 cm)
weaving width, ski shuttle

Technique Mock leno

Warp yarns 2¾ oz (75 g) 2/22 black
2-ply worsted wool (5,600 yds/lb);
2¾ oz (75 g) contrast yarn in superfine
kid mohair and merino

Weft yarn 2¾ oz (75 g) 2/22 black
2-ply worsted wool (5,600 yds/lb)

Reed 8 dents per in (2.5 cm)

Sett 12 ends per in (2.5 cm)

Selvedge 2 ends three times in each heddle
three times on each side. Omit space in
dent at selvedges, once on each side.
Floating selvedges

Width in reed 24 in (60 cm)

Weft sett 15 picks per in (2.5 cm)

Warp length 130 in (3.3 m)

Number of ends 288

Designer Helen Frostell

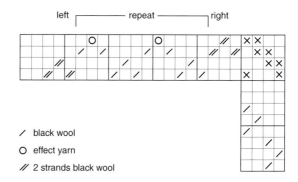

/ black wool

O effect yarn

// 2 strands black wool

THREADING

Sley three ends from each unit in
one dent, then leave the next dent
empty; for example, ends on shafts
1, 2, 1 dented together and ends 3,
4, 3 together, leaving an empty dent
between them.

WEAVING

Allow 8 in (20 cm) of warp at each
end for the fringe. Weave eight
picks to stabilize the weave. These
picks are removed as the fringes are
made. Weave for 95 in (240 cm), or
the required length. Weave eight
picks to stabilize the weave.

FINISHING

Remove the fabric from the loom.
Make a twisted fringe (see page 345)
before washing. Gently hand wash
and spin dry for 10 seconds. Roll
firmly around a tube for 12 hours.
Lightly steam press.

Note The contrast yarn used in the
pictured example is Alpine, a
multicoloured mohair from Touch
Yarns New Zealand, in turquoise
and red. A 12-ply (medium-weight/
aran) mohair may be substituted.

Furoshiki bag

Furoshiki is a Japanese word meaning 'wrapper'. This bag is simply but ingeniously constructed

from a folded rectangle woven of strips of kimono material on a cotton warp.

Size 17 in (43 cm) square, not including handle

Equipment Four-shaft loom, with 16 in (40 cm) weaving width, ski shuttle, throw shuttle

Technique Plain weave

Warp yarn Black 16/2 cotton

Weft yarn Kimono fabric cut into ½ in (12 mm) strips with the grain, and black 16/2 cotton

Reed 12 dents per in (2.5 cm)

Sett 12 ends per in (2.5 cm)

Selvedge 2 ends twice in each heddle on each side. Use floating selvedge

Width in reed 16 in (40 cm)

Finished width 13½ in (34 cm)

Weft sett 8 picks fabric strips plus 8 picks cotton per in (2.5 cm)

Warp length 75 in (190 cm), which includes 10 per cent shrinkage, ties, take-up and loom waste

Number of ends 200

Designer Helen Frostell

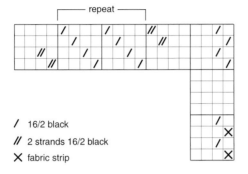

— repeat —

/ 16/2 black
// 2 strands 16/2 black
✗ fabric strip

WEAVING AND FINISHING

Weave a ½ in (12 mm) seam allowance with doubled 16/2 cotton. Then weave the bag, alternating 1 pick of fabric and 1 pick of 16/2 cotton. Weave so that the length is three times the width, taking shrinkage, take-up and seams into reckoning. Finish with a ½ in (12 mm) seam allowance. Secure the weave with some picks of cotton. Remove the fabric from the loom and machine zigzag each end to prevent fraying. Gently hand-wash. Press.

ASSEMBLY

Start with a rectangle of fabric three times as long as it is wide. Fold and sew the fabric following the diagram, A to A and B to B. Then pull up the two corners C and the shape will change.

For the handle, cut two strips of kimono fabric 13 x 1½ in (33 x 4 cm), or length and width desired. Having right sides together and raw edges even, and allowing a 1/4 in (6 mm) seam allowance, sew along both long sides and one short end. Turn through, press and attach to corners. Top stitch edges of handle. Bind the seams, or line the bag if desired.

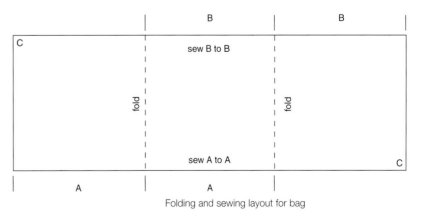

Folding and sewing layout for bag

Small fabric bag

Strips of fabric are woven with cotton yarn on four shafts to produce an appealing little bag.

The pictured example uses kimono fabric.

Size 9 x 7¾ in (23 x 19.5 cm)

Equipment Four-shaft loom, ski shuttle, throw shuttle

Technique Plain weave

Warp yarn 16/2 cotton, black

Weft yarn Fabric strips ½ in (12 mm) wide, cut with the grain, alternating with black 16/2 cotton

Other materials Stiffening fabric (for inner bag); lighter fabric (for lining); button or toggle

Reed 12 dents per in (2.5 cm)

Sett 12 ends per in (2.5 cm)

Selvedge 2 ends in each heddle twice on each side. Floating selvedge

Width in reed 10 in (25 cm)

Finished width 9 in (23 cm)

Weft 5 picks fabric, 5 picks cotton per in (2.5 cm) approximately

Warp length 50 in (127 cm), which includes take-up, loom waste and ties

Number of ends 120

Designer Helen Frostell

WEAVING

You will need cotton fabric, such as kimono fabric, for the fabric strips. Cut strips totalling 6 yards (5.5 m). These are folded in half, then ironed, giving ¼ in (6 mm) wide strips. Secure the weave at the beginning with a few picks of cotton. Weave a hem in plain weave (tabby) with doubled 16/2s cotton. Weave for approximately 20 in (50 cm). Weave another plain-weave hem. Secure the weave at the end with a few picks of cotton. Remove the fabric from the loom. Machine zigzag to reinforce the ends .

FINISHING

With wrong sides together, sew the side seams. From the stiffening fabric, make a firm inner bag, slightly smaller than the outer bag, and sew along the top edges; this inner bag gives stability to the bag. Make a lining from a lighter fabric. Attach a strap and a loop for the fastener. Sew the bag and lining together, right sides together, then turn right side out. Steam press. Attach button or toggle.

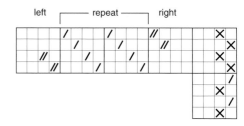

X fabric strips

/ 16/2 cotton

// doubled ends in each heddle

Monk's belt mat

Two subtly contrasting tones of linen are used here to form a striped band at either end of the weaving.

Size 17 x 12 in (43 x 30 cm)

Equipment Four-shaft loom with 13 in (33 cm) weaving width, throw shuttle

Technique Plain weave with monk's belt adaption

Warp yarn Unbleached linen 16/1, two ends used as one

Weft yarn Unbleached linen 16/1, and coloured linen 16/2 for the pattern

Reed 12 dents per in (2.5 cm)

Sett 24 ends per in (2.5 cm), using 2 ends as one

Selvedge 4 ends per heddle twice on each side

Width in reed 12½ in (31 cm)

Finished width 12 in (30 cm)

Weft sett 24 picks per in (2.5 cm)

Warp length 46 in (117 cm)

Number of ends 292 doubled

Designer Helen Frostell

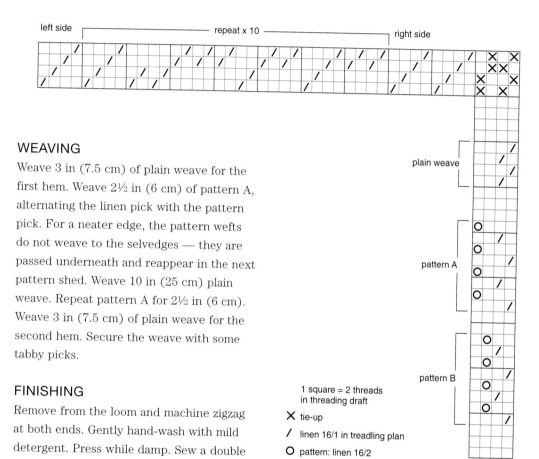

left side — repeat x 10 — right side

1 square = 2 threads in threading draft

X tie-up

/ linen 16/1 in treadling plan

O pattern: linen 16/2

plain weave

pattern A

pattern B

WEAVING

Weave 3 in (7.5 cm) of plain weave for the first hem. Weave 2½ in (6 cm) of pattern A, alternating the linen pick with the pattern pick. For a neater edge, the pattern wefts do not weave to the selvedges — they are passed underneath and reappear in the next pattern shed. Weave 10 in (25 cm) plain weave. Repeat pattern A for 2½ in (6 cm). Weave 3 in (7.5 cm) of plain weave for the second hem. Secure the weave with some tabby picks.

FINISHING

Remove from the loom and machine zigzag at both ends. Gently hand-wash with mild detergent. Press while damp. Sew a double hem with a finished depth of 1 in (2.5 cm).

VARIATION

Pattern B may be incorporated in the design if desired. Weave as for Pattern A.

Cushion covers

This complementary pair of cushions uses a damask weave in subtly contrasting shades or cotton and linen. The timeless design would enhance both contemporary and classic furnishings.

Finished size 17 x 17 in (43 x 43 cm)

Equipment Eight-shaft loom, throw shuttles

Weave Two-block, false damask on eight shafts. Block A on shafts 1 2 3 4, block B on 5 6 7 8

Warp yarns 1110 yds (1015 m) 16/2 cotton at 12,800 m/kg; three different blue to blue-grey colours of similar value. Wind a warp using three threads together, with a finger between each thread to prevent tangling. They are threaded through the reed randomly

Weft yarns 950 yds (869 m) 16/2 linen at 5,190 m/kg; three different dark blue to turquoise colours of similar value, woven randomly using 3 shuttles

Reed 10 dents per in (2.5 cm)

Sett 30 ends per in (2.5 cm)

Threading The colours are selected randomly when threading through the heddles

Selvedges 2 ends per heddle, twice on each side

Width in reed 19 in (48 cm)

Finished width 17 in (43 cm)

Weft sett 26 picks per in (2.5 cm)

Warp length 70 in (178 cm). Seam allowance of ¾–1 in (2–2.5 cm) included

Number of ends 548. This includes the doubled selvedge ends

Designer Helen Frostell

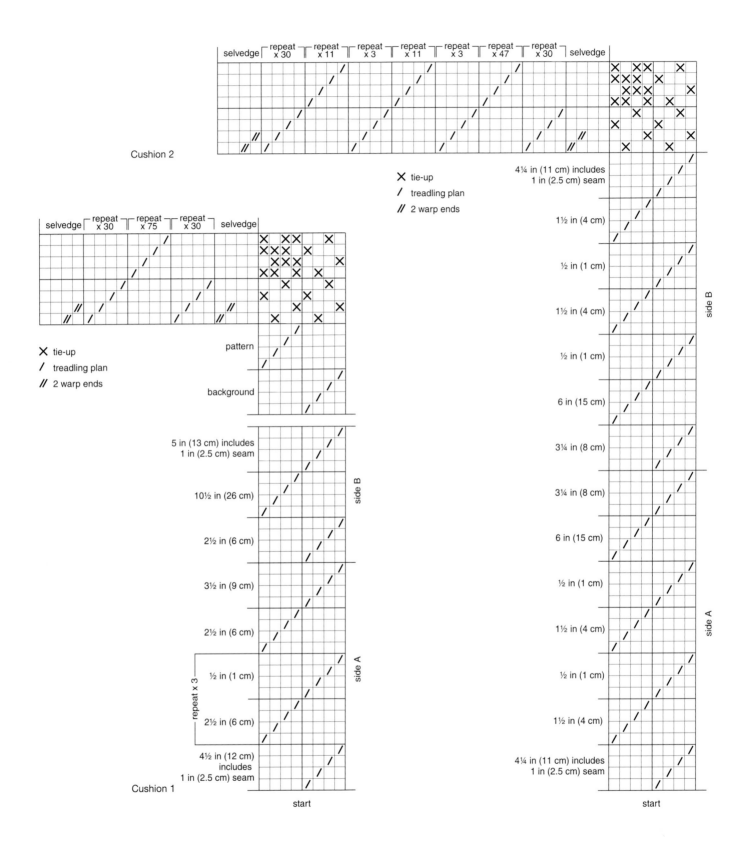

Cushion 2

	repeat x 30	repeat x 11	repeat x 3	repeat x 11	repeat x 3	repeat x 47	repeat x 30	
selvedge								selvedge

X tie-up

/ treadling plan

// 2 warp ends

4¼ in (11 cm) includes
1 in (2.5 cm) seam

1½ in (4 cm)

½ in (1 cm)

1½ in (4 cm)

½ in (1 cm)

6 in (15 cm)

side B

3¼ in (8 cm)

3¼ in (8 cm)

6 in (15 cm)

½ in (1 cm)

1½ in (4 cm)

½ in (1 cm)

1½ in (4 cm)

side A

4¼ in (11 cm) includes
1 in (2.5 cm) seam

start

	repeat x 30	repeat x 75	repeat x 30	
selvedge				selvedge

X tie-up

/ treadling plan

// 2 warp ends

pattern

background

5 in (13 cm) includes
1 in (2.5 cm) seam

10½ in (26 cm)

side B

2½ in (6 cm)

3½ in (9 cm)

2½ in (6 cm)

repeat x 3

½ in (1 cm)

2½ in (6 cm)

side A

4½ in (12 cm)
includes
1 in (2.5 cm) seam

Cushion 1

start

detail Back of Cushion 1

detail Back of Cushion 2

CUSHION 1

Two different treadling plans are given, 'A' for the front and 'B' for the back. These can be varied as you wish within the limits of the threading plan.

CUSHION 2

Cushion 2 is a variation of cushion 1. You can put on a warp for both cushions. When cushion 1 is completed, it is removed from the loom and a small variation in the threading is done. Ends from shafts 5 6 7 8 are transferred to shafts 1 2 3 4 to give small stripes in the opposite block. This is the threading given for cushion 2. When threading for cushion 1, position extra

heddles on shafts 1 2 3 4 to suit your plan for cushion 2, or make new heddles.

The treadling plan for side 'B' is the reverse of 'A'. This can be varied as you wish within the limits of the threading plan.

WEAVING

Weave a heading to stabilize the weave. Follow the treadling plan for 'A' (front) then continue with 'B' (back) for each cushion. When weaving side 'B', your own pattern may be designed within the limits of the threading. End with a header to prevent fraying. Finish the cushions, following the instructions at right.

Finishing

Remove the fabric from the loom. Machine zigzag the ends of each cushion. Hand wash in warm, soapy water. Rinse well, remove excess water and press while damp.

Fold in half and machine stitch the sides and a short distance on each side of the open end. Place an insert in the cushion and slip-stitch the opening.

Small table mats

These Japanese-style mats have an attractive ridged effect achieved by using two wefts, one thick and one thin, on a fine warp. Instructions are given for making a set of four mats.

Size 9¼ x 10¼ in (23.5 x 26 cm)

Equipment Four-shaft loom (see Note, below), ski shuttle

Technique Repp weave using four shafts and pedals

Warp yarn Cottolin, two threads used as one

Weft yarns Thick weft: Stranded cotton or ½ in (12 mm) wide rags; Fine weft: 16/2 cotton, similar colour to warp selvedge

Reed 12 dents per in (2.5 cm)

Sett 48 ends per in (2.5 cm)

Width in reed 9¼ in (23.5 cm)

Finished width 9¼ in (23.5 cm)

Weft sett 6 thick and 6 fine picks per in (2.5 cm)

Warp length 106 in (2.7 m) for 4 mats, including take-up, loom waste and ties

Number of ends 452

Designer Helen Frostell

WEAVING

Warp up with two ends of each shade. Weave a 2¼ in (5.5 cm) wide hem in 16/2 cotton on shafts 1 and 3, 2 and 4. Turn under twice to make a double hem.

The mat is woven alternating the thick yarn and the fine yarn. To get a firm edge, roll the thick yarn between your thumb and forefinger, making a firm twist. Enter the thick yarn from the right, then the thin yarn from the left. If the thin weft is under the outside end, enter the shed over the thick weft. If the thin weft is over the outside end, enter the shed under the thick weft.

FINISHING

Secure the weave with machine zigzag. Hand wash gently in warm water. Roll around a tube to remove wrinkles. Allow to dry, then hem.

Note A countermarch loom is ideal for this project, due to the firm beating necessary for the repp weave. Other looms may be used but the result will not be as sturdy.

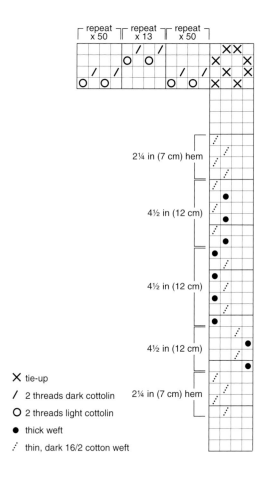

X tie-up
/ 2 threads dark cottolin
O 2 threads light cottolin
● thick weft
⁚ thin, dark 16/2 cotton weft

index